Reflexivity and Development Economics

Reflexivity and Development Economics

Methodology, Policy and Practice

Daniel Gay

First published 2009 by
PALGRAVE MACMILLAN

Palgrave Macmillan in the UK is an imprint of Macmillan Publishers Limited, registered in England, company number 785998, of Houndmills, Basingstoke, Hampshire RG21 6XS.

Palgrave Macmillan in the US is a division of St Martin's Press LLC, 175 Fifth Avenue, New York, NY 10010.

Palgrave Macmillan is the global academic imprint of the above companies and has companies and representatives throughout the world.

Palgrave® and Macmillan® are registered trademarks in the United States, the United Kingdom, Europe and other countries.

ISBN-13: 978–0–230–22016–4 hardback

This book is printed on paper suitable for recycling and made from fully managed and sustained forest sources. Logging, pulping and manufacturing processes are expected to conform to the environmental regulations of the country of origin.

A catalogue record for this book is available from the British Library.

A catalog record for this book is available from the Library of Congress.

10   9   8   7   6   5   4   3   2   1
18   17   16   15   14   13   12   11   10   09

Printed and bound in Great Britain by
CPI Antony Rowe, Chippenham and Eastbourne

To Jance and Alan

Contents

List of Figures and Tables

Figures

Tables

Acknowledgements

It is customary to begin with a bout of name-dropping, so I will begin by mentioning an important name. I am deeply grateful for the help and encouragement provided by Professor Sheila Dow. If, as I try to argue, subjective qualities matter in economics, then Sheila's open-mindedness and approachability contribute to making her a great economist, in addition to her large and important publication record. I am grateful that she was so often available for impromptu discussion and that she patiently indulged many of my ill-considered meanderings.

I would like to thank several lesser-known figures, some of whom are the subjects of 'development', and who helped me understand what economics means in the real world. These include, in Vanuatu Roy Mickey Joy, Tim Sisi, Tom Kalo Langitong, Moana Matariki, Nik Soni, Yurendra Basnett, Francis Hickey and Marcel Yawiko; and in Singapore Nora Latiff, Terence Kong and David Fullbrook.

Back to the academic name-dropping. Dipak Gosh was of great help with the development literature and with comments about structure. I also thank my supervisor at York, Bill Jackson, and Rodney Barker at the LSE. I had a useful discussion with Ravi Kanbur when starting my research, while Wendy Olson, Colin Danby and Jang-Sup Shin gave some valuable pointers for Chapters 3 and 4. Many others have helped, including my colleagues when I was at Stirling University. My work with the United Nations has since enabled me to keep visiting Vanuatu and other developing countries. Not last, and definitely not least, a scholarship from the Economic and Social Research Council (ESRC) funded my studies.

I am indebted to Geoff Harcourt for comments on an earlier version of Chapter 3 and for further comments and encouragement on the overall text. I also thank participants at the 2005 conference of the European Society for the History of Economic Thought, where an earlier draft of Chapter 3 was presented. A version of Chapter 4 is published as Gay (2007) 'Modernism, reflexivity and the Washington Consensus' *Journal of Economic Methodology* 14(1): 85–107 http://www.informaworld.com. For comments, I am grateful to participants at the November 2005 Stirling Centre for Economic Methodology workshop. I thank the publishers of the *Journal of Economic Methodology* for permission to reproduce parts of the article here. Chapter 6 draws on Gay (2004) "The

Emperor's Tailor: An Assessment of Vanuatu's Comprehensive Reform Programme", *Pacific Economic Bulletin* 19(3): 22–39, and I appreciate the permission of the publishers to publish material from this article.

Lastly, and most importantly, it remains only to thank Sula Young for her unstinting support. I am forever grateful.

1
Introduction

'I've got this scientist well-trained,' said one laboratory rat to the other. 'Every time I press the button, he gives me a peanut.'

The idea of reflexivity has long been the subject of discussion in philosophy. The origins of the term can be found in the 'Liar's paradox', a puzzle believed to have come from Eubulides, a pupil of Euclides in around the sixth century BC. Consider the sentence: 'This statement is false'. If the statement is false, then whoever said it was telling the truth. But if it is true, then it must be false because the speaker said it was. Therefore if it is true it is false, and if it is false it is true. The self-referential nature of the statement has even led some to question the absolute validity of classical logic.[1]

The word itself comes from 're' meaning back, against, or reversed and 'flectere', the Latin for bend. Grammatically, it denotes a pronoun that refers back to the subject of the clause in which it is employed. In logic it refers to a relation between a term and itself. The difference between reflexivity and reflection is that while the latter suggests looking in a mirror and seeing yourself, the former involves an action deployed on an object and that object reacting back, resulting in a changed situation. If the joke above about the lab rat is funny it is because the expected relation between subject and object is reversed. The scientist believes herself to be training the rat, while the rat has other ideas. The reader's perspective on the laboratory experiment is turned around. Reflexivity is as much about perceptions as about physical reality.

The idea of reflexivity has important implications for economic methodology, and it has featured prominently in the literature during recent years (for example Hands 2001, Davis and Klaes 2003). The intention here is to present a methodological argument as to why reflexivity is important in the study and practice of development economics. It is first important to define what methodology means, since the word is often mistakenly used as a synonym for method. Methodology has a specific, and important, meaning: the study of the framework within which methods are chosen (Dow 2002b: vii). As Fritz Machlup (1978: 61) points out, 'graphies' and 'logies' are different. Geography is description of the earth's crust. Geology is the study of what goes on beneath the surface. In the same way method (the word should really be 'methodography') is the technique used to tackle a question, while methodology is the deeper study of how to choose between methods. Arguably the word methodology has suffered so much slippage – it is now used so routinely as a substitute for method – that the debate is just semantics. The question then arises of what word should be substituted for methodology, something that undoubtedly exists. Either way, I choose to use the word methodology to mean the approach to knowledge which underpins the selection and application of methods. Methodology is not just abstract philosophical debate divorced from the real world.[2] Methodological discussions carry important implications for method, policy and practice. As Dow (1996) points out, the ways in which an economist chooses between methods, and in which school of thought an economist operates determine the kind of economics that is conducted, how it is used, what kind of policy recommendations result and even how they are carried out.

More specifically, the purpose of this book is to examine whether the concept of reflexivity helps transcend the methodological distinction between modernism and postmodernism in development economics. I focus on the Washington Consensus, which has formed the dominant, modernist, mode of mainstream development thinking since the 1980s. The Consensus has rigid methodological underpinnings which stem from its mainstream origins. In order to shed light on the theory and practice of the Washington Consensus, I apply some of the ideas of reflexivity from the last century of social and economic thought to the practical experiences of two countries at opposite ends of the development spectrum – Singapore and Vanuatu.

The Washington Consensus is not yet dead, even if considerable academic literature has criticised it and the global development institutions declare themselves to have moved on. The methodology behind the Washington Consensus persists, as do many of its policy prescriptions. The International Monetary Fund (IMF) and World Bank continue to provide loans to developing countries contingent on trade liberalisation, privatisation or corporatisation and lower public spending – as seen in the new round of IMF loans initiated during the global economic crisis which began in 2008. IMF conditionalities imposed on Pakistan required lower fiscal spending and increased interest rates. Latvia's government was required to cut public spending and lower wages. A $16 billion programme in Hungary carried the condition of deep cuts in government spending and lower pensions. In Belarus, according to the deputy managing director of the IMF: 'Key structural reforms, including price and wage liberalization, should follow the realignment of the currency. Broader measures to support private sector development – including reductions in the size of government, deregulation, and privatization – are also needed to underpin better medium-term growth, and should be undertaken as fast as market conditions allow'.[3] El Salvador and Serbia each faced fiscal austerity measures as a result of their standby IMF programmes. Ukraine was urged by the IMF to eliminate its fiscal deficit. All of these features are redolent of the earliest structural adjustment packages in the 1980s.

Reflexivity is often used to refer to any situation in which things affect themselves. The anthropologist Clifford Geertz (2004) has even suggested that methodology itself is reflexivity, as it involves discussing what you are doing. But reflexivity is more than this, as I aim to show. Rather than simply implying self-dependency, reflexivity can introduce an element of realistic unpredictability into the often deterministic world of modernist science. Within social theory, and therefore economics, the concept has implications for the subject/object divide as well as the idea of structuralism. In an era of increasing scepticism about human progress, some authors wonder whether the concept of reflexivity, further developed, might not constitute an entirely new way of thinking, just as Marx stood Hegel on his feet.[4]

One less ambitious interpretation of reflexivity, originating in the sociology of knowledge and discussed in the economic methodology literature by Davis and Klaes (2003), is that the author is implicated in her own text because she has a (usually unspoken) social background that affects what she says. Context and background affect all economics, including policy. The interest-rate decisions of the Bank of England, for example, depend heavily upon the particular composition of the nine-member Monetary Policy Committee and their interpretation of economic data and events, rather than being the straightforward application of models. Proponents of reflexivity suggest that presenting an argument or deciding policy therefore should involve making explicit the background, beliefs and possible biases to that decision or argument.

Any argument dealing with reflexivity should itself be self-reflexive in such a way. This does not mean being inward-looking or self-conscious.[5] Having your 'I's' too close together is an unattractive trait and self-analysis can be tedious. The declaration of predispositions, however, has value. To state theoretical leanings and to make explicit the context in which a text was written helps the author address the issue of subjectivity. As I show later, subjectivity matters. The scientism of much economics leads to the mistaken impression that the author's preconceptions are irrelevant; that as long as relevant methods are applied correctly the results of economic discussion are objectively true.

So here I will briefly explain the background to my enquiry (in an inevitably partial and subjective way, and doubtless leaving out details that others would consider important). Of course, acknowledging my own subjectivity risks qualifying my conclusions – a risk I am willing to take. After three years working as an economist and journalist in Singapore I returned to the United Kingdom to study for a mainstream MSc in economics. I felt critical about certain topics, and wondered why, unlike in the other social sciences I had studied, we were not encouraged to think *about* the subject. One of the first books on economic methodology I had read was Dierdre McCloskey's *The Rhetoric of Economics* (1985), which also re-ignited an earlier interest in postmodernism. Whilst writing my masters' thesis I was lucky enough to be accepted to study for a doctorate with Professor Sheila Dow. I began my studies and formulated my research question. At the same time I hoped to keep working in developing countries, and felt convinced of the need to continue learning about development through practice as well as books. I took an Overseas Development Institute economics fellowship working in trade policy with the government of Vanuatu in the South Pacific.

Two years later I returned to study full-time for my doctorate. As stated earlier my main research question was whether, within development economics, the concept of reflexivity helps in transcending the divide between modernism and postmodernism. To answer this question I developed a taxonomy, the final version of which is outlined in Chapter 4. The taxonomy is not supposed to be a final definition of reflexivity; it is an attempt to work out some of its implications for the practice of economic development. In the spirit of reflexivity it cannot be considered the final word on the matter and must be taken provisionally. I have since tried to put into practice some of the ideas of the taxonomy, and think critically about it, in my work with the United Nations in East and Central Asia and the Pacific island countries.

I cannot pretend that the case studies are a foolproof 'test' of whether the taxonomy works because I revised the taxonomy after writing the first case study. Equally the case studies were revised to make them better answer the points of the taxonomy, an initial version of which I drafted before I left for Vanuatu. Maybe some people would consider this approach to be bad science – but I suspect that in practice many authors switch between the bird's eye and the worm's eye view. It might be too much to aggrandise my approach as being in the Scottish political economy tradition (Dow and Dow 2005a) of alternating between the universal and particular, or as combining inductive and deductive methods, but I certainly find this sort of approach interesting and have a mostly Scottish education, in politics and economics. In a rather reflexive way, the kind of two-way approach I adopted is also required by the taxonomy, which advocates a revision of theory in the light of new evidence.

My critical, multi-disciplinary education and my time as a practitioner of development will inevitably colour my conclusions, just as the predominantly formal methods of mainstream economics influence the conclusions of those who think in such a way. Convinced formalists would argue that their approach is more precise (although we surely all think our own approach is correct), and that self-reflexivity is redundant. But as McCloskey points out, all science involves rhetoric, and pointing out certain leanings or predispositions helps the reader put the argument in context. I would argue that reflexivity also helps make scientific economic accounts more convincing, since economics is about humans, who are both the observers and the observed.

But a crucial assessment of whether conclusions are valid is whether they are believable – not only where they came from. Contextualising the enquiry moves the author only half-way to his goal. The other half of the journey is to present a convincing account, and this is what I have tried to do, with the assistance of case studies. This is also why reflexivity is about more than just the presentation of background and context. Beck *et al.* (1994), Bourdieu (1990a) and Bourdieu and Wacquant (1992) imply that the concept of reflexivity can contribute to the understanding of economic methodology.

My use of case studies was prompted partly by the possibility that some economists, heterodox and mainstream, do not tend to get their hands dirty enough. Recognising the interconnection of theory and practice, as realists do, for example, surely means doing case studies and perhaps even aiming at the physical transformation of economic activities in poorer countries. I suspect that there is an over-emphasis on 'the literature' rather than on 'the reality', meaning that development economics has a tendency to build an internally consistent academic discourse about a particular country without referring frequently enough to actual conditions on the ground. Acknowledging the importance of practical application throws into question the unstinting use of models, especially formal ones. Instead of always applying the results of established economic formulae, I wonder whether practical development economists may be able to behave in a more discretionary manner, depending on context?

Chapter 2 introduces the distinction between modernism and post-modernism. Economics has not engaged with the concept of methodological postmodernism to the same extent as have other social sciences, although signs of the concept exist in economic writings. I argue that the discipline of economics, the mainstream of which is modernist, would benefit from trying to address some of the questions raised by postmodernists, even if it does not accept all of their conclusions. Three open-systems approaches are presented: critical realism, the Keynesian tradition and the neo-Austrian approach, each of which can be seen as occupying the space between modernism and postmodernism. These traditions and projects have certain features in common, which can shed light on the discussion about modernism and postmodernism. The discussion in this chapter informs the discussion of reflexivity and the later case studies on Vanuatu and Singapore.

Other approaches, including the concept of reflexivity, have likewise tried to transcend the divide between modernism and postmodernism. Chapter 3 outlines five important ways in which the term has been used during the last century. Interdisciplinarity is necessary, partly because the discussion of modernism, postmodernism and reflexivity occurs throughout the natural and social sciences and the humanities. My multi-disciplinary education also prompted me to focus on a particular problem using a variety of approaches rather than to use a particular disciplinary toolkit. A good case can be made for cross-disciplinary approaches in development research (Harriss 2002) and there is a long tradition of 'trespassing' and 'crossing boundaries' (Hirschman 1980, 1998) in development economics. Discussions of reflexivity in the economic methodology literature originate with the sociology of knowledge, and it seems sensible to look within this field for ideas, which is why in this chapter I discuss authors ranging from Marx (1974), Tucker (1972) and Mannheim (1936) to Bourdieu and Wacquant (1992), Beck *et al.* (1994) and Giddens (1994b). Whilst important distinctions exist between the ways in which these authors use reflexivity, they also hold features in common. One of these common features is that because social research is unlikely to produce a final result valid for all time, and because the social context of knowledge changes, the way that economics conceives of knowledge may need to be revised periodically. The implication is that economics is a process of enquiry rather than a fixed set of tools.

In Chapter 4, I build upon the discussion of modernism, postmodernism and reflexivity to outline a taxonomy of reflexive development practice. This is aimed at establishing some ideas which might inform both the way economics is practised in developing countries and the process of conducting research in development economics. The first point of the taxonomy is that examining the influence of external values and norms would help make development practice more relevant to the national context. Certain ideas are likely to be acceptable across all countries, such as the provision of basic essentials. But beyond this, values and policy proposals vary considerably between countries, and it is up to the development economist to choose the theoretical framework and policies. Whilst not quite 'horses for courses' (Harcourt 1996; Lawson 1997b), it is true that considerable space exists for manoeuvre away from the standard 'one-size-fits-all' theoretical approach of the Washington Consensus.

The second part of the taxonomy suggests that it is worth making an implicit assessment of the importance of local context. 'Local context' means more than just governmental set-ups or exchange-rate regimes. Economic policy proposals must be tailored to take account of differences in behaviour, values and institutions. Without a solid grounding in the cultural context, policies are not only less likely to be successful but governments may feel insufficient ownership over reform. The experience of the last 20 years shows that externally imposed conditionalities have weakened governments' commitment to reform.

The third point of the taxonomy is that economic tools, concepts and policies can undermine themselves even though they were designed for greater control. This kind of reflexivity comes from the most simple use of the word – that things affect themselves. Remaining open to fallibility and accepting that policy ideas can be partly self-defeating helps deal with postmodern scepticism about scientific self-assurance, without descending into relativism.

The fourth and final point of the taxonomy suggests revising theory or policies if they prove inadequate or as circumstances change. Whilst most economists would accept the idea of theoretical progress, the wide-ranging and honest reappraisal of economic thinking is rarer than might be supposed. The influence of ideology in mainstream development economics has challenged the Popperian ideal. On the other hand, it would be a mistake to read critics of structural adjustment (such as Callaghy and Ravenhill 1993; Lensink 1996) as opposing any reform. It is important for alternative visions of development to retain the notion of agency, and in particular the ability of national governments to influence economic outcomes.

In Chapter 5, I outline briefly some of the reasons for choosing Vanuatu and Singapore as case studies. I realised from the start that the two countries are very different and that both countries are sometimes considered 'special cases' which do not tell us anything about development in general. I would dispute this view, but equally recognise that any lessons from the two countries are limited. The taxonomy is not intended to be a theoretical model to be applied everywhere. The aim here, modestly, is to try and show that it works in these two particular economies, and without proving it, maybe others. One of the implications of reflexivity is to be the observer and the observed at the same time – to involve yourself in the object of your research. Subjective details are important. My argument requires discussion of countries of which I have personal subjective knowledge.

Chapter 6 begins an examination of the ideas of the taxonomy in practice. I lived in Vanuatu when the country was emerging from a period influenced by a structural adjustment package initiated by the Asian Development Bank. The Comprehensive Reform Programme (CRP) was inspired by the Washington Consensus, proposing standard objectives such as reduced government expenditure, privatisation and current account liberalisation. After the programme started, the economy went into recession and per capita GDP fell. I suggest, following the ideas of the taxonomy, that had the CRP paid more attention to local context, including cultural and institutional peculiarities, it would have been more successful.

Next I examine the taxonomy in one of the other countries in which I worked, Singapore. I try to show that unlike in Vanuatu, the Singaporean government consciously maintained ownership of its development process. Certain outside ideas were accepted, such as the importance of foreign direct investment, but the government paid off external debt quickly and minimised the influence of international institutions. This self-reliance enabled it to accommodate particular domestic features, including values, institutions and behaviour. The government also remained beholden to no ideological framework, changing the development narrative as it saw fit. The combination of ownership, awareness of context and flexibility helps explain the government's economic success since independence.

Chapter 8 involves a comparison of the two economies, again using the taxonomy. Sometimes the kinds of comparisons inspired by the Washington Consensus tend to focus on the empirical, rather than considering wider methodological issues. Issues connected with the use of knowledge include the difficulty of knowing certain outcomes in advance and the importance of policy autonomy and ownership. An ontic issue is the use of money, which took a particular form in Vanuatu and influenced the success of privatisation and the role of the state. This is not just abstract academic dialogue, but the kind of discussion that helps establish economic policies that are more useful and compassionate.

Part I

2
Beyond Modernism and Postmodernism

2.1 Introduction

Science has long wrestled over the certainty of its claims. Can one scientific discovery apply equally to every situation and remain true forever? Are there absolute foundations to knowledge, or does truth depend on who is speaking? In recent years the philosophy of Lakatos (1976), Kuhn (1962) and Feyerabend (1975) has heralded a move away from foundationalism in science, accompanied by the 'postmodern turn' originating in the social sciences and humanities. Economics is no exception, even if it has come late to the debate.

The mainstream of economics can be placed firmly in the modernist tradition. Modernism is an early twentieth-century humanist move-ment in science and the arts that believes reality can be reduced to certain essential features discovered through rational enquiry. Method-ological postmodernism – in its various guises – broadly disputes these claims, asserting that realities are fractured and perhaps incommen-surate, and that therefore an independent assessment of the truth is impossible. Postmodernists are open to the charge of relativism and being anti-theory, but modernists must justify their foundationalism, scientism, determinism, essentialism and humanism.

Amid a minefield of 'isms', it is important to get definitions straight, and this is why I will spend some time reviewing the diverse fields of thinking represented by modernism and postmodernism. A distinction that has been touched on only briefly by the economics methodology literature is that between modernity and modernism. Within the social sciences, mainstream economics is in a sense the inheritor *par excellence* of the enlightenment project of modernity, a term which requires some illumination in itself. Are we living in an era of postmodernity, or is postmodernism a way of thinking about the world? In some parts of the world, the conditions of early twenty-first century capitalism are different to those of 100 years previously, but it is questionable whether a radical disjunction has taken place. It is equally true that we need new theories and tools to think about new developments in social life. But there is no need to opt wholesale for either side of the debate.

Within economics several approaches have tried implicitly to retain the useful features of modernism and modernity while pre-empting postmodern challenges. I will show that three of these approaches – critical realism, the neo-Austrian school and the Keynesian philosophical tradition – use an open-systems methodology in contrast to the closed-system tactics of modernism. Critical realists consider economics to be social theory, whilst Keynesians have often been better-disposed towards social economics than the mainstream. Using sociology to illuminate economic methodology is useful because it enables economics to rebut the charge of scientism, if this involves an over-reliance on static tools despite the changing subject matter of economics.

Pitching the argument at a more concrete level also complements the philosophical arguments advanced by critical realism and Keynes. All three open-systems approaches argue against a fixed theoretical definition of the economic agent outside human existence. Part of the problem with both postmodernism and modernism is that they operate at such a high level of abstraction that they place too little emphasis on what real people do, warts and all.

A position that moved beyond modernism and postmodernism might have amongst the following implications for economics. First, concepts originally used to understand economic life have themselves now become a part of economic life to be explained, and thus operate in a reflexive manner. Second, looking at the subject matter of economics as socially generated means economists themselves must be subject to the same social influences. Third, economics might try to conceive of its objects of enquiry – human beings – as in flux and somewhat unpredictable.

Achieving greater awareness of the changing nature of its own project would mean economics performs more self-critique. Taking account of these three implications would help economics to deal with the postmodern challenge whilst better equipping it to make scientific claims.

2.2 A review of modernism and postmodernism

Modernism and postmodernism are important for contemporary economics. The ideas that fall under each category are not just fashionable late-twentieth-century academic fads. They profoundly affect the way in which social science has been, and continues to be, practised. More than this, the concepts of modernism and postmodernism have fundamental historical and social significance, coming as they did during a century marked by ideological conflict and its associated political manifestations. It is no coincidence that an upturn in postmodernist writings accompanied the end of the cold war. Towards the end of the period which resulted in the collapse of the great belief-systems that had characterised the century, many came to espouse theories which emphasised discontinuity, fragmentation, openness and uncertainty.

Pigeonholing postmodernism is difficult since many of its various strands go against the practice of reducing a body of thought to one central feature. Many postmodernists (for example Foucault 1972, 1980; Lyotard 1984; Jameson 1991) try to replace this sense of conviction with a plurality of ways of conceiving of reality. Yet if the term is to be defined at all, it is perhaps as a series of categories which relate to its dual, modernism (Klamer 1995). Modernism is usually defined as a movement in the sciences and arts that originated around the First World War. In the sciences it was represented by figures such as Bertrand Russell (1991) and Paul Samuelson (1947), who appealed to rationality and logic in an attempt to replace what they saw as religious obscurantism and the rigid distinction between feeling and reason.

Cullenberg *et al.* (2001) provides the most complete discussion of modernism and postmodernism in economics in recent years. The authors argue that modernism can be seen as revolving around a number of features, each one of which has been criticised or highlighted by one or more dimensions of postmodernism. The first of these features is essentialism, the belief that every object can be divided into two levels, one 'apparent' and one 'true'. The enquirer uses tried and tested techniques to discover what is 'really' going on. For example language is held by many modernists (and others) to be at best only an approximation of the actual nature of reality, whereas some postmodernists argue that reality is constituted in language. Postmodernists charge that there may be no independent essence to discover and that the 'objective' tools of the scientist may be arbitrary or constructed. Discovery, for postmodernists, is best achieved through a variety of methods, implying that the reliance on mathematical techniques by those in the Samuelsonian tradition might be well complemented by other procedures appropriate to the situation.

Not only are postmodernists critical of privileging specific tools, but also they dispute modernism's foundationalism, the view that there is one single basis to reality that exists irrespective of how it is talked about. Some postmodernists (Lyotard, op. cit.) propose instead that there are a number of different realities, and that they depend on the situation of the speaker. Many postmodernists suggest that power relations underlie knowledge production, a stance which suggests relativism – that it is impossible objectively to evaluate competing truth claims. Michel Foucault (1980) has shown that power relations define most human behaviour; he thus uses power not pejoratively to describe a hidden facet of scientific misconduct, but as an everyday feature of knowledge creation.

Modernism also stands accused of scientism, the elevation of scientific practice to a privileged position above other lines of enquiry. This is not to say that postmodernists are anti-science or that they aren't interested in science, but that science should lay itself bare to its own techniques and should listen to other ways of knowing that aren't currently considered scientific. The non-scientist strain of postmodernism is to some extent a product of the critiques of essentialism and foundationalism. It reinforces the idea that the model-building and formal techniques used by mainstream economics are not alone sufficient to achieve an economic science; other lines of attack might enhance our knowledge of various economic worlds. I will mention later the criticisms of scientism proposed by Friedrich Hayek.

Some postmodernists also query modernism's determinism. Determinism refers to the linking of causes with effects in a specified relation under the umbrella of theory. An argument is determinist if one element within the system is said to be prior to others, and that element acts on other elements in a predictable and uniform way such that explanation always consists of seeking recourse to the prior element. Cullenberg *et al.* suggest that:

> The attack on determinisms of all sorts has been among the main contributions of postmodern critique. Alternative, specifically postmodern interrogations have emphasised the randomness of causation and the effectivity of chance, the indeterminacy of events, the multiplicity of possible causes, the fluidity of the relationship between seeming causes and effects.
>
> (Cullenberg *et al.*, op. cit.: 31)

A final angle to postmodernism's critique disputes the belief that humans should be the bottom line of enquiry. This anti-humanism is again exemplified in Foucault, who suggests that the desire to achieve perfect knowledge of the human body underlies much modernist philo-sophical thinking. He argues that there can be no single and timeless definition of the acting human subject. Rather, human beings behave in a range of complex and uncertain social ways.

Various postmodernists can accurately be described as discussing these five 'isms' of modernism – essentialism, foundationalism, scien-tism, determinism and humanism – but postmodernists can neither be homogenised, nor do their threads of thought even constitute theo-ries that can be placed in opposition to the modernist camp, since this would be self-defeating. If postmodernism is taken to its extreme it pre-cludes the possibility of theorising at all because no single thinker has better grounds on which to substantiate her claims. Rather than con-struct an image of postmodernism in unified opposition to modernism it is better to describe it as a diverse range of thinking that exists across the sciences, arts and humanities, and which is expressed in several ways.

Some think of it as a critique, meaning that it doesn't just propose ways of thinking but advocates what Cullenberg *et al.* (op. cit.) call a 'non-modernism'. Modernism falsely represents choices as being of the form 'either/or', thus some postmodernists advocate immanent critique, which means transcending some of the undesirable aspects of mod-ernism without rejecting the tradition in its entirety – postmodernism is to some extent a supercharged form of late modernism.

Postmodernism can also be conceptualised as a style. This is par-ticularly important for the subject at hand, for a number of theorists believe not only that all knowledge hinges on whatever assumptions are brought to the enquiry, but that theorists themselves should recognise the assumptions on which they base their analyses. This 'self-reflexive' style means that authors declare their values and beliefs at the out-set, meaning that they do not claim privilege over the objects of their enquiry.

For Jean-François Lyotard postmodernity is more than just a way of thinking; it is a condition. Lyotard's 'collapse of grand narrative' (Lyotard, op. cit.) rejects the overarching thought systems of enlight-enment thinking that have promoted normative programmes for the improvement of society. He argues that knowledge is not progressive and that attempts to employ technology and science to master nature are not only misguided but dangerous. Lyotard does not believe that human creations are always benevolent, and he disputes the idea that society has an identifiable past and a progressive future. This variety of postmodern thinking is among the most radical since it implies that human intervention in social affairs is fruitless and can only lead to worse outcomes.

If Lyotard is correct to suggest that modernity will self-destruct and that its methods are pernicious, then his findings are relevant for economics since modernism forms the backbone of much mainstream theory. Operationalism, the guiding principle of Samuelson's 1947 *Foundations of Economic Analysis*, is in a sense the very definition of the essentialism and foundationalism described above. Operationalism is the idea, originating in physics, that a term or concept only has meaning if there are a set of operations that can answer it definitively. Samuelson's suggestion that a theory is only operational if it can be empirically tested (Hands 2001: 62) is a rewording of the definition of logical positivism: that statements are only true if they can be tested.[1] Reality is 'out there' to be discovered, and the task is to find the correct tools to describe it. Mainstream economics also follows Samuelson's belief that mathematical methods applied to economic phenomena can replace ill-conceived ideology and unscientific dogmas to achieve a increasingly accurate representation of the world.

Although economics and the economics methodology literature contain a number of instances or discussions of postmodernism (McCloskey 1985, 2001; Dow 1991; Hoksbergen 1994; Dow and Hillard 1995; Kanth 1999; Cullenberg *et al.*, op. cit.; Ruccio and Amariglio 2003), there are few references to the difference between modernity and modernism. The distinction is both historically and conceptually important, since modernity is considered by most to have begun with the enlightenment rather than like modernism, a century ago. According to the *Oxford Companion to Philosophy*, ' "Modernity" and "enlightenment" tend to be used interchangeably, whether by thinkers... who seek to sustain that project, or by those – the postmodernist company – who consider it a closed chapter in the history of ideas' (entry by Christopher Norris in Honderich (ed.) 1995: 583).

The European enlightenment (as opposed to the Scottish enlightenment) can be seen as having its origins in René Descartes's search for a basic knowledge that is self-evident to reason and impermeable to the potentially damaging effects of scepticism. Since Descartes found his senses unreliable, the only way he could be sure he was alive and thus avoid the infinite regress of scepticism without descending into dogmatism, was the capacity for thought: 'I think therefore I exist.'

In answer to the question 'What is enlightenment?' Kant answers: 'Enlightenment is man's emergence from his self-incurred immaturity. Immaturity is the inability to use one's own understanding without the guidance of another.' Individuals should use reason to free themselves from dogmas, a difficult but not impossible process. The enlightenment of the entire public is more practicable, but comes with a precondition: 'Freedom to make public use of one's *reason* in all matters.'

Of the social sciences, it is perhaps mainstream economics that exemplifies the interpretation of the enlightenment project of modernity as an unchanging and reliable conception of human reason that can be applied across all cultures and circumstances. The mainstream tradition is interested, like Kant, in the use of individual reason publicly manifested – but mainstream economists believe this public manifestation of individual reason occurs in the market. As a contemporary example of the way in which economics interprets modernity consider a passage from the textbook *Macroeconomics* by N. Gregory Mankiw, in Chapter 1, entitled: 'The Science of Macroeconomics':

> Macroeconomists are the scientists who try to explain the working of the economy as a whole. They collect data on incomes, prices, unemployment, and many other economic variables from different periods of time and from different countries. They then attempt to formulate general theories that help to explain those data
>
> To be sure, macroeconomics is a young and imperfect science. The macroeconomist's ability to predict the future course of economic events is no better than the meteorologist's ability to predict next month's weather. But, as you will see, we do know quite a lot about how the economy works.
>
> (Mankiw 1994: 4)

Mankiw includes a quote from John Stuart Mill at the beginning of the textbook:

> The same persons who cry down Logic will generally warn you against Political Economy. It is unfeeling, they will tell you. It recognises unpleasant facts. For my part, the most unfeeling thing I know of is the law of gravitation: it breaks the neck of the best and most amiable person without scruple, if he forgets for a single moment to give heed to it.
>
> (Mill, 1867, in Mankiw, op. cit.: preface)

These four sentences are hardly representative of Mill's thought in general, but they portray economics as a science which can predict essential features of a single reality using data collection and Logic with a capital

L. Disputing Logic is equivalent to denying gravity. The use of reason, in the sense of Descartes and Kant, is the principal tool in building the undisputable foundations of knowledge.

The distinction between modernism and modernity is helpful because if economics can be shown to be attached to the longer tradition of modernity, as well as being modernist, it makes it harder to dismiss post-modernism as a reaction to a mere century-long cyclical trend, but on the other hand it implies that modernity might not be overcome quite so readily as many postmodernists suppose. It also suggests that it is useful to include within any analysis the wider neoclassical tradition, not just the mid to late twentieth-century modernism of Samuelson and others.

Postmodernism has been shown to have revealed serious shortcomings in the modernist approach, namely its mistaken belief that the object of study can be easily separated from the mode of analysis; the problem that no single representation or mode of analysis can be applied everywhere; its scientism, foundationalism and determinism. However postmodernism by its very nature is short on solutions, and where solutions are suggested they are often less than satisfactory. If there is nothing 'essential' or 'foundational' in economic reality or realities, then what independent criterion do we use to discuss economics? As we shall see, realists provide better answers to these kind of problems than many postmodernists. If, according to the arguments of some postmodernists, economics is a form of rhetoric or conversation, then surely its practitioners must be at least capable of addressing the same actual physical reality, or economists will surely be talking at cross-purposes? As Hodgson points out, 'there is no room for a philosophy of science in which "anything goes"' (Hodgson 2009: 186). Whilst postmodernists have developed sophisticated ways of tackling the problem of determinism, notably the Freudian and Althusserian idea of 'overdetermination' advocated in Cullenberg *et al.*, there is a risk of allowing *too much* role for the 'randomness of causation and the effectivity of chance, the indeterminacy of events, the multiplicity of possible causes, the fluidity of the relationship between seeming causes and effects'. If postmodern alternatives are to be seen as a challenge to modernist economics, then they may need to develop more structured ways of describing reality, and ones that might be appealing to a range of economics practitioners. For the task of examining and comparing developing economies, some kind of structure is needed, one that moves beyond randomness, chance, indeterminacy and fluidity. Structure, categorisation or provisional closure is evident in most human interaction, and it does not imply an inevitable universalism or essentialism. Without it, conversation, still less active recommendations about how to change reality (which is what development economics involves) can be extremely difficult.

Finally, for the purposes of doing development economics, which is about real poverty in actual situations, it may be useful to talk in terms of more than just critique or style. The issue of style is important, and will be addressed in some detail later on, but poverty is about putting food in mouths; it is not in the eye of the beholder, and it cannot be magically eradicated using different language.

2.3 Open-systems approaches

A fruitful way of approaching the distinction between modernism and postmodernism, and of trying to move beyond it, is to use the concepts of open and closed systems of knowledge. Mainstream economics has a particular unspoken epistemology, which contributes to its scientism and universalism. Certain modernist approaches, as well as schools of thought originating in the tradition of modernity, advocate what amount to closed-system conceptions. Seeing knowledge as a closed system means it is possible to pinpoint all the variables of interest in explanation, to discover the laws which link these variables and to determine whether or not the laws are capable of full knowledge or contain random elements. No unknowable non-random influences can affect the system since all variables can be isolated *a priori* as either endogenous or exogenous. Closure is achieved using constant event regularities that are valid continuously and which in the natural sciences are discoverable by experimentation. In the social sciences event regularities may be constructed through logical inference and supported empirically.

An example of a closed system is the general equilibrium approach, which aims to show how demand and supply simultaneously interact in several markets to produce prices for all goods. Prices are a product solely of components within the system and the way they behave and interact is rendered predictable by a number of restrictive assumptions. The general equilibrium method imagines that two price-taking, optimising consumers with perfect foresight buy or sell two goods under perfect competition. Closed-system approaches do not require assumptions to be realistic, since the concern is to isolate what they see as spatio-temporally fixed causal mechanisms not to explain existing states of affairs. Prediction matters most, rather than explanation (Friedman 1953).

Open-system approaches, in contrast, neither see the isolation and knowledge of all relevant variables as being feasible, nor assume that the objects of knowledge are fixed across time and space. The causal mechanisms that under the closed system are posited as laws regulating the interactions between elements are, in an open system, open to change; indeed they are not laws in the same sense. This does not mean that knowledge is impossible, but that the enquirer must look for tendencies that may change.

Because tendencies, and events, change, theories are allowed to change over time, and knowledge is fallible in the Humean sense that humans cannot discover the true character of the world in its entirety (Dow 2002c: 139–40). The open-systems approach should not be characterised as indeterminate and postmodernist in its questioning of the possibility of unchanging laws; it does allow for the existence of a single reality, even if it is at times obscured and can exist at different levels – unlike in the closed-system approach.

Most methodological perspectives that strive to avoid the pitfalls of modernism and postmodernism are based on an open-systems ontology. They aim to identify alternative ways of conceptualising knowledge beyond the simple foundationalism of modernism and the relativism associated with postmodernism. However the open-systems approach is compatible, although not coincident, with some strands of postmodernism. An open-systems theorist would be unlikely to depict herself as a postmodernist but a postmodernist might well follow a broadly open-systems approach. Three approaches within economics that emphasise the openness of systems are the neo-Austrian school, the Keynesian philosophical tradition and critical realism. The latter two approaches are not mutually exclusive – indeed they overlap – but they have different goals even if they are both critical of mainstream economics. The neo-Austrian perspective on open systems differs from the others primarily because it is methodologically individualist and has perhaps been more readily assimilated into mainstream economics. It does, however, share selected characteristics with both of the other approaches.

2.3.1   The neo-Austrian approach

Neo-Austrian thinking is represented by the work of Friedrich Hayek (1944, 1945, 1966), Israel Kirzner and Murray Rothbard. The work is less mainstream than that of the founder of the Austrian school Karl Menger (1963), and it can be contrasted with Hayek's near-contemporaries

Eugen Böhm-Bawerk (1970), Ludwig von Mises (1962) and Joseph Schumpeter (1944).

Of the three open-systems approaches the neo-Austrians draw closest to postmodernist tactics because they emphasise microeconomics and proceed on the basis of case studies (Dow 2002c: 124). Many neo-Austrians might assent to Jean-François Lyotard's 'Collapse of Grand Narrative' in their advocacy of a particularist approach. Neo-Austrian thought is perhaps the methodological opposite of Keynes's conception of a general theory since it disputes the notion that a single conception can approximate useful knowledge of an economic system. As we shall see, in contrast to critical realism or Keynes the neo-Austrians do not believe that the primary characteristic of knowledge is that it is socially generated.

Neo-Austrians think that systems are open because of the Hayekian belief that knowledge is inherently specific to the individual; no planner – even with the sophistication of Oscar Lange's supercomputer (Lange *et al.* 1938) – could ever know what every particular consumer knows. Because outsiders cannot access all personal knowledge, it is impossible to assign immutable tastes to a fixed theoretical consumer. The individualistic and shifting character of knowledge make it unpragmatic and undesirable to try to assign event regularities and laws to variables within a closed system.

From early on Hayek showed a desire to move beyond closed systems. In *Monetary Theory and the Trade Cycle* he identified money as the reason the market-clearing mechanism didn't work in the trade cycle. 'Money being a commodity which, unlike all others, is incapable of finally satisfying demand, its introduction does away with the rigid interdependence and self-sufficiency of the "closed" system of equilibrium, and makes possible movements which would have been excluded from the latter' (Hayek 1966: 44). The inclusion of a capital goods sector in his theory of the trade cycle meant that he could accommodate the way in which money affected other aggregates.

Chick and Dow (2001) point out that neo-Austrians allow for definitions of terms to vary in practice. Money, for example, cannot be encompassed by a closed, equilibrium approach because various agents think of it differently. It can be defined in general as those assets which are perfectly liquid, but specifically agents may think of various bank accounts as having different levels of liquidity and thus to try to identify monetary aggregates is impossible (ibid.: 710). Hayek is suspicious of statistical aggregates in general, believing them inevitably to agglomerate incompatible scraps of subjective information.

Hayek's thought changed in later years when he became more interested in methodological issues. In particular he showed antipathy towards what he called scientism, which consisted of amongst other failings historicism, collectivism and objectivism. Historicism was undesirable because it looked for unfaltering laws that govern human behaviour. He argued against collectivism for its attempt to analyse aggregates – like society or the economy – beyond the level of the individual. Objectivism meant looking at science as the examination of an observable, objective reality, and is mistaken because people differ in their subjective views. Scientism is thus inextricable from closed-systems methodology. However Hayek did believe economics to be a science, even if it studies complex phenomena and is limited in its ability to produce testable forecasts (Davis *et al.* 1998: 224).

His 1945 paper 'The Use of Knowledge in Society' buttresses the critique of scientism by arguing that:

> *If* we possess all the relevant information, *if* we start out from a given system of preferences and *if* we command complete knowledge of available means, the problem which remains is purely one of logic... The conditions which the solution of this optimum problem must satisfy have been fully worked out and can be stated best in mathematical form

> This, however, is emphatically *not* the economic problem which society faces. And the economic calculus which we have developed to solve this logical problem, though an important step toward the solution of the economic problem of society, does not yet provide an answer to it.

> (Hayek 1945: 519)[2]

The economic problem, in Hayek's view, is how to co-ordinate and use economic knowledge, which no single person or group can uncover in its entirety. State planning is doomed to failure because it cannot achieve full knowledge of all the interactions in an economy, and partial planning is condemned as a half-way house. Only price signals realised in competition can synchronize the innumerable fragments of non-scientific knowledge which exist in time and space. In response to a cutback in supply of a good even the 'man on the spot' need not know *why* prices rise; all that is important is that he reacts by reducing his consumption.

The neo-Austrians oppose a view of economics as the pure classical logic of choice, an approach encouraged by the Austrian-influenced Lionel Robbins. Brian Loasby shows that the neo-Austrians seek to examine what happens outside equilibrium, believing this approach to be more fruitful and realistic, rather than redefining rational behaviour, as neoclassical economists attempted to, in order to be able to represent the economy as a system of equations. Loasby attributes the following view to modern Austrians: '…the pursuit of rigour in rational choice theory has entailed ever tighter specification of the choice situation, with the result that what began as spontaneous human action emerges as fully programmed behaviour in which all problems of knowledge are expunged' (Loasby, cited in Mair and Miller 1991: 55).

2.3.2   The Keynesian approach

Keynes's economics involved a specific and overt methodological approach, developed prior to and during the writing of his most important work, the *General Theory of Employment, Interest and Money*. Keynes is not one of those economists who think that methodology is a waste of time or best left to secondary academic discussions. He purposefully developed a new way of thinking *about* economics, which is more than simply introducing a new set of ideas. In the final, oft-repeated sentence of the preface to the *General Theory* he says that: 'The difficulty lies, not in the new ideas, but in escaping from the old ones, which ramify, for those brought up as most of us have been, into every corner of our minds' (Keynes 1936: xii). A new way of thinking about economics was born – a methodological approach – and one which even Keynes himself had difficulty in grasping.

Keynes's methodological approach is bound up with his economics. It would be difficult to think in a complete manner about Keynes's work without acknowledging his methodology. In developing his vision of the acting economic subject Keynes develops new notions of money and uncertainty. Keynes argues that liquidity preference is partly a result of precautionary demand, an inherent conservatism amid uncertainty about the future direction of prices: '…our desire to hold money as a store of wealth is a barometer of the degree of our distrust of our own calculations and conventions concerning the future' (Keynes 1973: 116). Even though money may not be an interest-bearing asset, unspoken wishes act as a kind of defence mechanism against future fluctuations (the other two reasons for liquidity preference are the speculative and transactions demand for money).

Keynes's open-systems approach develops a specific approach to uncertainty. In the *Treatise on Probability* (1921) and elsewhere, Keynes starts from the view that there are certain kinds of human knowledge that cannot be known in advance. His targets are the utilitarian philosophers who provided a basis for classical economics. Keynes challenges the utilitarian tenet that human happiness is the presence of pleasures and absence of pain, and that in our moral behaviour we aim at the maximisation of utility as expressed according to the neoclassical comparison of preferences. As I will show in Chapter 4, the Polish economist Michal Kalecki, often described as 'Post-Keynesian',[3] similarly rejected the notion of utility, a stance which resulted from his 'commitment to "open-system thinking" [which] prevented him from formulating a comprehensive, fully-integrated and therefore closed system' (King 2002: 55). Kalecki's thoughts, as we shall see, are particularly relevant for the discussion at hand because his ideas about development are among the most well-formed of the post-Keynesians and open-systems theorists.

The prerequisite of the utilitarian approach is that we must be able to calculate the consequences of our actions with certainty. But Keynes believes this to be unlikely because much of the time we do not know what will happen in the future. The higher the level of uncertainty, the more agents prefer to hold money and the higher the interest rate. Thus his philosophical approach, which regards uncertainty as of central importance, is integral to his economics.

> The hypothesis of a calculable future leads to a wrong interpretation of the principles of behaviour which the need for action compels us to adopt, and to an underestimation of the concealed factors of utter doubt, precariousness, hope and fear. The result has been a mistaken theory of the rate of interest.
>
> (Keynes 1937: 222)

Keynes distinguishes this type of unquantifiable risk – when the outcome of actions cannot be known – from quantifiable risk when it is possible to make calculations about the future based on probability distributions. Echoing Marshall's misgivings about the role of maths, he makes it clear that discussions of the unquantifiable type of risk cannot be formalised whereas quantifiable risk can. Neoclassical economics is merely a special case, representing a situation where risk can be quantified. Keynes had for the first time identified more than one kind of economics, breaking the apparently unified stranglehold of scientism that had prevailed since Mill.

> It is a great fault of symbolic pseudo-mathematical methods of for-malising a system of economic analysis ... that they expressly assume strict independence between the factors involved and lose all their cogency and authority if this hypothesis is disallowed; whereas, in ordinary discourse, where we are not blindly manipulating but know all the time what we are doing and what the words mean, we can keep 'at the back of our heads' the necessary reserves and qualifica-tions and the adjustments which we shall have to make later on, in a way in which we cannot keep complicated partial differentials 'at the back' of several pages of algebra which assume that they all vanish.
>
> (Keynes 1936: 297–8)

Keynes was notoriously critical of what he saw as the inappropriate use of maths and statistics. Keynes described the first serious econometric analysis of the determinants of investment, by the Nobel prizewinner Jan Tinbergen, as 'charlatanism' and a 'mess of unintelligible figurings' (Keynes, in King 2002: 32) which produced 'false precision' (ibid.: 33). Keynes explicitly drew his dubiousness about econometrics from his own methodological approach, which saw economics as 'essentially a moral science and not a natural science. That is to say, it employs intro-spection and judgements of value' (ibid.: 33). Keynes saw economic science as riven with subjectivity and value-judgements, in opposi-tion to the physics-influenced view of economics propagated by Mill, Walras and others. Not everything could be captured using formalistic techniques, and a strong role remained for conventional rhetoric and argument.

Following the distinction between quantifiable and unquantifiable risk Keynes employed the concept of 'human' or 'ordinary' logic which uses intuition, distinct from classical logic which requires a rigid defini-tion of sets (Dow 2002c: 150–1). Rationality is a propensity anchored in the relation between acting human subjects rather than fixed for all time and derived from outside human experience. People do not make deci-sions based on a cold calculation of future likelihoods using universally available knowledge; their behaviour depends on individual peculiar-ities and social conventions. So Keynes's conception of open systems requires non-market ingredients.

As the post-Keynesians Chick and Dow (2001) point out, a second dimension of Keynes's open-systems methodology is that it has a temporal causal structure. Money, liquidity preference and long-term expectations cause, and therefore happen before, investment demand. This then inputs into aggregate demand. Short-term expectations, together with wages and other costs create output, while demand afterwards creates prices and profits, whereupon expectations are revised. Because it is not possible to be sure how all the elements in the system interact, an equilibrium occurs which reveals the nature of the interaction between all the components in the system. 'This equilibrium is a kind of temporary closure, which will break down as time goes on' (ibid.: 713).

Keynes's is a *general* theory because it is supposed to be a broad explanation of the nature of general economic activity, many components of which interact over time in a specified way and rely on each other to produce useful explanation. Extracting one feature of the *General Theory* and using it (for example in developing a mathematical formula) without accepting other dependent features would interrupt the temporal idea of the system. Keynes's General Theory is also general in that it covers unquantifiable risk (uncertainty) as well as quantifiable risk.

Where in the natural sciences it is possible to close the system completely by performing an experiment, Chick and Dow (2005) argue that social science is unable to close the system in a similar manner since its subject matter is always changing, making experimentation unreliable. Chick and Dow suggest that the use of temporary closure allows analysis to proceed even within an open system. Most discussion in the arts, humanities and sciences involves boundaries, which are a form of provisional closure. In economics Chick and Dow (op. cit.: 376) point to the example of *ceteris paribus*, a device which permits the temporary suspension of reality in order to help develop models. Importantly, the suspension of reality is only temporary, and subsequently such temporary devices can be lifted. In sum, for Chick and Dow, temporary, partial closure is allowed under Keynes's method, even if the tools used are human logic rather than classical logic, and inference rather than laboratory experimentation. This may lead to a messier picture of reality, but it is, in this interpretation of Keynes, more realistic.

2.3.3 Critical realism

Critical realism originates in the philosophical work of Roy Bhaskar (1978) and has been applied to economics by Tony Lawson amongst others.[4] Both critical realism and Keynes see knowledge and human behaviour as products of social relations. Like Keynes and the neo-Austrians, critical realists are sceptical about the use of formal methods, even if for different reasons. Bruce Caldwell (2009) draws parallels between critical realism and the work of Hayek. Lawson and Hayek identify a number of the same features of social reality as important: rule-following; the intentionality of social action; the existence of tacit knowledge; forward-planning; and the structure/agency divide (Caldwell, op. cit.: 13). All three open-systems approaches are a reaction to orthodox attempts to ascertain fixed laws and event regularities. It is worth pointing out, however, that unlike Chick and Dow (2001), Lawson argues that the property of closure defines closed systems, and that any system which involves closure, even if provisional, must by definition be a closed system. In his advocacy of a suitable method for social science, Lawson does not allow for even temporary closure.

Fullbrook (op. cit.) suggests that Lawson's work revolves around two main themes:

1. that success in science depends on finding and using methods, including modes of reasoning, appropriate to the nature of the phenomena being studied, and

2. that there are important differences between the nature of the objects of study of natural sciences and those of social science.

(Fullbrook 2009: 1)

According to Fullbrook and others, mainstream economics has borrowed the tools of nineteenth-century physics and insists on using these tools irrespective of whether or not they are appropriate to social reality. Lawson believes that the tools are inappropriate. Throughout his work Lawson insists that a proper approach for economics would be to look at ontology, or the nature of reality. The nature of reality should determine the tools used to study it, rather than the other way round, where preselected tools are employed to examine the world irrespective of what the world is like.

In his first book on critical realism, *Economics and Reality* (1997), Lawson highlights what he sees as a number of inconsistencies in mainstream economics (Lawson 1997a: 4–14).[5] Economists often do not practice the method they preach. For instance while econometricians claim to follow the classical model of inference, in reality, collectively, they run thousands of regressions to estimate their models. If events in the world really were as generalisable as econometricians imagine, it would not be necessary to complement one or a number of regressions with thousands more.

In addition to this inconsistency at the level of method, Lawson identifies a discrepancy on the plane of social theory. Economics claims it is 'choice theory', but by using a closed approach in modelling it really disallows choice by denying the possibility that individuals could have acted otherwise. Humans are reduced to the components of a machine in which there is no room for unpredictable action.

Lawson also highlights a third inconsistency. While economists pretend that they do not need to worry about methodology and instead should just get on with the job, in practice they do engage in philosophical arguments and they do use a specific methodology without acknowledging it. 'In summary, contemporary economics is not in a fit state. Most obviously, it fares poorly on its own terms; it neither provides particularly accurate forecasts of events nor illuminates the world in which we live. But of equal significance, the whole project is riddled with confusion and incoherence...' (ibid.: 14).

Removing the confusion and incoherence bred of deductivist closed-system economics is among Lawson's principal aims. Deductivism is not the same as deduction, a closely related but distinct type of argument whereby a set conclusion must follow from a given set of premises. Formally if Q is deducible from a set of premises $P_1, P_2, \ldots, P_n$ then $P_n \supset Q$ is deducible from $P_1, P_2, \ldots, P_n$, and $n = 1, P_1 \supset Q$ is a theorem. Deductivism adds to deduction the idea that general laws can be assessed by examining specific instances.

Lawson contests the proposition that the laws specified within a theorem are event regularities which always occur as unchanging states of affairs or probabilities in the form of 'whenever event x then event y'. This type of model is labelled 'deductivist-nomological' (nomos is the Greek for Law).[6] Lawson instead proposes the term 'demi-regularities' or 'demi-regs' to denote the periodic but not quite universal actualisation of a tendency or mechanism over time and space.

In contrast to the empirical realist tradition often associated with Hume,[7] Bhaskar and Lawson define realism as acknowledging the causal tendencies, mechanisms and powers that underlie the everyday apparent world. This is the first way in which transcendental realism differs from empirical realism. Second, it contends that three different levels of reality exist – the empirical, the actual and the real – which are out of phase with each other. No tendency, mechanism or power corresponds directly with each empirical event or sequence of events, rather 'non-isomorphism' means that events are co-determined by several influences. Objects can have powers even if these powers aren't used and tendencies can be seen as potentialities that aren't always realised in a specific outcome (Lawson 1997a: 23). For example gravity is a tendency that exists irrespective of whether or not I lose my footing.

Because systems are open and there are no constant event regularities, it is not possible to dig out causal laws using empirical methods. Instead critical realism proposes the use of retroduction, which means moving from the phenomenal level to a less superficial causal explanation:

> The central mode of inference is neither deduction nor induction. Rather it is retroduction. The aim is not to cover a phenomenon under a generalisation...but to identify a factor responsible for it, that helped produce, or at least facilitated, it. The goal is to posit a mechanism...which, if it existed and acted in the postulated manner, could account for the phenomenon singled out for explanation.
>
> (ibid.: 212)

Retroduction draws on existing, fallible knowledge of causal mechanisms to posit specific mechanisms in particular cases.

Relating to insights from the science studies and anthropological literature which will be discussed in the next chapter, knowledge is a produced means of production, meaning that it is constructed in social milieux and is fallible because circumstances change. 'Knowledge is a social product, actively produced by means of antecedent social products' (ibid.: 25). Rooting economic behaviour in society enables Lawson to deal with the second inconsistency in mainstream economics mentioned above, namely the way it deals with social theory.

Lawson proposes a social ontology that sees intentional human activity as the meeting point of structure and agency. Following Keynes, Lawson argues that tacit consciousness is a key motivator of economic behaviour. The later book, *Reorienting Economics* (2003), reinforces arguments for the centrality of ontology in economics. Neither the social nor the individual is more important for explaining rational motivation; instead individual behaviour produces social relationships and structures, but social relations also create and condition the actions of individual agents. Similarly to Anthony Giddens, whose later work (Giddens 1990, 1994a, 1994b) is discussed in the next chapter, rationality and logic are not abstract, unchanging phenomena implanted in people's brains, but constitute dynamic and ever-changing tools situated in specific social circumstances.

> The complex structures of the world are not revealed just by our sensing them directly. Nor is knowledge created out of nothing. Rather we start out, at any point in time, with a stock of knowledge, hunches, data, anomalies, suspicions, guesses, interests, etc., and through interacting with the world we come to transform our understandings. Knowledge, then, is found to be a produced means of production of further knowledge.
>
> (Lawson 2003: 92)

The social ontology of critical realism can be seen as presupposing a form of reflexivity:

> ...human beings not only initiate change in purposeful ways but also monitor and control performances (and indeed monitor the monitoring of performances; we are aware of our own state of awareness during the course of action)... Now it is clear that the social, including economic activity that each agent reflexively monitors is an ongoing flow, a continuous stream.
>
> (Lawson 1997a: 177)

> Through confronting 'objects' of study we learn not only about them but simultaneously about ourselves, including, in particular, the errors of our current thinking (as well, no doubt, as something of our social-cultural situations, values, and so forth).
>
> (Lawson 2003: 101)

We are aware of our awareness, and check it constantly rather than discretely. In a sense simply by admitting the distinction between epistemology and ontology (i.e. by highlighting the 'epistemic fallacy' that rephrases statements about being to statements about knowledge of being) a notion of reflexivity is permitted, in the sense of a two-way interplay between action and thinking about action. If economics were to make explicit its conception of ontology rather than trying to ignore the issue, it would be likely to re-evaluate its epistemology. Maintaining a distinction between epistemology and ontology might

require a periodic reappraisal of the interaction between what economics thinks about the world and what it believes about the nature
of reality. The question of agency and freedom, often overlooked by
much contemporary mainstream economic theory, becomes important.
If humans just acted mindlessly without continuously redefining the
way in which they acted, bearing in mind that a certain epistemology had meanwhile become part of what they did, then humans would
conform to reified thought patterns rather than continuously and self-
consciously created modes of thinking. Relative unfreedom is therefore
a possibility if the way knowledge is conceptualised is static rather than
dynamic.

Seeing knowledge as a social product, or as being a process, does not
mean a kind of truth relativism where it is impossible objectively to evaluate one piece of knowledge against another. One reason transcendental
realism does not dissolve into relativism relates to Karl Mannheim's
defence of his sociology of knowledge in his *Ideology and Utopia*, namely
that it involves a kind of relationism (Mannheim 1936). Relationism is
the idea that whilst knowledge is social, epistemology, or the way that
knowledge is understood, can advance, and hence we move towards
objectivity but never quite get there. Another of Lawson and Bhaskar's
defences against the charge of relativism, of course, is that a realist approach allows for the existence of only one reality, even if it is
multi-layered and may often be obscured.

Mannheim offers the earliest discussion of reflexivity and provides
some of the backdrop to the science studies research. *Ideology and Utopia*
tries, rather dubiously, to overcome the problem of relativism by suggesting that social enquirers need not be symmetric with the objects of
their enquiry, and instead identifies a separate intelligentsia which by
virtue of its standing outside normal class relations can perform objective analysis. This solution is arbitrary, and requires explanation as to
why the intelligentsia should not be subject to the normal rules. Critical realism would overcome the problem of arbitrariness by performing
self-critique: it realises that science itself is socially generated and thus
must be self-aware and constantly ready to change.

Critical realists have tackled the problems of essentialism, universalism and determinism encountered by modernism, and the critical realist
project attempts to improve upon postmodern responses to these difficulties. The challenge of essentialism – the mistaken identification of
'real' and 'apparent' domains which can be uncovered using particular
tools – is tackled by allowing for the possibility that theory and reality
can be inter-related in the sense that theory or language can influence

the way that reality is conceptualised (Fullbrook 2009: 281–3). Lawson takes on board the postmodern argument that the tools used to examine particular instances of social or economic reality affect the way in which that reality is construed. But he does not go to the extreme of Ruccio, who argues that: 'Economists literally see and analyze different economies, according to the discourses (or paradigms or theoretical frameworks) they use' (ibid.: 281). According to Lawson our conception of reality can be socially constructed, but not reality itself, of which there is only one. Our visions of reality may differ, and in this sense there is no 'essential' view of reality, but reality is singular. Thus critical realism can be seen to accommodate the valid postmodern assertion that visions of reality are affected by the way in which they are addressed, whilst avoiding the associated potential relativism: if reality itself is all in the eye of the beholder, then what independent criterion or criteria do we use to discuss it?

Critical realism also tackles the question of determinism. Rather than borrowing from nineteenth-century physics the notion that one element within a system is prior to others, and that element acts on other elements in a predictable and uniform way such that explanation always consists of seeking recourse to the prior element, critical realism, as shown above, uses the term 'demi-regs' under the banner of transcendental realism.

Because of its general openness towards pluralism and its self-positioning as 'underlabourer' for other heterodox approaches, Lawson believes that critical realism avoids universalism, despite the arguments of some feminist economists (van Staveren 2009) that he has a universal view of human nature. According to Lawson:

> There is nothing essential to scientific or ontological realism that supposes or requires that objects of knowledge are naturalistic or other than transient, that knowledge obtained is other than fallible, partial and itself transient, or that scientists or researchers are other than positioned, biased, interested, and practically, culturally, and socially conditioned.
>
> (Lawson 2003: 220)

As will be seen later, such an approach is useful in discussing the methodology of development economics because it helps avoid universalising standard economic prescriptions.

Certain authors, however (see Fullbrook 2009) have identified further inconsistencies in the critical realist project. For the purposes of the project at hand, it is worth highlighting here one of the critiques of Lawson's stance on practical research. Few authors have yet tried to perform critical realist-type economic research in developing countries, although a few have attempted to put Lawson and Bhaskar's approach into practice in developed countries. This is surely a shortcoming in the critical realist project. A perspective which suggests that there is one domain of reality, and which requires realistic assumptions rather than irrealist mathematical models, should surely show what sort of methods might be selected in order to produce practical research. Arguing that theory should fit more closely with conditions encountered in the real world requires a demonstration of *how* this should occur – and in all situations, particularly those parts of the world that might benefit from improved economic tools. Downward and Mearman (2009), whilst generally supportive of the critical realist project, suggest that Lawson's *Reorienting Economics* 'still leaves significant lacunae in its implications for what economists... are to do in their concrete research' (Downward and Mearman 2009: 139). The authors propose the use of 'triangulation', using as a metaphor the practice in navigation whereby a line is drawn from three geographical points in order to pinpoint a location. The use of multiple methods in no *a priori* order can help to cross-check results, hopefully making overall findings more accurate. Downward and Mearman argue that triangulation is consistent with retroduction, and indeed is an integral part of it. Lawson replies, in the same volume, by suggesting that those in social science who advocate the use of triangulation seem to have deviated from its original usage, and that he sees little reason to replace the term dialectic with triangulation. Ultimately Lawson feels that his proposal for critical realism to act as an 'underlabourer' for the social sciences places no onus on him to outline ways in which his ideas might be put into practice, and that critical realism should clear the path for other approaches to build a more useful economics. Heterodox approaches in general follow a division of labour under which each follows a roughly complementary line of enquiry, leaving critical realism to do the philosophical work.

However the point remains that a theoretical approach like Lawson's, which advocates plausibility of assumptions and which suggests that methods should follow ontology rather than the other way round, should surely promote practical research, even if there is no obligation on Lawson to do it himself. Marx asserts in the *Theses on Feuerbach* that:

> The question whether objective truth belongs to human thinking is not a question of theory, but is a *practical* question. Man must prove the truth, that is, the reality and power, the this-sidedness of his thinking in practice. The dispute over the reality or non-reality of thinking which is isolated from practice is a purely *scholastic* question.
>
> (Tucker 1972: 144)

For an approach which apparently bases itself partly on the Marx of the *Theses*, critical realism involves a surprising amount of theory and not much practice. Not all heterodox approaches see critical realism as their underlabourer, and still fewer mainstream economists know anything about critical realism. As shown earlier, alternatives to critical realism exist, and 'Lawson's moves are not the only ones available to us' (Ruccio 2009: 267). Other realist approaches have a practical bent – indeed realism may *require* practical research. As I show in Chapter 4, Pierre Bourdieu argues that realism is best served by the close involvement of the social researcher in the lives of the research subject, and Bourdieu himself conducts such research. Self-analysis can be an alternative means of overcoming the difficulties associated with essentialism and foundationalism. Case studies can also be a useful way of testing theoretical ideas, which is why in Chapters 6 and 7 I attempt to put into practice the taxonomy developed in Chapter 5.

Pointing out the need for practical grounding is by no means a damning criticism of the critical realist project, since there are examples of critical realist methods being used in practical analysis outside economics.[8] Yet further practical research in economics using some of the ideas of critical realism might help the project become more internally consistent, gain more widespread acceptance, and therefore achieve its aims, which are partly to modify the practice of contemporary economics. If not, there is a danger of Lawson leading his followers off into the wilderness and separating them off from the rest of economic enquiry, however flawed it may be. Lawson might reply that it is mainstream economists who refuse to talk to him, rather than the other way round. Yet stalemate is no excuse for refusing to make the first move. Dialectic means conversation; and perhaps the worst fate for the critical realist project would be for the mainstream to continue to ignore it.

2.4 Conclusion

The dilemma between postmodernism and modernism is crucial for contemporary economics. Should we continue with a discipline that believes its object of analysis is a closed system containing atomised individuals that act in probabilistic or predetermined ways? Or should we 'salute Nietzsche and all go our independent ways' (Giddens 1994a: 252), abandoning hope of useful science?

Neither. While postmodernism rightly emphasises the unknowable and reasserts the importance of the social sphere, modernism is a valued defender of science and a safeguard against relativism. This does not mean cultivating economic modernism's ambitions towards omnipotence, nor does it lead to the 'philosophy of flower power', as some have labelled postmodernism. Rather, better science means recognising the grey areas of social analysis; accepting our inherent inability to achieve universal knowledge; and understanding that we are the creators of the disciplines through which we understand the world. It also requires matching techniques to reality, rather than borrowing tools from the natural sciences and hoping that they will work in the economic domain.

If any social science is the progeny of the enlightenment, it is economics. Yet it is far from clear that the fathers of enlightenment thinking ever believed that pure reason would tighten our grip on the world. In the *Critique of Pure Reason* Kant adds an important caveat to his definition of enlightenment: 'Dogmatism is the dogmatic procedure of reason, without previous criticism of its own powers.'[9] In a sense reason is all the more potent if it recognises its limits. No science can stand still: it must constantly re-evaluate its tools, re-assess its own project and situate itself inside the world it purports to be discovering.

Most social sciences have acknowledged the internal contradictions of the enlightenment; that some attempts to control human life actually lead to greater uncertainty. Understanding that the institutions and concepts of modernity are biting back after originally being designed as tools for increased control requires that we improve and redesign these tools and institutions. Realising that previous ways of thinking no longer produce predictable outcomes places emphasis on human agency.

Lawson points out that: '...knowledge that proved to be revelatory when it was obtained, eventually takes on the appearance of the banal or of common sense' (Lawson 1997a: 223). It is not the revelatory knowledge that is at fault, it is an inflexible interpretation of it.

Avoiding banality means seeing modernity as dynamic and infused with reflexivity. If economics is a microscope through which we examine the economy, the magnification is no longer strong enough, the lens clouded and the slides dusty. We need to take our eye from the viewfinder, examine the wider picture and bring in new optics. As Skidelsky says of Keynes: 'He wholly endorsed Marshall's view of economics as "not a body of concrete truth, but an engine for the discovery of concrete truth" ' (Skidelsky 2003: 464).

The world is not just a series of snooker balls rebounding in probabilistic or predictable causal ways; some of it is unknowable. We employ different logics to discover it, from classical logic to Keynesian 'ordinary' thinking. Even the path of real snooker balls is subject to a chaos of physical influences. In the social sphere, various kinds of relations form an integral part of modernity, perhaps more so than in any other period of human history. If logic is not to suffer postmodern relegation to just another way of thinking, and if it is to lead to a more useful understanding of the world, economic enquiries must declare their allegiances, state their goals and examine their own projects.

Open-systems approaches – from the neo-Austrians through to Keynes and critical realism – see the object of enquiry of economics as ever-changing and open to unpredictability. Closed-system approaches resort either to the belief that individuals can act freely without outside influence, or to determinism – and result in the complete subsumption of individual autonomy by external circumstances. Their predominantly mathematical persuasions strip their subject matter of plausibility. It is not mathematical methods that are to blame, but the blanket application of formalism irrespective of context. As Keynes points out, some areas of thinking are incapable of calculation, and indeed achieving a realistic picture of uncertainty builds understanding.

It was suggested in this chapter that the category of open systems can be a more fruitful way of dealing with the problems of modernism than is postmodernism – although postmodernists may adopt an open-systems approach, and many of the recognitions of postmodernists remain valuable in assessing modernism. For this reason I continue to use the category of postmodernism in forthcoming chapters. The open-systems approach itself can be seen to some extent as a dialectical resolution of the distinction between modernism and postmodernism in that it adopts and builds upon postmodern ideas. It cannot, however, be considered as strictly 'superior' to postmodernism because it has different goals. Amongst open-systems approaches critical realism has proven among the most successful, especially in developing a workable ontology. Yet despite its realism, it has – intentionally – made few recommendations on practical research and may be difficult to apply. The next chapter goes further, looking at how the concept of reflexivity aims at developing an approach which goes beyond modernism and postmodernism; remains compatible with the open-systems tradition; and which has specific applicability to development economics.

3
Theories of Reflexivity

3.1 Introduction

It is not just open-systems approaches that have attempted to move beyond the methodological divide between modernism and postmodernism. Several theories of reflexivity are explicitly directed at transcending the divide, both on the philosophical and the practical levels. Indeed most theorists of reflexivity argue that philosophy and practice are, or should be, closely connected. This idea echoes the critical realist social ontology and the idea of retroduction, as well as the more socio-economic strands of post-Keynesianism.

Philosophers have grappled with word games like the liar's paradox (cited in the 'Introduction') for millennia, and will probably continue to do so. Some commentators have even dismissed the idea of reflexivity in a flippant manner – for instance Krugman mentions, 'the general principle of "reflexivity", which I take to mean that human perceptions both affect events and are themselves affected by them. Gosh, I never thought of that!' (Krugman 1998).

The term is more interesting than just the idea that human perceptions both affect events and are themselves affected by them. It has been developed in a number of complex ways during the last century of social science, and this chapter aims to trace the origins of the term in anthropology, the sociology of knowledge, social theory and economic methodology. The discussion is not exhaustive and excludes several treatments of reflexivity.[1] An attempt is made to assess whether the different manifestations of the term in recent social theory have features in common which may have relevance to current thinking in the methodology of economics.

First is a discussion of the Marxist origins of the term and Mannheim's development of the sociology of knowledge. Some of the anthropological literature on methodology draws heavily on Mannheim (1936) and Marx (1974; Tucker 1972). Second, Pierre Bourdieu's (1972) and Bourdieu and Wacquant's (1992) use of reflexivity is outlined at some length. Bourdieu has the advantage of having conducted anthropological research in developing countries (activity which has relevance for development economics) using what he considered to be reflexive methods. He has also commented on contemporary economic methodology. Third is a discussion of the quite different use of the term reflexivity in economic methodology, which itself uses the sociology of knowledge literature. Finally the idea of reflexive modernisation is introduced. Whilst its proponents Anthony Giddens (1990), Beck, Giddens and Lash (1994) are doing social theory in its grandest sense, the concept has methodological implications for economics.

3.2   Reflexivity and anthropology

In anthropology the concept of reflexivity can be traced to Marx's view in the *German Ideology* that economic class is a determinant of ideology. 'The ideas of the ruling class are in every epoch the ruling ideas, i.e. the class which is the ruling *material* force of society, is at the same time its ruling *intellectual* force' (Marx 1974: 64). Whilst this is Marx at his more determinist – other formulations of the ideology thesis are more subtle[2] – Marxist thinking generally implies that certain forms of accepted knowledge tend to support prevailing relations of production. For example economic inequality, which is in the material interests of the dominant class, might be portrayed as a universal good because it creates economic incentives, but to lower-income groups it simply manifests a poorer standard of living and is to be overcome. Thus knowledge does not pre-date human interaction, as a foundationalist might suggest, but is contingent on immediate social and economic relations.

Under Marx's version of materialism the relation between the subject and the object is dialectical in that the active subject transforms the passive object, producing knowledge in an active procedure. Knowledge is not a fixed substance (it is clear where critical realists draw their social ontology) but a process. To repeat a quote from the previous chapter, Marx suggests in the *Theses on Feuerbach* that: 'The question whether objective truth belongs to human thinking is not a question of theory, but is a *practical* question' (Tucker 1972: 144). Philosophers (including economists) who try to theorise in a vacuum, disconnected from the material conditions of society, are unlikely to produce results that have full practical relevance to everyday human existence. Whilst all mainstream economics cannot be dismissed as mere false consciousness (although some authors, such as Guerrien (2009), argue that economics is strongly ideological), and the idea of false consciousness itself is only one interpretation of the Marxian ideology thesis, Marxist thinking about ideology lends the insight that economic thinking is not hewn from granite, but must be seen against its (changing) historical and social backdrop.

Mannheim considered his sociology of knowledge to be a development of the Marxist method, although he is less concerned than Marx with economic relations and instead prefers to examine the social production of knowledge. In order to ground theory in the world of the practical, to anchor philosophy in the world of the everyday events of humans, Mannheim concurs with the Marxian notion that it is necessary to envisage knowledge as a product of specific circumstances. 'The principal thesis of the sociology of knowledge is that there are modes of thought which cannot be adequately understood as long as their social origins are obscured' (Mannheim 1936: 2). For Mannheim (as for Marx) there is no Hegelian 'Geist' which eclipses the individual, and nor is it accurate to see individuals as spontaneously producing knowledge in isolation. Instead, knowledge must be examined in the context of group existence.

Mannheim describes the central purpose of his project as the simultaneous examination of the subject as well as the object. He hopes to bring to the surface all the 'values and collective-unconscious' at work in any examination of the object, believing that it is necessary to be aware of the role of interests in order to achieve a 'new type of objectivity'. In his critique of past ways of thinking about theory Mannheim engaged in a project contemporary with that of Max Horkheimer, who in his essay 'Traditional and Critical Theory', published the following year (1937), laid out the foundations of the Frankfurt School belief that a theory which is critical must be self-reflective, capable of emancipation and aware of the social character of theory. Horkheimer concurred with the notion that 'theory' is not a passive, scholarly activity performed in the academy; it should be directed at changing our collective conditions of existence. This cannot occur unless its social embededness is understood: '... the insistence that thinking is a fixed vocation, a self-enclosed realm within society as a whole, betrays the very essence of thought' (Horkheimer 1937: 243).

Mannheim argues that self-reflection is a product of the European enlightenment. Before this time, ideas disseminated by the church and religion were simply taken as given without the realisation that they were a creation of human society. In general the production of ideas was the preserve of a certain social stratum and others were precluded from this. Amongst others, Marx is credited with the recognition that such thinking is one facet of alienation and as such is ideological.

For Mannheim, Marx's concept of ideology 'unmasks' the real motivation behind the thinking of a dominant class or stratum. In its classical form the concept of ideology showed that the interests of the ruling class cause it to promote certain ideas, ideas which it persuades the subordinate class are in its interests but which in fact perpetuate its subjection. Mannheim's working definition of ideology fits with Marx's but he focuses more on the pernicious implications of ideology for the dominant class itself: 'Ruling groups can became so intensively interest-bound in their thinking that they are simply no longer able to see certain facts which would undermine their sense of domination' (ibid.: 36).

Mannheim's decisive break with Marx comes with the corresponding idea of 'utopia', in a sense the opposite of ideology. Utopian thinking arises when groups or individuals wish to transcend the present social order and its accompanying categories and institutions. Such thinking achieves only a plan for action rather than objective explanation, since it is focused on a critique of negative social features to the exclusion of the positive.

For Mannheim, Marx's recognition that the ideas of the dominant stratum represent certain class interests is important but not sufficient. 'To-day, however, we have reached a stage in which this weapon of the reciprocal unmasking and laying bare of the unconscious sources of intellectual existence has become the property not of one group among many but of all of them' (ibid.: 37). Here, Mannheim is drawing on the Weberian recognition that historical materialism is not a tool to be used selectively by Marxists when they talk about the dominant class, but that the material contextualisation of thought applies also to users of historical materialism.

This is the core of the way anthropologists use the term reflexivity. 'To be reflexive, in terms of a work of anthropology, is to insist that anthropologists systematically and rigorously reveal their methodology and themselves as the instrument of data generation' (Ruby 1980: 153). In other words, like Mannheim, anthropologists recognise that it is not enough to highlight the social or contextual backdrop of societies under study: the same process must apply to themselves. The idea of reflexivity became popular in post-war anthropology partly as a reaction to the subjectivist approach of Bronislaw Malinowski in his studies of Melanesian society who, it is claimed, 'lived as a native among the natives for many months together, conversing with them in their own tongue...' (Malinowski 1978: vii). It became clear that while Malinowski believed he had embedded himself in the society he was studying, in fact he was unable to escape his own preconceived beliefs and cultural tendencies – such as the category 'native' itself.

Anthropologists, particularly in the neo-Weberian economic anthropological tradition (see Billig 2000) (it is sometimes forgotten that at Freiburg and Heidelburg Weber was a professor of economics, rather than sociology), subsequently argued that it was important to perform analysis on themselves; to lay bare their own motivations and social origins. Rejecting the foundationalist view that knowledge exists independently of human activity, they suggested that revealing the predispositions and preconceptions of the researcher tends to make research more believable and hence more valid.

3.3 Pierre Bourdieu

But this anthropological use of the term reflexivity was not without its problems. Some began to suggest that it led simply to introspection and stasis – too much time was spent on method, and not enough actually performing research. Pierre Bourdieu (1992: 72) writes that:

I must also dissociate myself completely from the form of 'reflexivity' represented by the kind of self-fascinated observation of the observer's writings and feeling which has recently become fashionable among some American anthropologists... who, having apparently exhausted the charms of fieldwork, have turned to talking about themselves rather than about their object of research.

Here he is taking aim at figures such as Geertz (1976), who understood reflexivity as self-analysis.

Bourdieu (1972) argued in his famous structuralist analysis of the Algerian *Kabyle* house that it is not possible for the researcher to attain an outside, objective picture of reality without immersion amongst the objects of examination, but neither is the subjective experience of the examined alone enough for complete understanding. Bourdieu redefined Malinowski's term 'participant objectivation' to show that researchers impose their own predispositions on a subject-matter; they tend naturally to objectify a situation, and yet they must also recognise that this objectification applies equally to themselves. As with the anthropological method researchers must perform self-enquiry; to turn the tools of examination upon their own activity.

Bourdieu differs further from the anthropological version of reflexivity in that he suggests that enquiries, rather than the author, should be the focus of attention. He expresses justifiable scepticism about the rather self-obsessed and inward-looking character of much reflexive enquiry in the anthropological literature. Instead of entirely doubting the possibility of theory, science should simply be aware of its boundaries, and any theoretical account of social phenomena should possess self-awareness. In its greater optimism about the possibilities for scientific enquiry and its explicit avoidance of relativism or nihilism this position perhaps represents an advance on the introspection of the reflexive anthropologist.

> The upshot of this is not that theoretic knowledge is worth nothing but that we must know its limits and accompany all scientific accounts with an account of the limits and limitations of scientific accounts: theoretical knowledge owes a number of its most essential properties to the fact that the conditions under which it is produced are not that of practice.
>
> (Bourdieu 1992: 70)

Bourdieu is particularly relevant for the subject at hand because he proposes a method that tries to transcend the modern/ postmodern divide (if indeed there is a 'divide' in the modernist sense), and he simultaneously criticises the universalising methods of mainstream economics and in particular what he calls 'rational action theory' on the grounds that economists wrongly substitute one, material, self-motivated interest for the plurality of 'interests' that motivate human behaviour. In *The Social Structures of the Economy* (2005) Bourdieu uses a study of the French housing market to argue that people buy houses not just because of price or individual preference, but because of a network of social influences including advertising and state power. Because markets are socially constructed, the methodological individualism of neoclassical economics and its abstract mathematical tools are alone inappropriate for achieving full understanding. For Bourdieu, sociology must accompany economic analysis. A specific epistemological stance underpins this critique, elaborated in *An Invitation to Reflexive Sociology* (1992), *In Other Words* (1990a) and *The Logic of Practice* (1990b).

Whilst it would be reductionist to talk of modernism/objectivism versus postmodernism/subjectivism, the latter dual tends to be grouped together and modernist thought frequently implies that an objectivist view is possible. The Washington Consensus, which will be discussed in the next chapter, revolves around an epistemically objectivist picture of reality, whereby economic facts can be unearthed and data analysis performed using known 'laws'. The tools of investigation are the same wherever they are used, while axioms are derived from basic premises. Axioms depend on a logic which is user-independent. The outside analyst can therefore visit a country with the intention of curing economic problems, free from the questionable influence of his or her own prior values. Epistemic objectivism is different from ontic objectivism, a term which realists use to describe a deeper level of reality which it is the task of social science to discuss. In other words it may be possible to 'be objective' without necessarily being objectivist about knowledge.

Objectivism is sometimes allied with structuralism, in the sociological sense (Levi-Strauss 1964; Althusser 1996, 2001), which concerns the analysis of social structures that transcend individual behaviour.[3] The Washington Consensus contains features of structuralism, identifying ahistorical aggregates that extend beyond the individual, and which can be used by the observer to explain and alter the system being analysed.

Epistemic subjectivists, in contrast, would deny that an objective view is possible, instead pointing to the role of human values in interpretation. This is not simply to acknowledge that subjective views of economic phenomena exist. Most economists would surely accept this. It is to promote the idea that it is not possible to analyse or assess a particular situation without the viewpoint of the observer intruding on the results. What appears to be an objective, clear-cut account may be coloured by the perspective of the author, and therefore the 'objective' 'structures' identified by structuralists are not really there. Advocates of the Washington Consensus may present it as yielding objective advice but it is heavily influenced by the values of its architects and practitioners. The materialist worldview of Washington may not translate, for example, to traditional societies where spiritualism and communalism predominate. It is not possible fully to understand the experience of another – to 'put yourself in their shoes'.

Subjectivism can be illustrated by the unlikely trio of economic marginalists, existentialists and post-structuralists. For the marginalist school, prices depend on the value individuals ascribe to things rather than an objective foundation such as the labour theory of value.[4] For Jean-Paul Sartre, an inter-subjective break precluded the identification of overarching social structures; experience was irretrievably personal and the external world had at best limited bearing on the course of life, which is determined largely by individual volition. Post-structuralists in the Derridean mould criticised Levi-Strauss for, amongst other mistakes, imposing foreign standards on the societies he examined. Any attempt to 'get inside' the society being scrutinised, without examining the system of knowledge-production, is doomed to failure. According to the epistemic subjectivist's position, an outsider would be unlikely to solve an economy's problems because even the conceptualisation of those problems – never mind the proposed solutions – would inevitably depend on the values of the observer rather than the observed. Doing economics would surely be a difficult task.

For Bourdieu, an ontological realist, the opposition between the objective and the subjective is analytically valuable in that it advances the discussion to a certain stage, but it is a divide which must be transcended.[5]

> One of the central themes of Bourdieu's work is the attempt to understand the relationship between 'subjectivity' – individual social being as it is experienced and lived from the personal inside out, so to speak – and the 'objective' social world within which it is framed and towards the production of which it contributes. This theoretical project is a key aspect of Bourdieu's attempt to develop a sociology which can transcend the subjectivist/objectivist dichotomy.
>
> (Jenkins 1992: 25)

This echoes Marx and Mannheim's attempts to examine simultaneously the subject and the object. The practical melding of the subjective and the objective emerged in Bourdieu's study of the Kabyle in Algeria, where he aimed to achieve subjective understanding but into which elements of an objectivist approach intruded. Using the guile of the embedded anthropologist, he wanted to portray the real, detailed life of the peasant as he or she might experience it; but in digging beneath the surface he revealed hidden features such as the categorisation of the outside of the house as male and the interior female, and the gendering of domestic items, including furniture and food. Such findings clearly have wider significance which is intelligible only from outside. While discoveries like these are fascinating from the observer's point of view and might take the appearance of objective reality, they cannot be expressed in anything but subjective terms. The maleness of the outside of the house might change over time, not every house might be similarly divided, and the finding only makes sense in terms of the way gender is perceived by the Berber people. Bourdieu's analysis is neither objectivist nor subjectivist; it is both.

Bourdieu's concern with reflexivity can be seen in his discussion of the Béarn region of France, where he was brought up and subsequently returned to study. He was simultaneously, and purposefully, the researched and the researcher, directing analysis towards something of which he was a part. He considered this situation to carry the advantage of academic training applied to a situation of which he had intimate personal knowledge. A further example of reflexivity in practice came with Bourdieu's analysis of the French academic community in *Homo Academicus* (Bourdieu 1988) – a community of which he was a member, but on which he was also a commentator. Many different versions of reflexivity exist, and Bourdieu is at pains to show that his is not of the navel-gazing variety. His point is that achieving useful explanation and epistemological integrity means combining insider knowledge and external detachment; the subjective stance of the observed complements the objectivity of the observer, and it is possible for the researcher to approximate a position which is simultaneously both insider and outsider. The scientific techniques of the outsider help to 'see things with fresh eyes', whilst few can possess the tacit knowledge of the insider.

Bourdieu specifically addresses the purported objectivity of some social science and anthropology by showing that attempts to achieve detachment from the object of analysis distort understanding. The values, norms or ideals under scrutiny begin to take the appearance of rules, to which it is imagined a community always conforms. These 'rules' might change, and may only be identified as unchanging symbols because they were prominent at that particular moment, and because the researcher was unconsciously looking for certain traits. For example Captain Cook began the myth of the licentious Tahitian after witnessing a sexual display between a middle-aged man and a young girl. Later research sheds doubt on the perceived regularity of such behaviour, suggesting that the locals had decided to put on a show for their visitors. To the outside observer the behaviour may have appeared normal, but in reality it was not routine.

This is the type of analysis to which Bourdieu refers when he says that it is necessary to:

> call into question the presuppositions of the 'objective' observer who, seeking to interpret practices, tends to bring into the object the principles of his relation to the object, as is shown for example by the privileged status he gives to communicative and epistemic functions, which inclines him to reduce exchanges to pure symbolic exchanges.
> (Bourdieu 1990a: 27)

An important dimension of Bourdieu's writing on epistemology is the emphasis on the need to marry theory and practice. Here, like critical realists, he draws on Marx's famous statement in the eleventh Thesis on Feuerbach that 'the philosophers have only *interpreted* the world, in various ways; the point, however, is to change it' (Tucker 1972: 145). For Bourdieu it is impossible to conduct empirical research, epistemology or theory separately: Research is blind without theoretical structure and pure theory is redundant if not informed by the facts or some strong connection with reality. As Jenkins puts it: '... only insofar as one does things is it possible to know about things' (Jenkins, op. cit.: 69). Bourdieu can therefore be used to deal with the problem that much contemporary economics, including the theoretical underpinnings of the Washington Consensus, has become far removed from practical reality. The idea that a theorist of development economics must *practice* development economics is a step beyond the concern of contemporary critical realists with ironing out philosophical nuance – and highlights the drawbacks of their apparent lack of concern with research or practice. Bourdieu's advocacy of praxis demands that any theoretical project reflexively interacts with the real world, in a more profound sense than a case study (although such an approach is not to be discounted), but by the intimate involvement of development economists in the everyday lives of their target audience.[6]

Bourdieu's approach suffers inconsistencies. He rightly highlights the validity of different kinds of knowledge, be they the findings of the 'expert' outsider or the inside knowledge of the group under study. In an effort to remain practical he gives special privilege to statistics, believing they offer better description than other methods; a trait which dates to his account of the Berber. But this privileging of statistics forgets that all data are produced. The subjectivist ideal type, even if it cannot be separated analytically from objectivism, has the benefit of showing that statistical categories are not neutral or objective and that they can be used to reflect the aims of the statistician. Giving special consideration to descriptive statistics is not necessary in order to remain practical and it undermines Bourdieu's attempt to stress the importance of a mode of analysis which is both local and universal.

Bourdieu's project is central to social theory, which concerns overcoming the 'fallacy of composition' which says that what is beneficial for an individual is beneficial for the community. His discussion is therefore highly relevant for economics. His examination of the social influences on behaviour such as upbringing, class background, culture and surroundings – including what he calls 'habitus' – leads to an explanation of how humans are at liberty to pursue action outside such constraints, and indeed how structure and agency interact. Whilst structuralism is valid in the sense that structures exist that extend beyond the individual, subjectivists are also right to throw doubt on the purported neutrality of objectivists. Bourdieu considers himself to have reduced the tension between, or gone beyond, structure and agency, and to that end is highly critical of contemporary mainstream economics, which he considers (in common with critical realists) to have excluded room for human agency.

3.4   The sociology of scientific knowledge

The sociology of scientific knowledge (SSK) emerged roughly contemporaneously with Bourdieu, and was represented principally by Steve Woolgar (1992, 1988), Malcolm Ashmore and David Bloor (1976). Along with the general trend towards postmodernism in the social sciences, Woolgar, Ashmore and Bloor were influenced by social constructivism. SSK also evolved from the Marxist literature and drew on Mannheim, but it evoked reflexivity differently. SSK sees science as influenced, like every other activity, by social interests and undeclared predispositions. No independent criterion exists from which to achieve scientific knowledge. Highlighting the social backdrop of scientific enquiry enables SSK to contextualise some of the positivist claims put forward by scientists and social theorists.

Woolgar and Ashmore define two varieties of reflexivity which operate on a continuum: constitutive reflexivity and 'benign introspection'. The latter type involves a marked difference between the author and the topic (or between object and underlying reality). Authors should be aware of their potential biases and predilections. At the other extreme constitutive reflexivity means that the author and topic are inextricably linked; there is an intimate inter-relation between the object and underlying reality, similarly between representation and object. In other words, it is almost as interesting to find out about the author as it is about what they are writing.[7]

But for SSK, although Woolgar and Ashmore appear to deny it, constitutive reflexivity becomes a problem. If scientific knowledge is a product of social relations, then for SSK to claim scientific knowledge it must also be produced. In other words, SSK was subject to the very social influences that it is trying to analyse, but if this is the case, then why should we believe SSK? It must claim some sort of superior status outside society, but then surely this disputes the whole claim that knowledge is socially constructed? Mannheim's idea of relationism – or the evolution of how knowledge is perceived – will not suffice, because the intelligentsia which is supposed to identify this evolution are arbitrarily given a position outside normal social relations.

Esther-Mirjam Sent examines the issue of reflexivity with reference to the work of Thomas Sargent on rational expectations (Sent 1998). Macroeconomic predictions may actually affect the behaviour of agents, making predictions self-fulfilling or self-defeating. Sargent believed that he could overcome this problem of reflexivity by replacing adaptive expectations with rational expectations. Agents, in making decisions, use the same macroeconomic predictions as economists. Sent, does not, however, believe that Sargent's solution – adopting a vector autoregression model over the restricted distributed lags approach – overcomes the problem of reflexivity.

Sent also acknowledges her own dilemma: 'If sociologists of scientific knowledge are *symmetric* with scientists, then, why should we take their word over that of scientists? If sociologists of scientific knowledge are *asymmetric* with scientists, then, what kinds of standards can they employ to establish their privileged position' (ibid.: 122)? Why should we believe Sent any more than Sargent? And if readers of the book have an equally valid view of Sargent as that of Sent, does reading the book take them any further? At this stage, we become subject to the same sort of relativist aporia as in the liar's paradox. If all views are equally valid, then why should any be believed more than another? Why, in fact, should anyone be interested in what is being written here?

A way of addressing this type of reflexivity problem, Sent argues, is to see Sargent as rewriting his own history and at the same time to believe that it is entirely acceptable also to rewrite his history, without being influenced by the way in which Sargent latterly tells his story. As long as Sent states the dilemma and outlines her objectives, she could be seen as having something useful to say about Sargent. The dilemma may not be resolved, but as John Davis and Matthias Klaes (2003) point out, a kind of 'second best' answer has been achieved. The identification of different types of reflexivity can help resolve the difficulty of relativism.

Davis and Klaes propose rescuing the situation by distinguishing between three different types of reflexivity: endogenous, epistemic and transcendent. 'Reflexivity can be seen as benign if the endogenous reflexive relation that includes us as observers can be epistemically investigated without jeopardising our status as observers' (ibid.: 5). Endogenous reflexivity is the type of reflexivity that operates within the text, that can be contained and talked about without compromising the objectivity of the observer, even if the observer is subject and object at the same time. This was the type of reflexivity suffered by Sargent when he found that predictions can become self-fulfilling or self-defeating.

The second, epistemic, kind of reflexivity is further-reaching: it transforms the subject into an object. This involves the relation of the text to the creator of the text. Instead of looking into a mirror and seeing a reflection, it is as if the mirror somehow reaches back and twists your features. The subject/object distinction is thereby reversed or dissolved, and instead of subject A acting on object B, end of story, subject A acts on object B then B transforms into a subject that objectifies A. Davis and Klaes might say that even if Sent is implicated in her own analysis of Sargent, it is still possible for her to produce valuable analysis if we can find out about the way in which she is conducting her project. It becomes imperative that Sent, as enquirer, declares her assumptions and performs self-critique.

A third type, transcendent reflexivity, encompasses epistemic reflexivity, which in turn includes endogenous reflexivity. The epistemic sort of reflexivity presupposes a strict division of subject and object, but it may not be possible in reality to enforce this distinction. For example a painter may include herself in the picture, and thus as a subject simultaneously turn herself into an object. 'Put differently, endogenous reflexivity is wholly internal to the text..., epistemic reflexivity topicalises the author–text relationship, and transcendent reflexivity alludes to the social context surrounding both' (ibid.: 3).

In sum, Davis and Klaes believe that Sent displays a kind of endogenous reflexivity towards Sargent and avoids the self-defeating, epistemic type. She makes explicit her relation to her own text and to Sargent's, thereby becoming self-aware. Although this may not have overcome the problem, it at least achieved a second-best solution in that it could leave the reader to decide whether or not to accept or reject the findings. To an extent any act of evaluation involves asymmetry and perhaps this kind of reflexivity problem is not as damaging as it might at first seem. If knowledge is social, then it is up to neither the interpreter nor the author to decide on the final interpretation of the text, it is up to social individuals who read the text.

3.5 Reflexivity and modernity

The theory of modernity developed by the sociologists Ulrich Beck, Anthony Giddens and Scott Lash involves a different use of the term reflexivity. Aiming to overcome the sometimes sterile contest between modernism and postmodernism, Beck *et al.* aim to portray a new way of thinking about modernity. The introduction to *Reflexive Modernisation* suggests that: '...the protracted debate about modernity versus post-modernity has become wearisome and like so many such debates in the end has produced rather little' (Beck *et al.* 1994).[8]

Despite his weariness Giddens's analysis of modernity responds to postmodern attempts to situate schools of thought in their histori-cal and social milieux. A well-known charge levelled at postmodern approaches is that they, like some forms of reflexivity, can lead to rel-ativism and ultimately nihilism – if knowledge has no independent foundations, fact becomes the same as opinion and nobody can say anything. Action becomes pointless. Giddens aims for a more sophisti-cated approach by arguing that modernity is historically dynamic rather than a fixed entity that exists for all time; it follows that progress and knowledge are possible and that human action can change our condi-tions of existence. The scientific disciplines that retain old ideas about modernity are neither utterly mistaken nor completely correct. Rather, they should adapt constantly as modernity evolves. This implies that existing economic tools should be selectively reassessed and modified. Giddens's idea of structuration (Giddens 1984), for which he is perhaps best-known, disputes the notion of agency and structure as unchang-ing opposites, and instead sees the one as being constituted within the other. Structure is a process, rather than a substance, and agency both conditions and is affected by structuration.

Another advantage of Giddens's schema is that it operates dialec-tically. Postmodernism is faced with the problem that it has argued against normative programmes for understanding human existence and therefore cannot suggest that anything comes 'after' modernity. But if nothing transcends modernity, then why should we give credence to postmodernism? As Sheila Dow suggests, it is better to think of postmod-ernism as the antithesis to modernism's thesis (Cullenberg *et al.* 2001: 61). Both categories are being eroded by similar processes and will lead to a new synthesis. The concept of reflexive modernisation is pitched as a sociological contribution to that synthesis.

In *The Consequences of Modernity* (1990) Giddens starts from the premise that modernity has been wrongly understood as a fixed period of history with a uniform character. An analysis of the rup-tures and dynamism of the process is missing. Even conceptions of history such as Marxist historical materialism, which emphasised discontinuity and change, saw history as an evolutionary process that puts contemporary human society at an advanced stage. Giddens disputes this evolutionism:

> Modernity, as everyone living in the closing years of the twentieth century can see, is a double-edged phenomenon. The development of the modern social institutions and their worldwide spread have created vastly greater opportunities for human beings... But modernity also has a sombre side, which has become very apparent in the present century.
>
> (Giddens 1990: 7)

The sombre side, in Giddens's view, consists of the spread of degrading labour practices, the development of mass political control and the industrialisation of military power. The view of modernity as leading to a benign outcome is therefore mistaken, but rather than adopt the view that history goes nowhere and that the creations of modernity are all dire, Giddens wanted to develop an analysis that accommodates the double-edged character of modernity by focusing on institutions and emphasising the role of human agency. In arguing that in late modernity we are faced with a dynamic opportunity to shape our economic and social environment for the better, there is an echo of Mannheim's mention of: 'the ascent of human beings from mere pawns of history to the stature of men' (Mannheim, op. cit.: 82). Giddens believes that the notion of reflexivity is one of the key drivers of this dynamic conception of modernity.

Giddens accepts the Marxist and Mannheimian use of the term reflexivity to mean that the discoveries of social science cannot just be applied to a static subject matter but must be refracted through the self-knowledge of social agents. However Giddens goes further, pointing out that the social sciences create concepts using everyday knowledge, but that these concepts themselves are subsequently used in everyday life.

> Concepts like 'capital', 'markets', 'industry' and many others, in their modern senses were elaborated as part of the early development of economics as a distinct discipline in the eighteenth and early nineteenth centuries. These concepts, and empirical conclusions linked to them, were formulated in order to analyse changes involved in the emergence of modern institutions. But... they have become integral to what 'modern economic life' actually is and inseparable from it.
>
> (Giddens, op. cit.: 41)

Humans relate reflexively to the concepts/institutions created by human society. This reflexive process leads to a degree of obfuscation, and it precludes the positivist view that social theory (and therefore economics) gradually accumulates knowledge about the world, but it also permits a continual arranging and rearranging of social relations as new knowledge emerges. Giddens proposes a picture in which we are at one and the same time able to influence and understand our collective destiny but are also subject to self-created, but unpredictable, risk and uncertainty. Reflexivity consists in institutions of enlightenment thinking – including some of the tools developed by economics – reacting back on modernity and in turn shaping that process. Modernity is a dynamic process rather than an inert period of history.

Giddens suggests that: 'There is a fundamental sense in which reflexivity is a defining characteristic of all human action. All human beings routinely "keep in touch" with the grounds of what they do as an integral element of doing it' (ibid.: 36). But in modernity reflexivity assumes greater importance – it becomes intrinsic to the process of modernisation. Tradition, meaning routinised ways of acting and thinking, can no longer be defended for its own sake because we are compelled to reconsider the way we behave. Institutions and the way the world is perceived are constantly open to re-evaluation. It is important to contrast this role for human action with simple modernisation where reason appeared to replace dogma with a sense of certainty. Instead scientific knowledge, which is achieved through reason, is periodically revised and open to uncertainty. As Giddens (1994a) points out, even Karl Popper said that all science is founded on shifting sands.

Giddens shows in *Reflexive Modernisation* how social reflexivity forces the pace of manufactured uncertainty on an individual level (Beck *et al.*, op. cit.). His conception complements other, more philosophical discussions of the debate between modernity and postmodernity because it focuses on what real people do at a concrete level. Both postmodern and modernist approaches tend to operate at a high level of abstraction, far removed from practical behaviour. Some currents within postmodernism question the notion of the modern 'individual' (for example Foucault 1980) and suggest that agency is a product of social forces acted out within certain group structures. Many modernist approaches have such a fixed notion of individuality that they preclude unpredictable behaviour.

For Giddens individuals act in ways peculiar to a specific social and historical period. Today, individuals are compelled to act on an array of information hailing not just from within the locality, not only from inside the nation, but from all around the world. This information must be screened, arranged and the important pieces picked out, resulting in a widening of 'intelligence'. Knowledge is no longer available only to a privileged caste of ivory-tower intellectuals, it is understood, used and shaped by increasing numbers of people.

This opening up of knowledge means that it is difficult to conceive of the human agent in a fixed, reified way, and instead human behaviour is rendered more unpredictable but at the same time choice becomes widespread. Institutions and tools initially created by humans with the intention of asserting more control are now reacting back unpredictably on society, leading to unintended effects.

The vision of reflexive modernisation is summed up with the metaphor of a juggernaut which collectively we can control at times but which threatens to run off the road. 'The juggernaut crushes those who resist it, and while it sometimes seems to have a steady path, there are times when it veers away erratically in directions we cannot foresee' (Beck *et al.*, op. cit.: 139). Giddens thus prefers to talk not of postmodernism, with its connotations of nihilism and despair, but of radicalised or high modernity. The latter terms suggest that we live in modernity but that our view of modernity should change to accommodate reflexivity. The concept of reflexive modernisation revives the role of collective human agency because it refutes the teleological and evolutionist views of history and therefore is not deterministic. It arguably places yet more emphasis on human agency by disputing the concretised, modernist, theoretical view of the human agent as entirely free to exercise its subjective powers.

3.6　Conclusion

The concept of reflexivity has been used in many different ways. It is difficult to compare some uses of the term, and any attempt at grouping them together too closely would lead to misrepresentation. Although there has not been an unbroken, linear progression in the use of the term, the idea has travelled a long way from its early twentieth-century manifestation, and a number of different and incommensurate reflexivities can be identified. Marx never used the word and the Marxist usage of reflexivity only developed during subsequent discussion. Mannheim's project concentrated on epistemology; for anthropologists, the emphasis was more on practical method. Bourdieu tried to extend the reflexive method to other areas of social science, whilst he opposed the self-orientated approach of earlier thinking that considered itself reflexive.

For SSK reflexivity was a problem rather than a solution, although not, it has been suggested, an insurmountable one. Whereas reflexivity is a side-issue for some analyses, Giddens's project is perhaps the most ambitious, aiming at a new theory of modernity of which reflexivity is a central feature. To relate the discussion to Chapter 2, in critical realism the idea of reflexivity is not a key concern, although the Marxian origins of the particular notion of social ontology can be seen. It is also clear that the postmodern vision of reality as *entirely* socially contingent is as far from transcendental realism as it is from Giddens and Bourdieu.

Yet at the risk of simplification, it has been implied here that certain characteristics unite most uses of the term, from Marx, Mannheim, anthropology, Bourdieu and the science studies literature, to Giddens.[9] All uses of the term derive in part from the Marxist recognition that ideas are generated within a certain class or socio-economic position. All involve a social conception of the human agent, one for which self-awareness is an important part of human activity. According to each version, by pointing out the social nature of thought and therefore the possibility of a plurality of ways of thinking, it is necessary to perform self-analysis. Most definitions allow for the possibility of progress in human history, although there is no inevitability about this progress, unlike the more deterministic interpretations of Marx.

Lawson's social ontology, which sees intentional human activity as the meeting point of structure and agency, plainly has a Marxist heritage and therefore holds features in common with Bourdieu's attempt to look for a solution to the problems of objectivity and subjectivity. Both Bourdieu and Giddens look for a way of 'transcending' the objectivist/subjectivist distinction and indeed appear sceptical about dualism in general, a suspicion they share with Dow (1990). Bourdieu's discussion of reflexivity has perhaps the most relevance for the methodology of development economics because it deals with methodological issues in anthropology and because he expresses firm views about mainstream economics.

One of the implications for economics is that because there can be no final word on the object of examination, and because the social context in which knowledge is attained is constantly changing, economists must remain open to the possibility that the way they look at the world may need to be revised. For all the versions of reflexivity portrayed here, social science, including economics, appears likely to be a dynamic process of enquiry rather than a static set of tools, even if at times a certain set of tools may be relevant.

Chapter 4 attempts to apply some of the themes from this chapter to the contemporary practice of economic development, in particular the Washington Consensus and its revised version. The central part of the chapter is the four-point taxonomy of reflexive development practice, which draws together some of the insights of the discussion until now and which is examined in the context of the case-studies in Chapters 6 and 7.

4
Reflexivity and Development Economics

4.1 Introduction

Acknowledging the argument that theory and practice are inter-related, this chapter aims to apply some of the ideas of reflexivity to development economics, and in particular to the dominant mode of development practice of the last two decades. The policies of the Washington and 'Post'-Washington Consensus have been the subject of much debate. Their underlying methodology has received relatively little attention despite the wealth of literature on methodology that has emerged over the same time period.[1] A methodological dimension helps discern why particular schools of thought achieved prominence, as well as why certain policies were recommended rather than others.

The Consensus has a distinctive modernist methodological character. John Williamson, who coined the phrase, suggests that it has absolute truth and that its veracity cannot be challenged. Even with the amendments proposed by Joseph Stiglitz in the 1990s, advocates consider it to apply universally, irrespective of context. Economists in Washington can, given the correct data and targets, design specific policy programmes for developing countries. It is just the kind of modernist project with which social theorists have engaged critically over the past half-century or more, and the notion of reflexivity is therefore a useful theoretical framework within which to discuss it.

Several theorists of development have criticised the methodology behind the Washington Consensus. Methodological postmodernists (rather than those who identify postmodernity as a historical stage, such as Jameson, op. cit.) have been among the most vocal challengers. Policy proposals, they suggest, are influenced heavily by the interests and social backdrop of those who design them, so a single specific set of policies cannot apply universally. Critics of essentialism, scientism, foundationalism and determinism charge that no fixed basis exists on which economic advice can be constructed, and that policy outcomes are difficult to predict. Instead, development practitioners should address the differences between countries and social experiences, focusing on the various forms of oppression that face men and women in the global south.[2]

The postmodern critique is valuable, but postmodernists, despite their protestations, remain vulnerable to many of the charges levelled in Chapter 2. Many postmodernists appear reluctant to apply their ideas in practice, whilst the spectre of relativism refuses to fade. An opposition to the idea of historical progress is incompatible with the notion of development, limiting the use of postmodernism for the task at hand. Several other important theorists of development, including Kalecki, Sen and Hirschman, either pre-empted the methodological concerns over the Washington Consensus or implicitly cautioned against the kind of modernism implicitly assumed in its methodology, without suffering the kind of difficulties encountered by those in the postmodern tradition.

Bourdieu's approach to reflexivity, perhaps more than any of the versions of reflexivity discussed in the previous chapter, can contribute to development economics since it helps take into account subjective differences between societies but at the same time retains scope for generalist analysis. Bourdieu is, amongst other things, an anthropologist and therefore has insights about developing countries. He also discusses the methodology of mainstream economics.

The final section of the chapter, and the core of the book as a whole, outlines a taxonomy of reflexive development practice, derived from the discussion in this and previous chapters. The taxonomy suggests that, acknowledging reflexivity, successful development practice and understanding of that practice would be informed by the following characteristics: a self-reflexive examination of values and norms; an assessment of the extent to which local context is important; a recognition that policies are fallible and can sometimes worsen the problems that they set out to solve; and the suggestion that theory and policy might be revised periodically as circumstances change.

4.2 The Washington Consensus and after

The Washington Consensus originated in the early 1980s but was coined as a popular phrase in 1989 by John Williamson, who outlined a universal, 'positive' set of economic policies to be adopted by all countries at all times. There is debate over how important Williamson's contribution is to the definition of the Washington Consensus and over whether his position has changed over the years, but it is clear that he developed a framework that relied on a distinctive methodological position, and which underlay the structural adjustment programmes carried out across the developing world throughout the 1980s and 1990s (and into the next millennium) whereby the World Bank and IMF delivered loans conditional on the adoption of prescribed policies.[3]

Williamson (1993) suggests the phrase 'universal convergence' as an appropriate synonym, and overtly tries to define the policies advocated as being beyond debate. The universal convergence is simply good practice:

> the sooner it wins general acceptance and can be removed from mainstream political debate, the better for all concerned ... The proof may not be quite as conclusive as the proof that the Earth is not flat, but it is sufficiently well established as to give sensible people better things to do with their time than to challenge its veracity.
>
> (Williamson 1993: 1330)

Dissenters are described as 'cranks' who ought to be indulged by the democratic process but whose views are to be disregarded when designing policy.

In his original (1990) article Williamson details 10 sets of policies which he believes most Washington policymakers of the day would accept. The list includes cutting budget deficits and public expenditure; lowering taxes; liberalising financial markets and the exchange rate; reducing import tariffs; abolishing barriers to foreign direct investment; privatisation; and fostering competition (Williamson 2004–5: 196). He is clear that officials and analysts in that particular city at that particular time could pre-design a detailed economic programme for any country, irrespective of whether its politicians or officials are part of the consensus and whatever the country's circumstances. Williamson declares that his intention is not normative, or to promote his own desired policy mix, but to identify the cumulative accepted wisdom of development practice as expressed in the locale at that time. Economic growth comes first. Social development is seen as a secondary consequence.

Rodrik (2002a) suggests that the programme is neoliberal, although Williamson denies this in an attempt to claim political neutrality. In a series of subsequent articles (Williamson 1990, 1999, 2002, 2003, 2004a, 2004b) Williamson makes minor amendments, acknowledging that certain sets of policies, such as trade liberalisation, might prove more controversial than his original article suggested. He also lists policies which lie outside the so-called consensus.

Williamson (2003) claims that the term was initially only intended to apply to Latin America, while he 'never thought of the Washington Consensus as a policy manifesto, for it omitted a number of things that seemed to me important, most notably a concern for income distribution as well as for rapid growth' (Williamson 2003: 1476). He also says that a further generation of reforms should concentrate on crisis-avoidance and institutional change, and that: 'One blueprint will not be right for all countries' (ibid.: 1481). This stance constitutes a change of emphasis from his 1993 statement that proof of the Washington Consensus is almost akin to proof that the earth is not flat. To a certain extent it does not matter what Williamson himself meant, or whether he backtracked; the Washington Consensus undoubtedly became an agenda for global policy used by the World Bank and the IMF. Whether Williamson makes amendments or not, the initial list of 10 points became concretised in the 1990s as a policy agenda urging reduced government expenditure, current-account liberalisation and privatisation on most developing countries. This policy agenda has been discussed, with little reference to Williamson in, for example, Gore (2000) and Fine *et al.* (2003). My use of the term is based on this generally-accepted position. In any event, Williamson (2004–5) continues to defend most of the core features of the Washington Consensus as well as its universalist methodological standpoint.

A number of shortcomings had already been identified by the late 1990s, particularly because structural adjustment in practice was more radical than the theory behind the Washington Consensus. Joseph Stiglitz, then chief economist at the World Bank, initiated a revision (Stiglitz 1998a, 1998b). Prompted by a shift in perspective ranging from his neoclassical textbook to the more radical *Globalisation and its Discontents* (2002), World Bank staff were encouraged to rethink the presumed welfare benefits of the free market that had coloured policy for the last two decades, substituting the theoretical work that won Stiglitz a Nobel Prize in 2001. Informational asymmetries between market participants and unavoidable transactions costs caused market failures. Institutions began to take a more prominent role, particularly in light of the experience of rapid privatisation in the Soviet Bloc and Eastern Europe. The concept of social capital was brought into the mainstream in order to deal with the non-economic nature of many dimensions of development. This 'post'-Washington Consensus adopted a more human face and used less free-market rhetoric, widening its aims beyond the merely material.

The augmented Washington Consensus is *less* universalistic. Yet it shares certain crucial characteristics with its predecessor. It retains the notion that in all economies, developing and developed, market equilibriation will bring about optimal outcomes. It assumes that outside intervention by centralised institutions using a roughly similar pattern is the best means of achieving better development outcomes. Above all, as Dani Rodrik points out: 'It is too insensitive to local context and needs' (Rodrik 2002a: 1). It still attempts to apply economic blueprints to developing countries and retains common features such as inflation targets, independent central banks and balanced budgets. Rodrik argues that even with institutional, poverty-orientated and social measures, it is 'infeasible, inappropriate and irrelevant' (ibid.: 1). Some, such as Cammack (2002) suggest that there have been serious and avoidable consequences for poverty in developing countries.

Ha-Joon Chang shows that the ethos of the Washington Consensus reflects methodological changes inside the whole of development economics:

> acquisition of knowledge of particular countries' economic structures, institutions, politics and socio-cultural factors that used to be regarded as a highly-valued – even essential – asset for development economists in the early days of the subject, was denounced as a waste of valuable training time. Indeed, many of those who hold the 'economics-as-a-universal-science' view would go a step further and argue that the possession of detailed knowledge about a country is a sign of intellectual failure. In their view, it is a sign that the researcher has sought refuge in the intellectually 'soft' areas like languages and other social sciences because he/she was incapable of dealing with the 'hard' logical concepts required of rigorous economic analysis.
>
> (Chang 2003b: 5)

Adding caveats to the original Consensus has not altered its modernist methodological character. It focuses on those targets deemed important by its architects, who believe themselves to be catering for the interests of developing-country inhabitants. Because mainstream development policy remains wedded to the universalising inclinations of neoclassical economics, and its preference for abstraction and idealisation rather than specificity and nuance, it has not engaged with postmodernism as have other social sciences. This has been at the expense of practical policy. As Fine *et al.* (2003: xx) point out, 'the post-Washington Consensus remains remarkably remote as far as policy stances in Africa, Eastern Europe and elsewhere are concerned. The dissonance between rhetoric and practice has already been felt within the World Bank with the resignatio[n] of Joseph Stiglitz...'

4.3 The modernism of the Washington Consensus

The Washington Consensus and the post-Washington Consensus encourage rational, material progress towards a single human goal – increased income, and as a result well-being – using principles that differ little according to context. It can be seen that it conforms in some degree to most of the 'isms' of modernism discussed in Chapter 2. The approach propagated by the Washington Consensus is essentialist in that it suggests that there is a hidden level of reality which can be, or already has been, discovered using the tools of economics. From this viewpoint all economies possess an 'essence' which exists independently of local knowledge or the tools used to describe or analyse the economy.

A critic of essentialism might charge that the predominantly formal and Western methods of the IMF, World Bank and regional Development Banks that carry out the Washington Consensus, rather than 'revealing' any hidden layer of reality, discover only what they are looking for. If, as social constructivists argue, knowledge is socially generated both by the outside agency and by the local inhabitant, a more complete understanding would be achieved using a variety of methods, such as the adoption of local traditional knowledge or the immersion of development economists in local culture. As Rodrik suggests, 'post'-Washington Consensus attempts to achieve a more human face have amounted to little more than window-dressing; the context-immune core of the consensus remains intact.

A second dimension of the Washington Consensus's modernism is its foundationalism, the view that there is one basis to reality irrespective of how it is discussed. Economic knowledge and policy prescription can be built upon a secure knowledge base, in the Cartesian sense which claimed to have distilled the basic nature of reality through enquiry. A policy such as the 'provision of secure property rights', for example, is based on the 'stylised fact' that all economic actors are individually-motivated and respond to the incentive of property ownership by working and consuming more.

Postmodernists might charge that there is no fixed foundation to knowledge about human behaviour, and that those who claim to have discovered it are only reflecting their own rhetorical position. Foucauldian analyses of development such as Ferguson's (1990) *The Anti-Politics Machine* emphasise the role of power relations in reinforcing what are seen as development 'problems'. Such arguments, as well as others within the broad postmodernist tradition, imply that economic actors in many developing countries cannot be assumed to be self-orientated or as materially-motivated as those in other countries, and that other, collectivist, spiritual, cultural or environmental ends might take precedence.

A strong strain of scientism permeates Williamson's discussion and that of most proponents of Washington Consensus-type views of development from Lal (2000) through to Lucas (2003). The privileging of a specific type of scientific practice and the exclusion of other methods are a consequence of the essentialism and foundationalism described above. If there is only one reality and context is unimportant then development economists become impartial scientists dispensing advice from an objective standpoint, much as laboratory technicians inject an enzyme into a rat in order to make it grow faster.

Postmodern approaches would emphasise non-formal methods in order to tailor analysis to the local situation. Critics of the teleological view of science might charge that there is no inherent superiority in a perspective on development that happened to predominate at the end of the twentieth century. Rather than reflecting a 'universal consensus' the dominant policy ideas reflect the material interests which influence the thinking of the Bank and Fund. Stiglitz (2002), for example, argues that Wall Street representatives of financial capital influenced the IMF into bailing out countries that owed them money.

The methodology of the Washington Consensus appears to assume a somewhat deterministic relationship between policies and development outcomes. In contrast to the postmodern or critical realist argument that interaction between elements within a system cannot be reduced to timeless laws, the neoclassical underpinnings of the Washington Consensus result in the belief that outcomes will be relatively predictable – and therefore few alternatives are considered. For instance the financial programming model, the main tool of the IMF during the 1980s and 1990s,[4] emphasised the restriction of domestic credit in the belief that this would usually address balance of payments problems. Fiscal policy was considered less important, even in economies where balance of payments problems were not due to excessive domestic credit creation. The shortcomings of this approach, and the unpredictability of outcomes, were starkly illustrated during the Asian financial crisis, particularly in

South Korea where IMF-inspired monetary austerity turned a short-term liquidity problem into a real economic crisis.

The basic model used by the World Bank in structural adjustment similarly corresponds with the goals of the Washington Consensus, although its policy implications are more open than the financial programming approach. The World Bank's model is based on the Revised Minimum Standards Model formulated by Hollis Chenery in the 1970s. A useful summary is provided in Bergeron (2006: 111–115). The model sets targets for foreign capital and savings, and closure is achieved by targeting specific levels of foreign investment. Growth is considered a function of the capital/output ratio, as a result of the model's Harrod-Domar origins. An estimate of the capital/output ratio is used to assess current and future efficiency levels, while the marginal propensity to import and the predicted export levels are also predicted. Following this, the necessary levels of investment and imports are calculated, with each disaggregated appropriately. The next step is to calculate the feasible level of consumption. Finally the balance of payments is brought in with an assessment of the capacity of the country to finance imports. The overall implications of the model are, like under the financial programming model, that development will be capital-intensive, while liberalisation and integration with global markets will lead to higher output.

Arch modernism underlies the Consensus and its amended version, which have failed to take account of the abundance of social science literature criticising modernism. Whilst the models underlying the Washington Consensus and its successor are held true deterministically for most countries at most times, there are many instances where they have proven counterproductive, throwing doubt upon the determinism in their methodology. Proponents of the Consensus, or some revised variant of it, have continued to advocate development policies that assume away context, the randomness of causation, the role of chance, the indeterminacy of events and the changing role of causes and effects. To some the Washington Consensus may appear comparable with proof that the earth is round, but to others, most notably many recipients of the advice, it merely reflects the interests and perspectives of its proponents.

4.4   Other theories

Here, I present several theories of development which contrast with the theory underlying the Washington Consensus. Since my argument focuses on the distinction between modernism and postmodernism, the discussion concerns those thinkers who can be used to provide method-ological insights in this direction rather than on all those who oppose the Washington Consensus. A range of theories can be highlighted, par-ticularly those which have an interesting methodological bent, rather than one preferred theory singled out. Whilst theory is crucial in doing development economics and it is not true that 'any theory goes', specify-ing a single theory and asserting that is true everywhere risks making the same universalising, essentialist mistakes as modernists. It may be that different theories apply at different times and in different contexts. The taxonomy presented in the next section is pitched at the methodolog-ical level, and is intended to allow a range of overlapping possibilities. It does, however, rule out several approaches such as the use of single models like the RMSM or financial programming. One of the underly-ing motivations behind the taxonomy is to suggest that it is necessary to start thinking about practice as soon as a methodological position is adopted. In other words methodological discussions – which are about the approach to knowledge which underpins the selection and applica-tion of methods – require a consideration of what the world is like, and how it might be changed. This kind of methodological/practical discus-sion can, and arguably must, occur alongside the selection of theory.

4.4.1 Postmodernism

According to modernists, development issues as conceived by those in Washington can be tackled scientifically, based on a universal under-standing of what is essential in economic behaviour. The Western development 'expert' can solve the problems of developing economies. Postmodern critics have focused particular attention on technical approaches, which they believe to be a product of modernism. Parpart (1995) shows that the notion of expertise is embedded in Enlighten-ment thought and the subsequent specialisation of knowledge. Certain strands of Enlightenment thinking involved the view that science can, through its trained practitioners, overcome the problems of the natural world: human society is no longer vulnerable to the will of God. A tech-nical, expert-driven approach pervades mainstream economics, which has increasingly 'turned inwards' (Klamer 2002), excluding anyone who is not well-versed in its complex formal techniques.

Parpart addresses the issue of scientism by suggesting that the 'prob-lem' of female poverty in the so-called third world is constructed by experts from the global North who often know little about the subjective experience of local inhabitants. Women are seen as helpless victims, subject to uniformly similar forces. Parpart approvingly draws attention to approaches which emphasise empowerment and diversity: 'development theory and planning for women must exhibit greater sensitivity to difference and an awareness of the multiple oppressions – particularly race, class, ethnicity and gender – which define women's lives in the South' (Parpart 1995: 237).

While Parpart is right to question the infallibility of Northern expertise and to disaggregate the object of development economists' intentions, her approach suffers drawbacks. In arguing for the wholesale rejection of an economics-orientated approach in favour of 'empowerment' it is difficult to understand the purpose of promoting development. Focus groups, indigenous participation and sensitivity are all very well, but what should people actually *do*, apart from perhaps advocate for piecemeal local change? The postmodern emphasis on method rather than progress surely ignores what is implicit in the promotion of development – the implication that large-scale action must be taken to improve the situation of groups, whether on their terms or by the criteria of the outsider. It might be argued on philosophical or moral grounds that development is an inherently Western concept and should be rejected, but Parpart does not do so, and it should be noted that few postmodernists resort to such extremes.

Bergeron (2006) argues that the national economic state has been constructed, and that both left and right, statist and non-statist, tend to talk about the state as if it is a natural economic unit. She draws on Benedict Anderson's idea of 'imagined communities' in questioning the desirability of directing theory at arbitrarily constructed collections of groups. 'The process of disaggregating the economy for sectoral analysis does not lead to a fundamental questioning of the national economy as an object of authoritative intervention' (Bergeron, 2006: 52). Bergeron rightly points out that in any discussion of policy it is worth asking whose interests are being represented, and who is party to economic policy discussions. It should not be assumed that focusing development on national government policy is in the best interests of the poor, not least because governments do not always represent the interests of marginalised groups.

Like Parpart, Bergeron talks of the 'illusion of expertise' (ibid.: 115), doubting whether objectivity is possible – it is a 'view from nowhere'. Bergeron appears to question the possibility of controlling the economy at all, either in a neoclassical Washington Consensus way or the old statist fashion. However her preferred responses, which involve empowering women's groups to work on overlapping levels at the local, national and global levels, appear modest in their ambition. It is quite possible that directly confronting 'nation-centred, economistic and globalistic discourses' (ibid.: 163) serves to reproduce existing power relations, but as for Parpart, the alternative, if it involves only the reconceptualising of discourses and empowerment of women's groups, may prove almost as conservative.

Other postmodern approaches to the Washington Consensus focus on the possibility of different kinds of development. The 'Western' truth is only one among many. Kanth (op. cit.) is critical not only of the Washington Consensus but of what he terms 'Euro-centred epistemologies' in general, including mainstream economics. He suggests that 'even if economic theory were true, and its "science" valid, in some acceptable sense, *it would still only represent only one manner of interpreting the myriad facts of social life*' (ibid.: 190, italics in original). According to this line of argument, mainstream economics leads to policy approaches which tend to impose foreign values on the object of study.

Escobar (1995) suggests that the imposition of foreign-led development unintentionally involves a top-down, technocratic approach which excludes the voices of its target audience. The type of approach offered by Escobar can be criticised for being too general – not all aid is top-down or technocratic – and being difficult to use as a plan for action. Some broadly postmodern authors try to go further. Parfitt (2002) proposes a 'principle of least violence' which is supposed to be a guide for overcoming the pernicious impacts of aid and other development efforts. Whilst the sociological thrust of this argument means that it is heavy on analysis of the postmodern influence on development policy, again there is little practical or technical concern with change in the lives of ordinary people. Little practical advice is given beyond the idea that development should involve the 'least violence'. Lee (1994) highlights the irony that whilst developed-world culture is engaged in a questioning of modernist precepts, most developing countries forge ahead with a modernist agenda. He argues that the postcolonial world is characterised by different patterns of economic and cultural development. We should not think of development as a linear process.

Keynes showed signs of anticipating some of the contemporary criticisms of the modernism of the Washington Consensus. Klaes (2006) shows that as a member of the Bloomsbury group Keynes had a well thought-out relation to modernism, which may be thought of in terms of immanent critique. Klaes regards McCloskey (2001) and Klamer

(1995) as allowing that Keynes might be a postmodernist. Keynes is not a postmodernist, because as Skidelsky shows, his life's work was dedicated to the modernist project of showing how economic science could advance the human condition. In *The Economic Consequences of the Peace*, written when Keynes had most contact with Bloomsbury, 'Keynes asserted not only his own claim to attention but the claim of economic science to shape the future. The princes of the old world had left a dreadful mess; it was the task of the scientists to clean it up' (Skidelsky 2003: 249). Further, Keynes permitted the notion that agents might act as if they were certain about future economic outcomes, even if they were not:

> the necessity for action and for decision compels us as practical men to do our best to overlook this awkward fact [of uncertainty] and to behave exactly as we should if we had behind us a good Benthamite calculation of a series of prospective advantages and dis-advantages, each multiplied by its appropriate probability, waiting to be summed.
>
> (Keynes 1973: 114)

Yet it is possible to identify non-modernist traits in Keynes's thought. Ruccio and Amariglio (2003) argue that Keynes's notions of uncertainty and probability represent postmodern moments. Keynes can be seen to emphasise in both his early work on probability and in his later economic writings the impossibility of certain knowledge and the centrality of uncertainty. This contrasts with the neoclassical treatment of probability and uncertainty, which assigns probabilities to future events. For Keynes, such calculation is not the only way of arriving at probabilities. Other means can be used, such as intuition.

This position has postmodern hallmarks firstly because it shows that economists, like other people, can face limits to their knowledge. Certain things are simply unknowable, and the knowledge of the 'expert' economist may be no better than that of the economic agent (Amariglio and Ruccio 1993: 341–2). Second, it suggests that people cannot always act according to rational motivation; 'animal spirits' may be responsible. This contradicts the modernist idea that action is exclusively based on rational activity which originates in the mind. Third, it undermines traditionally modernist economic concepts, like equilibrium, which are associated with certainty, accuracy and numerical precision (Ruccio and Amariglio, op. cit.: 71–3). Instead, 'whim or sentiment or chance' may sometimes motivate economic action.

Uncertainty is not relevant only to Keynes's theory of interest. The existence of uncertainty and a lack of scope for rationality relate to the theory of effective demand and the need for intervention in order to bring the economy back to full employment. If economic agents cannot know about the future with certainty, and still further if these uncertain agents act together in such a way that may lead to economically undesirable outcomes, it may make sense for government to intervene to bring about a more useful economic situation. Likewise Keynes's ideas about the Bretton Woods system were intended to insure against uncertainty about the future, as well as to help engineer global economic prosperity. As his first biographer Roy Harrod points out, Keynes '... disliked reverting to the law of the jungle. His instincts were for international cooperation' (Harrod 1972: 621). The centrality of uncertainty to this system and the resulting need for co-ordination from non-market agencies can be contrasted with the modernist standpoint of the Washington consensus, where the belief that economic systems operate deterministically and that future economic outcomes can be calculated with some certainty mean that the global economy is largely unregulated.

All this is not to suggest that Keynes was a postmodernist; simply that he engaged with modernist questions, and that it is significant that he did so long before the emergence of the Washington Consensus, and before modernist economics became dominant. The different role of rationality in Keynesian economics and the resulting difficulties with predicting the future undermine the self-confidence of modernist economics.

4.4.2 Kalecki

Michal Kalecki's ideas about development represent a particularly relevant alternative to the methodology of the Washington Consensus. Although much of Kalecki's work was devoted to socialist or developed capitalist economies, and he was no postmodernist, he wrote an important series of essays on development with important implicit methodological underpinnings that can be interpreted as relating to the divide between modernism and postmodernism. He can be considered a Post-Keynesian (although in a sense he was 'pre-Keynesian' because he pre-empted Keynes's theory of effective demand) with an open-systems approach, who would have considered the universalism of the Washington Consensus to be misplaced and inappropriate. Many of the drawbacks of modernist-type thinking had already been recognised in his *Essays on Developing Economies,* a collection published posthumously in 1976. Kalecki had a distinct style of thinking which would have precluded him from an essentialist or determinist approach. Moreover, as we shall see, with respect to development economics his approach had certain advantages over Keynes's. As Joan Robinson puts it in the introduction to the *Essays*: 'Kalecki had never learned the orthodox doctrine, and had no need to escape from it' (Kalecki 1976: 7).

Kalecki's methodology possessed four defining characteristics. First, he used an open-systems methodology and believed that a model's assumptions should be realistic; second, he understood that the kind of economics appropriate in the developing world[5] was different to that in developed economies; third, he recognised the importance of politics; fourth, he never used the concept of utility and rarely employed the idea of equilibrium.

Eschewing positivist methods, Kalecki appeared to believe a final 'answer' to the problems of development was unlikely. As one of his collaborators puts it: 'Kalecki was always suspicious of too sweeping formulations and excessive reliance on one single "miracle" solution. He would always emphasise the importance of analysing concrete solutions and bringing into the picture all relevant factors be they economic or not' (Sachs 1977: 54). This approach can be seen in the differing advice he gave to the four main countries with which he was involved: Israel, India, Cuba and Bolivia. It would be wrong, however, to see Kalecki himself as a pluralist in the broadest sense because he identified two main models of the economy – one for developed countries and one for developing – rather than a multitude of ways of thinking about development.

Kalecki did not see it as possible to isolate all relevant variables in any given scenario, rather his approach was to model a real situation as best as possible, drawing tentative conclusions with a particular aim in mind. He rarely talked of economic 'laws' and did not believe himself to have arrived at a concrete developmental truths valid for all time. His

> theorising was usually directed towards some fairly immediate purpose, such as the explanation of economic fluctuations, the level of unemployment etc. His theorising was usually directed towards the explanation of real world phenomena which he regarded as important, and his abstractions and assumptions were related to the concrete conditions of the world he sought to explain.
>
> (Sawyer 1985: 147)

and '...in most of his theorising, Kalecki had a clear objective in mind...and whilst the assumptions would be attuned to the purpose at hand they were also based on observations of the real world. Thus assumptions are specifically chosen for their apparent relevance and importance' (ibid.: 271). Kalecki appreciated that the objects of knowledge were not fixed across time and space – and understood the need to adapt the theory of effective demand (his major innovation) to the context of developing countries, where capital was scarce and labour relatively abundant. Kalecki was, however, much more convinced about the possibilities for maths and econometrics than Keynes, and he placed more emphasis on the role of objective analysis rather than the subjective.

The second defining characteristic of Kalecki's approach was his distinction between the economics appropriate to developing and developing economies. Like Albert Hirschman he disputed the notion of a 'monoeconomics' which would work everywhere. He pointed out that a government-induced increase in effective demand would be less likely to reduce unemployment in developing economies, which are constrained by capital rather than by labour. In a developed economy the government may borrow to increase expenditure, with the aim of raising employment, which can then be put to effective use alongside previously underutilised capital equipment. This he termed a 'sort of financial trick' (Kalecki 1976: 21). However given the shortage of capital stock in developing countries, the main task was to increase productive capacity rather than to raise employment (although he acknowledged that a lack of effective demand was possible), 'the main problem here being the deficiency of productive capacity rather than the anomaly of its under-utilisation' (ibid.: 23). The difficulty thus lay with the supply side of the economy rather than the demand side.

Kalecki, although an advocate of trade, would have had no truck with the export-oriented model of the Washington Consensus, which concentrated on the elimination of barriers to trade, including tariffs and non-tariff barriers. Because of the Consensus's neoclassical belief in the substitutability of capital and labour and its advocacy of privatisation, its exponents believe that markets in poor countries will automatically adjust to the increased market access that came with trade liberalisation. Companies would produce more of the desired type of goods and services, leading to a more efficient overall outcome. According to supporters of the Washington Consensus, since the market would take care of things, there was thus little point in enacting measures aimed at developing the demand side.

Kalecki, in contrast, argued that developing countries should first place priority on expanding agricultural activity, a process which required some degree of planning. Unlike some of his contemporaries, such as Nurkse and Myrdal, he did not advocate a large-scale transfer of surplus labour into industry, and nor was he a proponent of full state ownership. Because of the inelasticity of supply of agricultural goods, the increase in incomes that would result from higher employment would lead to inflation. Unlike the essentially monetarist financial programming approach, Kalecki did not believe that restriction of the money supply would reduce inflation. Likewise better technology and productivity would be likely to raise efficiency only in urban areas, and would be likely to reduce employment elsewhere. It might be argued that countries could import food instead of growing it themselves – but Kalecki suggested that this argument applied only to countries with significant natural advantages such as mineral deposits, which could be exported to pay for food imports.

Kalecki believed that foreign aid would be necessary in the absence of a country's ability to generate foreign exchange, but that aid should be evaluated on at least two criteria. First, does aid improve a country's balance of payments position? Ideally the improvement should increase investment in capital goods, social services or essentials rather than luxuries or intermediate goods. Second, do the additional resources raise investment above the rate of domestic savings, or are they diverted into consumption? Some economists continue to argue that foreign direct investment is preferable to aid because it comes with fewer strings attached and is non-distortionary. The RMSM uses foreign investment as the main way of closing the gap in the balance of payments. Kalecki, however, believed that the profits of foreign enterprises would be likely to be repatriated, with a resultant drain on the balance of payments, and that foreign investment may not go into areas of priority for development.

Theoretical solutions, Kalecki realised, were all very well, but their implementation would encounter political difficulties. 'At no time would Kalecki indulge in what might be called pure economics. The adjective "political" weighed high in his brand of political economy' (Sachs, op. cit.: 55). The need for planning to bring about the desired long-term increase in investment in agriculture was, Kalecki understood, likely to bring political opposition. Feudal landowners would be unlikely to give up their rights quickly and they often held significant power in government. Increasing the rate of investment should not be achieved by taxing the poor, so taxes have to be levied on the rich – which is often politically unpalatable. For Kalecki, government spending to restore a higher rate of effective demand could be on poverty reduction, an objective which may conflict with the priorities of industrialists. In the United Kingdom it has been argued that one of the reasons Keynesianism was accepted was the need to expand arms spending for the Second World War. 'Overcoming the resistance to such institutional changes by the privileged classes is a much more difficult proposition than the financial trick which solves the problem of effective demand crucial for the develop economies' (Kalecki 1976: 26).

Neither Kalecki nor Keynes were utilitarians, but one of their key differences was that Kalecki performed analysis at the level of the social class rather than the individual. Keynes's approach was more easily adapted by those who wished to use utility functions. Like critical realists Kalecki saw that social classes influenced individual behaviour, and that individual agency both affects and is conditioned by social interaction. Because of his emphasis on social ties rather than autonomous individual behaviour, Kalecki rarely used the concept of equilibrium, preferring a picture in which competition was always imperfect and prices the product of the relative changes in the degree of monopoly and costs. Capitalist economies were in constant flux, their dynamism their interesting characteristic. Unlike Keynes, Kalecki saw little role for Marshallian supply and demand, believing perfect competition to be so unrealistic as to be barely relevant to the analysis of either developed or developing economies. Again, he had no need to escape the orthodox doctrine.

4.4.3 Sen

Nobel Prize-winner Amartya Sen is the figurehead of the human development approach, which amongst other things aims at overcoming the shortcomings of the kind of simple income-based or utilitarian measures of growth used by proponents of the Washington Consensus. One of the main benefits of his approach is that it allows for different development outcomes, avoiding any attempt to impose a tight monetary-based definition of development. Human development can be defined as the flourishing of humanity in its widest sense: 'human freedom is both the main object and the primary means of development' (Sen, 2000: 53). What Sen terms the 'evaluative reason' (ibid.: 4) for this is that development should be assessed according to whether freedoms have been enhanced. GDP growth is of little use unless it helps people gain more choice over how they live. The 'effectiveness reason' is that development depends on people's agency. Freedom, Sen argues, is both the aim of development (the 'constitutive role') and instrumental in achieving it.

> The constitutive role of freedom relates to the importance of substantive freedom in enriching human life. The substantive freedoms include elementary capabilities like being able to avoid such deprivations as starvation, under-nourishment, escapable morbidity and premature mortality, as well as the freedoms that are associated with being literate and numerate, enjoying political participation and uncensored speech and so on.
>
> (ibid.: 36)

The various interconnected types of freedom – political, economic, social, transparency-related and those related protective security – are not only ends of development, they are instrumental in achieving development. The political freedom to vote out an incompetent government, for example, can help improve economic policy. The economic freedom to use resources for production or exchange helps advance wealth and in turn improves people's lives. Social goods like health care and education promote development because, amongst other reasons, people live longer and may be more productive. Guarantees of transparency can help avoid corruption and financial irregularities, each of which is economically damaging. Protective security refers to social safety nets, which can help avoid severe deprivation.

'Functionings' are those things that a person might value, like being adequately fed or disease-free, or being part of a community. These functionings are specific to a particular person, and no set of functionings can be said to be universal. The capabilities approach pioneered by Sen suggests that development should be a process of establishing various combinations of feasible functionings, which together amount to capabilities. Human development involves expanding individual capabilities through improved health, knowledge and skills, and it involves the ability to achieve what is valued, using these capabilities. Poverty, for Sen, is a process of capability deprivation rather than only an absolute material level of income or inequality. Relative poverty in a rich country can feel a lot worse than the same level of income in a country in which everyone is at a similar level of income. Sen thus avoids the charge of universalism – that it is inappropriate to set one substantive standard of analysis for all countries – whilst avoiding the kind of relativism that would suggest that all experiences of poverty are different, and that the independent observer cannot judge the subjective feeling of one person's life experience. The capabilities approach is seen as a value-free way of assessing poverty and development in all countries. Despite its conservationist credentials and the value placed on various alternative ways of living, the concept of human development is not conservative. Like Stiglitz's vision of development as social transformation, it is about changing people's lives for the better.

The theory behind the human development approach has been readily converted into practical usage. The United Nations Development Program (UNDP) has translated the concept into a composite measure known as the Human Development Index (HDI), published annually since 1990. The three primary indicators that form the HDI – education, longevity and income – are used as proxies for knowledge, a long and healthy life and standard of living. The processes of improving these proxies are viewed as 'enlarging people's choices' (UNDP 1990: 10). The HDI has been criticised for failing to capture the multi-dimensionality of human development. The weightings given to each indicator in the index may also be considered arbitrary, and a slight alteration in one can have a significant impact on a country's HDI ranking. Whether or not one is an advocate of the HDI, and despite its inevitable shortcomings, it broadens the scope of development and gives due recognition to non-monetary indicators. The HDI has been acclaimed as a welcome addition to a debate under which conventional understandings and measurements placed economic growth as the sole manifestation of development.

Sen points out that human development is not a

> luxury that only richer countries can afford. Perhaps the most important impact of the type of success that the East Asian economies, beginning with Japan, have had is the total undermining of that implicit prejudice. These economies went comparatively early for the massive expansion of education, and later also of health care, and this they did, in many cases, *before* they broke the restraints of general poverty.
>
> (ibid.: 41)

This view is supported by the available evidence. In the fast-growing Asian economies, overall public investment grew rapidly in the 1980s and 1990s. In the early days of its development the Republic of Korea, for example, placed high priority on tertiary education and linked university research with industry, much of which was export-oriented.

Korea had the world's highest rate of university enrolment in 2004 and tertiary enrolments in technical areas were over twice the OECD ratio. These strong human development policies were necessarily state provided. In Korea the public investment to GDP ratio grew by 14 per cent between the 1970s and the 1980s and by an additional 14 per cent between the 1980s and the 1990s. During the same period, Thailand's ratio grew by 16 per cent and 14 per cent in these two periods, and in Malaysia the ratio rose by 60 per cent.[6]

Following this line of argument, the empirical work of Ranis, Stewart and Ramirez postulates a 'strong connection between economic growth and human development' (Ranis *et al.* 2000: 197). The authors develop two causal chains, stressing that while both economic growth and human development should be promoted jointly, human development is not just an end in itself. The first causal relationship (how economic growth supports human development) is that economic growth generates resources which in turn can be used for human development purposes such as greater investment in health and education. The second causal relationship (how human development fosters economic growth) shows that education and health can enhance labour productivity and ultimately growth. As for Sen, the direction of causality can run from human development to economic growth, and from economic growth to human development. The findings of Ranis and Stewart support Sen's contention that many successful developing countries, such as Singapore and Hong Kong, invested in health and education at an early stage in their development, implying that a healthy and educated workforce is a precondition for economic growth.

4.4.4 Hirschman

Like Kalecki, Albert Hirschman disputed the notion of 'monoeconomics' and his work crossed the border between economics and politics. Although he did not use the word methodology, Hirschman made frequent methodological statements alongside his economic insights, believing that it was important to discuss his approach to economics rather than conducting research using only pre-established ideas. Hirschman's economics was innovative as a result, and he did perhaps more than any other post-war thinker to establish the discipline of development economics, inventing important new ideas and concepts, many of which have subsequently enjoyed widespread usage.[7] Hirschman's economics is broad-ranging and varied, and it is impossible here to do justice to the full range of his work. But with respect to the task at hand, three methodological characteristics stand out: his identification of the existence of more than one kind of economics; his self-criticism; and his belief in the importance of learning by doing and local knowledge. Accordingly, like Kalecki and Keynes, he can be seen to have cautioned in advance against the kind of universalism and essentialism that characterised the Washington Consensus.

Written at the start of the decade which heralded the birth of the Washington Consensus, Hirschman's essay 'The Rise and Decline of Development Economics' (1980: 1–24) traces the path of the subject since its beginnings in the 1940s and 1950s. Hirschman identified two basic ingredients of economics: the monoeconomics claim and the mutual-benefit claim. Monoeconomics implies that underdeveloped countries are no different to developed economies and that the same approach can be applied to both. The mutual-benefit claim is that economic relations can benefit both developed and underdeveloped economies. This typology reveals amongst other things that the conventional Marxist approach held a belief in monoeconomics in common with the orthodoxy (even though Marxism had in mind a different economics and disputed the mutual-benefit claim). This opposition to development economics from two otherwise opposing angles partly explains the discipline's relative decline by the late 1970s.[8]

Hirschman goes on to explain that development economics came to prominence as a result of Keynes's establishment of two kinds of economics – the special neoclassical case applying to full employment and under which risk can be quantified, and the other, under which labour and capital are underemployed and assessments about the future are made using ordinary or human logic. 'The Keynesian step from one to two economics was crucial: the ice of monoeconomics had been broken and the idea that there might be yet another economics had instant credibility...' (Hirschman, op. cit.: 6). Like Kalecki, Hirschman understood that redundancy of capital is less common in developing countries because the capital stock is much less advanced, and that underemployment of labour is more likely. Rural underemployment is thus more widespread in developing economies, and a different approach was needed to overcome it.

Hirschman cites the work of Gerschenkron in affirming the different approaches to industrialisation used by orthodox and development economics. Delayed industrialisation, the entrenchment of staples production and the inability of modern capital-intensive industry to absorb agricultural labour are some of the reasons given for the inappropriateness of orthodox economics in development situations. Gerschenkron '...showed once and for all that there can be more than one path to development, that countries setting out to become industrialised are likely to forge their own policies, sequences, and ideologies to that end' (ibid.: 11). Hirschman's work in political theory and philosophy led him to use the Hegelian notion of dialectic, which he identified in the process of contact between the ideas of development economics with orthodox economics. It turned out that many of his strategies for overcoming underdevelopment (Hirschman 1958), aimed at more fully using human and capital resources, were also applicable to developed countries. 'Our understanding of the economic structures of the West will have been modified and enriched by the foray into other economies' (Hirschman 1980: 9). The final result was not reunification, but two versions of economics, each of which was enriched through contact with the other.

A further defining feature of Hirschman's thought was his self-analysis. Like Geertz and others, he believed it was important to discuss his own predispositions and subjectivity, and in this sense Hirschman can be seen to display a form of self-reflexivity. Acknowledging his own fallibility, and the fallibility of economics – as in the collection *A Propensity to Self-Subversion* (1995) – prompted Hirschman towards the recognition that it was unlikely that the application of a single universal logic would lead to timeless truths. Instead, useful views about development economics were more likely to be attained through dialectical argument, the revision of ideas and conscious self-criticism. The likelihood of being wrong, even slightly, led Hirschman towards the view not only that no single approach towards development should be promoted, but that there probably is no single route to development.: '...I can lay claim to at least one element of continuity in my thought: the refusal to define "one best way"' (ibid.: 76).

Hirschman sounds very like a critical realist when he says that

> Whether the sun turns around the earth or the earth circles around the sun, we are certain that both of these propositions cannot be true at the same time. We tend to forget that, in the social world, things are much more tangled and ambiguous. Here any connection we have established convincingly between events, as though it were a universally valid law, could be found simultaneously to hold and not to hold (or to hold in a very different form) in various subsections of human society.
>
> (ibid.: 91)

In distinguishing between the methods of the natural and social sciences he almost directly disputing Williamson's later use of the natural metaphor concerning the truth of the Washington Consensus as 'akin to proof that the earth is flat'. As we shall see in the case of Singapore, paradigms can overlap, and pragmatic governments can use contrasting economic theories in the same development situation.

A final feature of Hirschman's economics that pre-empted methodological concerns over the Washington Consensus and implicitly cautioned against the kind of modernism implicitly assumed in its methodology was his belief in the importance of local knowledge. According to Santiso: 'For Hirschman, the most important thing is learning by doing' (Santiso 2000: 99). Similarly to Bourdieu, Hirschman believed that only by doing things was it possible to know about things, and knowing fully about things requires local knowledge. In some cases a government may not even have preconceived objectives: it must be allowed to fail, and must be permitted to try out different avenues. In opposition to the relativist views of postmodernists, Hirschman believed it was important to learn lessons from past development experiences – but that it was also important to contextualise these lessons. Development experiences must involve the beneficiaries of development programmes in design, monitoring and subsequent assessment. The subjects of development must be permitted to say what they want from the process, to be involved in enacting programmes and to own the outcomes. Hirschman is unlikely to have believed that such things could be decided from Washington.

4.4.5 Preliminary conclusions

Acknowledging Keynes's position and that of some postmodernists, it is possible to see that development 'experts' may have little more (and perhaps less) knowledge about the economy than economic actors or national policymakers with particular insights about the economy. Yet outsiders tend to bring useful external detachment, which may complement the situatedness of economic actors. Given this situation, ceding control over economic policy decisions to local economic actors and policymakers with particular insight into the development situation (as suggested by Hirschman) helps overcome the problem of uncertainty. The more devolved are economic policy choices, the less likely they are to succumb to the problems associated with essentialism and foundationalism. A more pluralistic development policy spectrum, which permits a multitude of approaches and economic relationships, is likely to be less deterministic. Similarly it is unlikely that economic reform programmes can predict outcomes with the confidence assumed under the Washington Consensus. Instead, it is worth bearing in mind that people sometimes act according to whim or animal spirits.

Kalecki, an economist with no postmodern leanings, brings to the debate the valuable realisation that economic theory can be open-ended and yet still capable of achieving useful concrete solutions. Disputing monoeconomics, and focusing on immediate cases rather than trying to achieve general abstract truths, he showed that an economics is possible which rejects even some of the most revered totems of the mainstream – utility, preference curves and equilibrium. Like many realist economists, he crossed the boundary between the economic and the political, understanding the fallacy of composition.

Sen, perhaps more than most other development theorists, develops a vision of development that is compelling and wide-ranging yet avoids the universalising claims of modernists. Sen's ideas are so valuable because they allow the economist who is interested in transcending the difficulties of modernism and postmodernism to perceive what development might look like. Seeing development as the enhancement of capabilities does not require a rigid or tight definition of the specific goals of human advancement, and it can accommodate different sets of values; yet it is not conservative. Unlike some postmodernists, who allow little role for wide-ranging social or state action, Sen sees development as the transformation of society and as the progression of freedom.

Ironically, despite Hirschman's call for greater modesty in economics and his identification of the 'decline' of his discipline, after the 1980s economics became *less* modest, not more so, and development practice was not a series of unrelated technical processes. The formalisation of economics became allied with its ascendancy over other disciplines. After the 1980s, there was really only one economics. Development 'experts' believed that scientific economics could slay the dragon of backwardness. Yet Hirschman's ideas were prescient, crystallising the doubts about one-size-fits-all recommendations that would later bedevil the Washington Consensus.

The thinkers discussed here offer a non-universalising view of economics that gives greater voice to the inhabitants of developing countries. The insights of these thinkers suggest that academic abstraction and idealisation can only go so far – and that the wide-ranging, sometimes inconsistent reality of lived human experience forms a more solid basis for development economics, even if it may be less satisfying in that it provides no blueprints. Rather than abandon economics altogether for an entirely particularist approach which avoids active policy, a better solution may be to reform the practices of the development economist so that he becomes more aware of diversity and the multiplicity of experiences in the global South. Both modernist and postmodernist economic approaches tend to show scepticism about intervention in human affairs; the postmodernist because she expresses scepticism about 'grand theory', the modernist because he believes that reducing government intervention in markets will progressively increase wealth. Surely a middle ground is possible, which retains economic intervention, but tempered by the recognition that intervention can take radically different forms, depending on context?

4.5   Why reflexivity matters

Whilst theory is essential in the practice of development economics, a methodological approach, which examines the framework within which methods are chosen, helps anchor the selection of theories on solid foundations. Bourdieu's epistemological project, which is useful for the job at hand, has important implications for contemporary development economics and for the methodological divide between modernism and postmodernism. His suggestion that the subjective and the objective cannot always be disentangled during analysis of other societies means that it is difficult actively to promote development without bringing in outside values or trying to identify abstract meanings. The entanglement of subjectivism and objectivism is not in itself a problem, it is simply an often-ignored reality which, unless it is acknowledged, can weaken the results of policy advice.

An example from development economics of the difficulty of separating the subjective from the objective concerns the issue of employment. In many developing countries, and most developed nations, paid employment is considered a necessity for survival. In neoclassical terms this might be dealt with in some function of the form $Y = f(K, L)$ or $Y = f(AK, L)$, etc, where Y is income, K capital and L labour. Labour, paid its marginal product, combined with capital (perhaps augmented by technology, A), produces income.

It is well known that cash employment is either peripheral or non-existent in a number of traditional societies. Paid work can be sporadic, temporary or part-time, and unpaid work is often a matter of survival. Outsiders seeking an objective analysis tend to use conventional categories in order to generalise. This ignores the problem that people may value ends other than income, or that labour often cannot be distinguished from leisure, or capital from technology. In other words it is difficult to represent labour as just L, or technology as A, or capital as K. These categories have local subjective meaning that it is difficult for the outsider to comprehend. Not only do traditional societies treat labour differently; all societies may have slightly different ways of approaching work. Adopting what is imagined to be an objective approach may be inappropriate anywhere. To homogenise income, capital or labour such that they can be represented as a letter is legitimate as a heuristic technique aimed at highlighting an abstract relation, but when applied to policy it may not fully capture local subjective meaning and therefore might not produce convincing, or complete, explanation. The aim is to avoid what Graham Greene wrote about the character Cubitt in the novel *Brighton Rock*:

> He was like a professor describing to a stranger some place he had only read about in books: statistics of imports and exports, tonnage and mineral resources and if the budget balanced, when all the time it was a country the stranger *knew* from thirsting in the desert and being shot at in the foothills.
>
> (Greene, 1978: 185)

It might be argued that objectivism is not necessarily a quality of the outsider, in this case the international financial institution. According to this line of thinking the World Bank or IMF might merely portray its own, subjective viewpoint and it is wrong to talk of a dualism between the outsider-objectivist and the insider-subjectivist. Users of the Washington Consensus are at pains to portray their approach as scientific and relevant to any situation. Attempts by the international financial institutions to harness subjective knowledge have often made little practical difference to policy and have conflicted with the overall universalist approach. The Consensus's self-identification as objectivist is good reason at least provisionally to consider it part of this category.

A more pertinent apparent objection is that the 'insider' – the inhabitant of a developing country – is perfectly capable of accumulating objective knowledge. Much post-colonialist literature has sought to overturn the idea that only foreigners can be objective. Increasing access to education, travel and the recruitment of developing country nationals into international institutions have broken down the racist notion that it is impossible for non-Europeans to have a worldview that extended beyond their immediate horizons. This point is not really an objection. The notion of reflexivity derived from Bourdieu aims exactly for a reconciliation of the objective with the subjective. In development this implies further assimilating developing countries into development theory and practice, which means that developing-country nationals, in conjunction with those of other nations, should run the global development organisations.

Critics might object that drawing attention to the gap between the objective and the subjective drives a further wedge between developed-country inhabitants and their developing-country counter-parts. According to this argument development is a common enter-prise and participants should collaborate on equal terms irrespective of their origins. It is impossible, for practical policy purposes, to draw a distinction between objectivity and subjectivity, so the sta-tus quo should remain. But arguing that development is a common endeavour obscures the reality that the wealthy nations finance and control the major global development institutions, that they are run by developed-country nationals[9] and that they are staffed mostly by those trained in the developed world. Although to some observers the development institutions may appear to work in harmonious collaboration with developing countries, developed nations, like any-where, hold their own interests uppermost. Bourdieu's aim, to repeat, is to propose a method with which to reconcile the benefits of the objective and the subjective, and to make theory more practical. The reality is the reverse of what this apparent objection supposes. Ignoring reflexivity allows the gap between the advice of the global development institutions and the needs of developing countries to persist.

Highlighting the continuity between subjectivity and objectivity underlines the importance of policy ownership. The fact that outside institutions find it difficult to understand other forms of knowledge means that it is important to cede ownership of any economic transi-tion to local authorities and to local people. Moulding subjective reality into any plan for economic development better fits economic policy with reality.

But there must *be* policies to manipulate. Policy space is crucial in ensuring that the promotion of development fits with national pri-orities. Chang (2005) points out that the major international finance institutions have an increasing influence on national government pri-orities, particularly trade and industrial policy. A form of 'mission creep' has meant that the World Bank, IMF and WTO now push for specific targets such as independent central banks, inflation targets and a binding agreement to reduce non-agricultural tariffs towards zero. All of these trends are more than just changes in policy; they are changes in the way that policy can be formulated and they deprive government of policy autonomy. Trade policy provides an interesting case study. Although discussion at UNCTAD XI, the organisation's biennial conference held in Sao Paulo in 2004, centred around the concept of policy space, the concept has yet to be applied in any meaningful sense. The WTO around the same time began to talk of 'Collective Preferences', in other words national values that trade negotiations should not compromise (Lamy 2004). The Ministerial meetings in Cancun during 2003, Hong Kong 2005 and the mini-Ministerial in Geneva 2008 involved little practical use of this concept. Given the subsequent moves at the WTO towards further market opening in developing countries, and the intransigence of developed countries on so-called special safeguard mechanisms, which a number of developing countries argued that they needed to protect domestic industries in times of crisis, the discussion amounted to little. When international institutions deny that choices exist, and portray the Washington Consensus as akin to 'proof that the earth is not flat', accompanying advice with large loans, many developing countries are persuaded that there is, in fact, no choice. Policy autonomy is reduced by the denial that it exists.

It might be suggested that developing countries benefit from a reduction in policy space. The main idea is that governments engage in a 'race to the bottom', during which they reduce their remit in an effort to improve market confidence and to attract trade and capital. Ideal policies are considered to be minimal social insurance, flexible labour markets, deregulation, privatisation and restrictive monetary policy. This type of thinking is exemplified in Thomas Friedman's (1999) 'Golden Straitjacket' argument:

> As your country puts on the Golden Straitjacket, two things tend to happen: your economy grows and your politics shrinks... [The] Golden Straitjacket narrows the political and economic policy choices of those in power to relatively tight parameters. That is why it is increasingly difficult these days to find any real differences between ruling and opposition parties in those countries that have put on the Golden Straitjacket. Once our country puts on the Golden Straitjacket, its political choices get reduced to Pepsi or Coke– to slight nuances of tastes, slight nuances of policy, slight alterations in design

to account for local traditions, some loosening here or there, but never any major deviation from the core golden rules.

(Friedman 1999: 87)

Closer examination of various development success stories – from the East Asian Tigers to contemporary China – reveals a wide variety of policy options. Democratic Taiwan is the site of fierce political debate over economic policy. South Korea, which only passed a law fully permitting foreign investment in 1998, routinely violated Friedman's 'golden rules' during its development, and many consider the country to be one of the most successful examples of economic development in history (see, for example, Wade 1990; Chang 2007). China's state-owned enterprises, fixed exchange rate and capital controls suggest that rapid economic growth can occur without full liberalisation. Malaysia's capital controls and currency peg appear at best to have helped stave off further financial-market volatility in 1998, and at least did no harm.

Rodrik (2002b) has pointed out that a number of countries, such as Argentina in the 1990s, have engaged in a 'race to the bottom' with disastrous results. Whilst the Argentinean president and finance minister aimed first and foremost to satisfy international investors, eventually this policy became unsustainable because it was wreaking social harm. Markets anticipated the popular backlash, prompting a fresh exodus of capital, and the ministers were forced to resign. Rodrik's point is that in democracies, politics can be the deciding factor in determining international investment confidence: 'When push comes to shove, democracy shoves the Golden Straitjacket aside' (ibid.: 15).

4.6   A taxonomy of reflexive development practice

The aim here is to show how the exclusively modernist approach of the Washington Consensus was inappropriate, and to show that a methodological position which explicitly tried to overcome the problems of modernism and postmodernism holds benefits. An advantage of discussing the methodological framework is that it ameliorates controversy over political bias and narrows the debate over method.

'Going beyond' two perceived opposites, whatever they are, involves the danger of a rhetoric that ends up with the same misguided objectivism discussed above. If the impression is given that the opposite poles are the only two available and that the new resolution is unique, then the synthesis can be falsely accorded a higher truth status than its predecessors. In reality, though, a number of resolutions to polar opposites are usually possible, and the content of the resolution depends on what the poles are and how they are described. Although a dialectical analysis of modernism and postmodernism in the Washington Consensus *helps,* the risk remains of giving too much legitimacy to the result. The kind of synthetic policies arising out of the engagement of modernism with postmodernism are not appealing simply by virtue of eclecticism. Policies must have advantages over their predecessors and have real-world applicability rather than forming a new, fixed, theoretical dogma. With careful analysis, it should be possible to build the methodological foundations for the kind of theoretical approach that interacts with the real world. Engagement with the real world becomes the touchstone of theoretical validity rather than dialectical reconciliation. This recognition frames the discussion in the following section, which outlines a possible methodological framework for a reflexive development process. The taxonomy is aimed at economic development theoreticians, practitioners in the global institutions, and national policymakers.

Acknowledging reflexivity, successful development practice and understanding of that practice would be informed by the following five characteristics:

1. An examination of the influence of external values and norms. Partly, the idea of being reflexive simply means having an open mind and looking at your own project, as suggested in the writings of Bourdieu and other theorists of reflexivity. Being socially reflexive at an institutional level would require that the agents of a development process ask to what extent 'grand theory' is useful, distinguishing between objective advice and what is simply a reflection of interests or a projection of a different worldview. To this extent, the ideas of those in the postmodern tradition, such as Foucault (op. cit.) and Lyotard (op. cit.) are difficult to ignore. Yet extreme interpretations of such arguments go too far in dismissing the idea of *any* universals. In trying to dismiss grand theory, it is easy to end up back with the same level of abstraction and idealisation that was the object of criticism in the first place. One of the advantages of realist approaches such as that of Lawson (op. cit.) is that they recognise that abstraction is necessary, whilst arguing for the grounding of theory in practical reality. By looking at the practical, nitty-gritty detail of development, it is possible to see that certain objective universals hold true.

The kind of objectivist or universal input that is valuable usually aims to empower national policymakers to achieve national goals, often using lessons learnt from other countries. This might mean enlisting international assistance to improve statistics to a basic level and teaching government officials how to understand them; technical advice aimed at enabling participation in, or rejection of, international trade agreements; assistance with public finance; or help with the design of nationally-driven macroeconomic policy. Examples of this kind of approach include the largely self-determined economic adjustment processes of Singapore (discussed in Chapter 7) and Malaysia, which drew on outside support in the form of the technical know-how of foreign companies or international agencies.

The desirability of an outside approach highlights the reality that development is a common human endeavour; and to that extent the postmodern questioning of *all* universals and *all* essentialism is misplaced. If development is desirable at all, it is a process that involves certain universals such as basic essentials including food and water, housing, education and health. For all its shortcomings, the Millennium Development Goals approach[10] acknowledges that total national autonomy is unlikely to produce the required results, and that a 'global partnership for development' is required. Sharing the analysis of development in a number of countries builds up expertise and economies of scale in knowledge. Using an outside agency can shift the blame for unpopular decisions away from national policymakers. Countries may not have the skills required for rapid development, importing administrative and technological know-how.

Values and norms do not spring from a vacuum. Pressure from vested interests and social influences can prompt international institutions to favour certain policies (Bøås and McNeil 2004). For instance the IMF policy of providing large loans to Russia during the late 1990s was influenced by the desire of US financiers for an exit strategy (for example, see Wedel 1998; Stiglitz 2002). Financial incentives such as loans can make it difficult to question accompanying conditionalities. Often, countries have had reform packages thrust upon them unnecessarily. To this extent it is important to examine whether reform is necessary at all.

The existence of material compulsions towards certain policy conclusions makes it unrealistic to expect all development institutions to perform a regular and unlimited assessment of values and norms. But perhaps the influence of material influences such as the desire of US financiers for an exit strategy makes it all the more important for development practitioners to be self-reflexive. Some attempt to examine values and norms is always possible, and the process highlights the reality that Washington Consensus-type policies are not compelled by global forces, but are open to choice.

Bourdieu and others (from Kuhn, op. cit. to Woolgar, op.cit.) show that science is affected, like every other activity, by social interests and undeclared predispositions. It is difficult to establish independent criteria from which to assess scientific knowledge, and highlighting the institutional backdrop of scientific enquiries makes it possible to contextualise scientific claims. Economists and policymakers are subject to social influences. For example the exclusive environment of early twentieth-century Cambridge may partly explain Keynes's elitist political views. This contextualisation applies to all within the development chain, from theorists, to those who devise policy, to practitioners and civil servants.

Exposing social or economic context does not automatically disprove the resulting ideas. The IMF worldview might have cogency whatever the material compulsion underlying it, and it is best challenged through argument and counter-evidence rather than only, for example, by revealing hidden interests. Room always exists for manoeuvre away from apparent economic interests, and a range of theories could be chosen as a result of one ideological position. For example the IMF financial programming model remained in widespread use for at least a decade after monetarism fell out of favour in the domestic policy context (Killick 1995b). The persistence of the model was a result not just of ideology, but of a modernist approach that believed that the answer to developing countries' problems had already been found, and that success lay in more focused application of the model.

Even if the link is not deterministic, context can help explain why people tend towards certain general theoretical influences rather than others. For example it is unlikely, given their location, training and close relation with US financial capital (described in Stiglitz 2002) that IMF economists would advocate socialisation of the means of production. Exposing social or economic interests can also help shed light on how appropriate policies are for certain value-systems or contexts. Applying a foreign approach which is not self-reflexive can result in the prioritisation of ends which may be inappropriate to the local situation. For instance short-term contractors – often the main agents of structural adjustment – do not have the opportunity to learn about important customs and culture. They may impose inappropriate foreign values and beliefs on economic policy proposals.

2. **An implicit assessment of the extent to which local context is important.** Together with point 1 this corresponds with the discussion of objectivity and subjectivity. If the existence of reflexivity

is acknowledged, the process of self-scrutiny suggested by Bourdieu requires questioning the importance of local context as well as external values and norms. Economics can learn from the bottom-up approach of anthropology, the aim of which is a detailed description of a culture rather than to squeeze the facts into an externally-created model. It is perhaps no surprise that the discipline of anthropology was one of the first to deal with the question of how researchers' values affect their output. Context, in this sense, becomes all-important. Most criticisms of the Washington Consensus revolve around its lack of attention to context, which matters for at least three interconnected reasons:

(a) People in different societies might behave in different ways. Economic theory must involve certain generalisations about human behaviour, and exaggerating behavioural differences tends to obscure the role of policy.[11] But social context creates important behavioural variations which in turn have implications for relations assumed in traditional models. For example some explanations of East Asian economic success highlight the importance of the work ethic and a desire to provide for subsequent generations. Although there are other, more important explanations for the East Asian boom, this idea relates to recent attempts to understand consumption and saving. A lack of appreciation of differences in economic behaviour partly explains why during the Asian financial crisis the IMF vastly over-estimated the threat of inflation, prescribing restrictive monetary and fiscal policies. The IMF also misunderstood the extent to which economic actors within a developmental state act against what might appear to be their own immediate interests for the benefit of the common good.

(b) Values might vary. As subjectivists would argue, values underlie theory even when it is couched in technical language. Not all inhabitants of developing countries aspire to the same goals as those within developed nations: Washington policymakers have different ideals to South Pacific subsistence farmers. Keynes, among others, has shown that the framework of utility maximisation is insufficient to accommodate wide variations in values. Many people are not utility-maximisers, while it can be difficult to assign numerical probabilities to future events. A basic standard of living is probably a universal goal, but beyond this it is difficult to generalise about the desire for more material wealth, as pointed out by Sen, who shows that development should be a process of securing basic functionings, some of which are specific to the individual or group, rather than only the attainment of riches.

(c) Institutions might be different (Schmid 2005). The economic anthropology literature (such as Hefner 1990; Billig 2000; Danby 2002) shows that even an institution like the market is constructed, and that it works in different ways. In some subsistence communities, for instance, a relative lack of scarcity means that the profit motive is minimal, and where markets exist, prices are similar because competition can be seen as unsocial. Even institutions like private property and money can take various forms. When the necessary institutions do not exist for deep-rooted cultural reasons, they often cannot be implanted in a short space of time. Assessing the extent to which institutions differ from conventional assumptions requires a corresponding adjustment of policy. In countries with no commercial tradition, rapid privatisation can make little sense because the private sector is too undeveloped to provide the service, and foreign companies are often reluctant to participate unless for a price that may not be worth paying.

These three features interact. Variations in values can cause behaviour that is unexpected from the outsider's point of view, while institutions may work differently because of diversity in behaviour or values. The importance of context underlines the need to build local ownership into sdevelopment experience. This means more than just consultation meetings or seeking consent from politicians: such processes can be manipulated or misunderstood. The country must itself be in charge of choosing and adapting theory, deciding what kinds of policies it wants and executing those policies, with the international institution in a supporting role.

3. **A recognition that economic tools, concepts and policies can undermine themselves, even though they were designed for greater control.** One of the main objections to modernist theories is their over-confidence. 'Grand narratives' claim to have created a system of thinking that is capable of explaining diverse events from central axioms or precepts. Given correct application of these axioms or precepts, using deduction, outcomes can be predicted with some degree of accuracy. Clearly the axioms need to be valid, but it is increasingly clear, moreover, that economic systems are open-ended and that some events are unpredictable. Even if they differ in important ways, the open-systems approaches of critical realists, Keynesians and the neo-Austrians lend

support to the broad tradition of reflexivity. In this sense, reflexivity means being modest about models and predictions.

If theory does not produce policies that have direct relevance to on-the-ground experience, these same policies can worsen the very problems that were identified in the first place. For example introducing Western notions of governance, with the introduction of powerful public service officials into close-knit, traditional societies, can institutionalise the very problems that they set out to solve. It may be better to use traditional methods of decision-making which deal with nepotism or corruption in consensual, devolved ways. Rigidly employing the same tools despite the existence of an ever-changing and differentiated reality can lead to a mismatch between policy and the economy, while policy in turn becomes part of that changing, open-ended reality. This is the kind of process that Giddens refers to when he discusses the concept of reflexive modernisation.

An important contribution is Paul Ormerod's argument in *Why Most Things Fail* (2005) and *The Death of Economics* (1994) that governments and businesses cannot possibly predict future outcomes with certainty because of the inherent randomness produced in economic systems. This kind of unpredictability is different to the Keynesian and critical realist notions of open systems discussed in Chapter 2, because it refers to stochastic unpredictability and draws on chaos theory, rather than emphasising the impossibility of knowing certain economic outcomes. A complete picture of GDP, on Ormerod's argument, is impossible because too many elements exist, and they adopt varying degrees of importance at different times. Collecting and analysing more statistics will not solve the problem: '... even when we have all the data and all the information that exists in a particular context, uncertainty can still prevail' (Ormerod 2005: 57). Ormerod probably goes too far in his scepticism about government policy, failing to recognise that reducing the size of government, especially in small developing economies, can often worsen uncertainty. Market failures, in many economies (for example during the Asian economic crisis), can be at least as destabilising as government failures. An understanding that all outcomes are uncertain, using an open-systems approach, should enable governments to design better policy, rather than implying that attempts to shape the economy should cease.

This said, the idea of reflexive feedback mechanisms is based on the principle that many parts of social reality affect themselves, and that cause-and-effect is only one way of conceiving of the relationship between entities in an economic system. It is possible to go deeper than a statement that policy making can fail; instead reflexivity implies that purported 'cure-all' policies are highly fallible, that policies must be applied in combination and that many policy recommendations are partly self-defeating. A parallel is the Lucas critique (Lucas 1976), which suggested that microfoundations to macroeconomic models were crucial, since aggregated data do not accurately capture individual behaviour. Policy advice succeeds or fails by virtue of its ability to deal with changing individual behaviour, while policy advice can change individual behaviour. Part of the challenge lies in disaggregating policy measures, and their outcomes, and taking action to rectify or avoid the negative consequences. One task of the practitioner of development economics is to minimise the extent to which aspects of policy undermine themselves and to remain alert to the possibility that once-successful policies might become outmoded.

4. An allowance for theory to be revised if it proves inadequate or as circumstances change. This should be obvious, but for all the teleology of mainstream modernist economists, many are reluctant to allow wide-ranging epistemological progress. The methodology underlying mainstream development economics during recent decades has remained somewhat stationary. Confronting the postmodern challenge does not mean accepting that methodologically 'anything goes'; rather it means an openness to fallibility, allowing for the possibility that theory which might have been appropriate previously, may, as circumstances change and enquiry proceeds, turn out to be inadequate. The honest reappraisal of theory becomes important, as, possibly, does its augmentation or replacement. This is more than just Popperian falsificationism; competing theories may subsist simultaneously in the same context. Moreover theories may become inadequate because social circumstances change rather than because science makes new discoveries.

An understanding of policy and economic theory which was self-scrutinising, recognised the importance of context, was aware of the potential for policies to undermine themselves and understood the social influences on policy, would be more likely to lead to a revision of development advice to make it more closely tailored to local circumstances. The arguments of Bourdieu imply that economics might periodically re-assess its methods. Economists such as Marshall and Keynes believed that economics is not an ever-enlarging body of knowledge, but a way of thinking. Some pluralist economists would go further, disputing the uniform nature of economics and arguing instead that it includes several ways of thinking.

As Chapter 7 shows, successful developing countries such as Singapore have proven able periodically to change their development narratives, with the government altering its theoretical stance. Rather than operating exclusively within a developmentalist paradigm which shifted resources into areas of apparent comparative advantage, leaders began to talk in Schumpeterian terms, promoting entrepreneurship and highlighting what it saw as the benefits of a process which was pushing unemployment to historic highs. Not all states are as small, adaptable or in control of policy as Singapore, but the experience shows that the self-conscious reassessment of theory and policy can produce positive results, and that developing countries must retain policy autonomy to be able to cope with change.

4.7 Conclusion

An excessive concentration on style or form to the exclusion of action can be frustrating to the development economist who is interested in change. Some postmodernists do not consider themselves to be contributing anything more than stylistic variations, in the belief that proposing substantial alternatives commits the sin of modernism. Postmodernists, in particular in the tradition of Lyotard, that deny the possibility or even meaning of progress, or that suggest any social outcome is as good as another should perhaps be left to one side; such views are incompatible with the promotion of economic development on any definition.

The social sciences that are concerned with methodology can, however, contribute to the way that economists theorise and practise development. It would seem a profitable exercise for development economics to confront the challenge of postmodernism, even if it is to rebut it. Such exercises are not without precedent: John Maynard Keynes defined his relationship to modernism, and in so doing discussed issues that are now considered outside the boundaries of economics. He recognised that addressing fundamental philosophical questions, such as the role of the particular versus the universal, or the limits of human knowledge, are part of progress in economics.

The ideas of Sen, Hirschman and Kalecki offer examples of the kind of economics that can avoid the universalistic tendencies of modernists. Hirschman and Kalecki pre-empted concerns with the Washington Consensus and put political economy at the heart of their thinking. Sen offers a vision of development that allows for the pursuit of differing goals, and which may not be solely about the accumulation of material wealth. Hirschman was an advocate of pluralism, understanding that the Keynesian revolution heralded a shift away from 'monoeconomics'. The methodological insights of Bourdieu and other thinkers in the tradition of reflexivity are compatible with these thinkers. Bourdieu's approach, like Hirschman's, is inter-disciplinary, and points to the conclusion that economics is social theory rather than methodologically individualistic. Bourdieu proposes a research method that combines the objectivist stance of the outside researcher with the subjective angle of the local inhabitant. Purposefully performing self-reflexive analysis and positioning yourself inside the society that you are examining leads to more complete explanation. This affects method. It can be difficult to perform subjective analysis or research using an exclusively formal approach, and Bourdieu is critical of what he calls rational action theory. His approach urges caution in making recommendations or predictions, or the likely consequences are subject to uncertainty.

The kind of approach put forward by Bourdieu is at odds with the current methods of the international financial institutions, which are non-reflexive, do not recognise the social origins of theories of economic development and which have not engaged methodologically with the issues of modernism and postmodernism. Moreover, they do not take into account the importance of peculiar national social and economic details. These absences have made policy during the last two decades less effective than it otherwise might have been.

In proposing an outline of development practice, there is the danger of falling into the very prescriptivist trap that reflexive approaches try to avoid. The postmodern critique of the Washington Consensus shows that it has tried to force a tight straightjacket on to countries, irrespective of context. The taxonomy involves an implicit normative question: what are 'successful development processes'? The intention here was not to try and answer this question in any specific way, but simply to point out theoretical principles which might lead countries to choose their own development paths, thereby allowing them to discover successful development processes for themselves. It is hoped that the proposals are general enough to avoid defining development in a way that simply reflects the author's prejudices, whilst retaining some sort of theoretical purchase. I, as the author, plainly have a social background (discussed in the introduction) which affects what has been written, but at least acknowledging the existence of this background gives the reader some criterion with which to accept or dismiss the proposals. In any case it was acknowledged in point 1 above that exposing material or social motivations does not by itself disqualify the consequent ideas or behaviour.

The taxonomy is supposed to be more than just a wish-list. It may be all very well to argue for a change in the thinking behind the practice of contemporary development economics but the international institutional set-up may preclude methodological change. As suggested above, however, room always exists for theory to manoeuvre away from a simple reflection of material interests, and opponents of change often wrongly try to portray it as impractical, not just undesirable. The Washington Consensus can be replaced by self-aware, context-sensitive alternatives, based on methodological principles that lead to a close interaction between theory and practice.

Part two examines the taxonomy in the context of two developing countries, Vanuatu and Singapore. The next chapter outlines some of the reasons for choosing these two countries and discusses the issues of comparative study and contrastive explanation.

Part II

5
Introduction to the Case Studies

The two economies under discussion have peculiarities which make them very different from each other and from other developing countries. The differences between the two countries also means that any results from a comparison will prove limited. Vanuatu is officially 'least-developed', geographically isolated, poor and recently independent, while Singapore is richer than many developed nations, lies on a major trading route and has a long commercial history. Some postmodern-influenced views might suggest that comparisons between national economies are difficult anyway, and that such differences make the task even harder. Many mainstream modernist economists might also reject a comparison, since econometric studies often involve roughly similar countries, in the same geographic region, with the aim of isolating particular features which it is believed will contribute to cumulative economic knowledge.[1]

The discussion in Chapter 4, however, implied that *many* experiences of economic development hold lessons for each other, if sometimes limited, and that successful comparison lies in establishing objective points of comparison. Reflexivity implies thinking explicitly about methodology and perhaps revising it – rather than leaving methodology unspoken and unchanging – in order to help derive useful lessons. In line with the kind of approach suggested by the taxonomy, comparative studies help discern interesting results, but without giving them the appearance of timeless, concrete laws derived from within a closed system. Moreover unusual comparisons can produce surprising results.

Lawson highlights the value of contrastive studies when he notes that:

In short, it is through recognising that generalisations about concrete social circumstances and processes will usually have limits, and through exploring how specific generalisations break down in areas where our current understanding suggests (most reason for supposing) they could nevertheless have held, that we can learn, by way of contrast explanation, of hitherto unknown or insufficiently understood factors that make the difference.

(Lawson 2003: 100)

In a sense all science is about learning of hitherto or insufficiently understood factors, but in social science and some other areas this cannot be done in a laboratory environment. Lawson (ibid.: 88) illustrates his point with the example of plant breeding, under which researchers try to determine whether a particular chemical compound is responsible for increased crop growth. These experiments take place in an open field rather than in laboratory conditions. It would be difficult to perform a valid experiment on one plant in a laboratory and draw conclusive general results, so the researcher treats some plots in the field with the chemical compound and some without. If the plots treated with the compound grow faster, the compound can fairly be considered responsible. Lawson suggests that this kind of experimentation, partially modified, can be used in the social domain. The key point is that 'there is no presumption that any causal factor, including the compound under investigation, interacts with other causal factors mechanistically/atomistically' (ibid.: 89).

The case studies of Vanuatu and Singapore differ from the kind of contrast explanation recommended by Lawson in several important ways. First, the objective is not to apply critical realism, although there are, as noted earlier, points of similarity between critical realism and the realism of certain thinkers who promote a reflexive position. I do not make an explicit attempt to determine underlying causal mechanisms or demi-regs that might explain economic phenomena. Second, the case studies concern comparisons of entire economies – perhaps controversially, since some authors (such as Bergeron 2006) dispute the notion of the national economy – rather than discrete economic processes. Third, the purpose is not primarily to highlight new findings that are valid everywhere; it is to examine whether or not the taxonomy holds true in these particular economies.

Yet it is still worth acknowledging the general point that development economics does not take place in laboratory conditions, and that control experiments are not possible. Whilst the arguments of some postmodernists might go as far as to suggest that this means no lessons can be learnt, and that economics is fatally flawed, this is too extreme a view, and it is the purpose of this book to argue that a middle ground is possible. Lawson's suggestion is useful: that limited results can be derived from contrastive explanation, as suggested by the example of plant breeding. Whilst it may be inappropriate for economists to try to isolate constant event regularities and it is impossible to hold all other factors constant in an attempt to find incontrovertible results, limited lessons can be derived from more general experiments, where the specific explanation may not be known but where the results can be taken as valid. Looking at developing economies – perhaps two countries that would not normally be compared – alongside each other can yield surprising and interesting findings.

It is therefore worth establishing what kind of comparisons are worth discussing and learning from, and whether the taxonomy helps in this task. According to some strands of reflexive thinking, particularly the approach adopted by Bourdieu, analysis is most useful when it focuses on something of which the researcher is part. To *really* know about an economy means that you have to spend time there. Comparing countries in which I had not lived would have been unreflexive and would have involved a rejection of the need for involvement with the subject under study. The argument of authors who write on reflexivity, and others, that practice is inseparable from theory implies that it would have been self-defeating to theorise about reflexivity without examining the ideas in practice.

A further reason for selecting these particular case studies was to focus on the details of the countries in which I had lived. I wanted to recount the nitty-gritty details of economic life in the places that I knew, including the impact of political decisions and social trends. Did Singaporean cultural mores matter for economic policy-making? Were Vanuatu farmers as self-interested as mainstream models supposed? I also wanted to discuss the peculiar minutiae of which only the country inhabitant is aware, such as the impact of news, unusual habits or unspoken ways of behaving. After two decades of one-size-fits-all policy, do such features have repercussions for development economics?

This might seem an arbitrary way of selecting case studies, but it may be equally arbitrary to adopt the usual tactics, which are to select case studies on the basis of the quality of data, population, per capita GDP, size of the economy or even whether they fit well with a favoured theoretical approach. The approach of mainstream comparative economics often seems to take place using a series of standard data, using generic tools. In this sense the neo-Austrian view is worth considering: that statistics can aggregate incompatible scraps of information, and that apparently impartial statistical analysis can miss pivotal subjective details such as cultural habits, the everyday flow of news, people's reactions to that news and knowledge of flaws in data.

Although acknowledging the subjective is important, it does not mean abandoning statistics altogether. Selected descriptive statistics can be complemented with important subjective details. To reject the use of statistics entirely would mean that little could be appraised according to transferable criteria. Certain descriptive statistics, if accurate, such as balance of payments data, debt and GDP, can lead to helpful comparison – although limits must be acknowledged. Selected statistics are even more useful when subjective discussion establishes their validity and complements them with qualitative analysis.

Some statistical series can have more or less the same meaning in most countries. The balance of payments is calculated using a standard accounting method, which is why I use it in both chapters. Even if the data on which it is based can be unreliable, the IMF flow of funds analysis is often able to cross-check where problems occur and take remedial action. Debt statistics in various countries can also be compared, with some degree of caution, partly because they are subject to confirmation by the lender and the borrower. Trade data can be confirmed by an analysis of the mirror statistics, so that if US data show garment imports from Vanuatu, this can be checked with the home country's export data.[2] Although none of these uses of data is without its problems, they do provide rough benchmarks from which to make limited comparisons.

Contrary to the approach suggested by many modernists, and particularly positivists, it is questionable whether economic science is progressively building up knowledge about developing economies. This is not to say that economies and the processes that drive development cannot be understood better, but that knowledge about development must be thought of as subject to periodic revision, that it can be contradictory, and that knowledge of developing countries may deteriorate. Tools and findings that once were considered finalised may become less useful. A Kuhnian perspective would suggest that what are regarded as truths might quickly become invalid as a paradigm changes. Further, as will be shown in the case of both Vanuatu and Singapore, new circumstances make new theories and policies relevant.

Comparison is a useful device because it avoids wide-scale generalisations about economic development and throws certain explanatory features into relief without suggesting lessons that are true for all time and across all developing countries. Comparison also allows that different peoples understand the world differently, and that understandings of the world are continually evolving. Achieving 'results' that are only temporary and limited may feel unscientific, but in fact this kind of approach mirrors developments in many natural sciences, where, as shown earlier, in recent years caution about modernism and positivism has increased.

The discussion of Vanuatu and Singapore shows that lessons can exist on different levels, including at least the methodological and practical levels. Discussions of developing countries frequently occur exclusively at the empirical or practical level, and theory is selected only insofar as it generates a set of final, positive results. The researcher may run a regression of GDP growth rates against some explanatory variables to which numerical values have been assigned, such as corruption, ethnic fragmentation or inflation. Once these findings have been 'established', it may be asserted that therefore corruption or ethnic conflict or inflation are always, in general, bad for economic growth in developing countries. Apart from the problems of assigning numerical values to qualitative data; or the difficulty of establishing timeless results in an open, evolving system; or the different ways in which variables combine across economies, approaches which produce purely empirical results are unnecessarily particular and may miss valuable methodological findings. Vanuatu, for example, is ethnically homogeneous, has no history of inflation and corruption was not the problem it may be in other countries. Analysis of such a unique economy must involve a higher level discussion.

An exclusive focus on practical specifics can mean that knowledge is conceived in a closed way, and that alternative ways of thinking about knowledge are not considered. Focusing on accuracy, specificity and measurement omits the subjectivity that is sometimes necessary when discussing open economic systems. Over-specificity can also lead to overconfidence, particularly in the prescriptions of the international consultants involved in economic reform programmes. This was certainly true in Vanuatu. As Erik Angner has recently argued, 'economists-as-experts are likely to be victims of significant overconfidence, and ... the consequences can be dramatic' (Angner 2006: 2).

The IMF or World Bank's self-criticisms of structural adjustment only go so far. The institutions may say that interest rates were too high or that reforms were carried out too quickly. A lack of attention to methodology (as opposed to method) means that moving beyond the monetarist financial programming approach is rarely considered, still less qualifying the use of models or even occasionally replacing models with subjective analysis. The focus of the analysis underlying such programmes of intervention is often so narrow that desired results are assumed in advance. Avoiding this problem would require a more widespread and open-minded discussion about how knowledge develops, including the possibility that economists cannot know about some outcomes with any certainty. Comparative case studies can highlight such epistemological concerns. Issues like policy autonomy and ownership, which were so important in Singapore, are more to do with knowledge of how *any* policies work, than about the policies themselves.

When a comparative discussion moves beyond the merely empirical, the importance of ontology likewise becomes clear (Lawson 2003: 28–62). In the case of Vanuatu close attention to the use of money in traditional communities would have required questioning the generic nature of the structural adjustment model and its standard conception of money. This kind of discussion would have had important implications for assumptions about how markets work in that particular society, and in turn for privatisation, public expenditure and even the role of the state.

Development practitioners are not usually philosophers, and they do not use words like ontology and epistemology, but this kind of discussion is not complicated: it involves basic ideas like 'can money be defined the same way here as in other countries?'; 'should the results of this economic model be interpreted rigidly?'; 'should we abandon the model if it does not work?'; 'Might the institutions in this country not be compatible with rapid privatisation?' To repeat a point made earlier, help with answers to these kind of questions usually comes from listening to local people.

Contrary to positivist approaches, which tend to assume that one school of thought is valid until superseded, the case studies presented in Chapters 6 and 7 show that different theories and schools of thought can prove valid even within the same country. The case of Singapore does not show that the early developmentalist paradigm failed, but that after a certain stage of development and in a new international context, other influences such as a Schumpeterian emphasis on entrepreneurship and the new growth theory were held to be increasingly relevant. This is hard to cope with from a deductive-nomological, closed-systems methodological perspective. The different schools of thought are partly incompatible, and results cannot be derived using established laws from a central system of axioms. To this extent the postmodern critique is valuable in that it recognises the possibility that contradictory ways of thinking may operate simultaneously, and that not all understanding proceeds on the basis of rational calculation. But it is not necessary to resort to irrationalism or relativism; pluralistic conceptions of knowledge allow for the partial co-existence of different schools of thought.

The next chapter is the case study on Vanuatu. It follows the general outline of the taxonomy in order to make an assessment of whether the taxonomy is an adequate framework within which to examine development theory and practice in this context.

6
Vanuatu: The Anti-Crusoe Economy

6.1 Introduction

Having discussed various definitions of reflexivity and drawn out some of their implications for the methodology of development economics in the form of a taxonomy, I attempt here to examine these ideas in practice. The idea that theory and practice are linked is central to reflexivity – and reflexivity itself requires practical application. Since the taxonomy is partly based on a critical discussion of the Washington Consensus there is also a need to examine the validity of the Washington Consensus. Vanuatu is a particularly good case study, for if the Consensus is to claim valid universality, it must apply not only to well-known less-developed states, but also to the global periphery.

This chapter examines Vanuatu's economic experience between 1997 and 2004, a period during which the Asian Development Bank (ADB) initiated a Washington Consensus-inspired[1] structural adjustment package known as the Comprehensive Reform Programme (CRP). The aim is to examine the points of the taxonomy in this context.

If there is any country that is at the periphery of the world economy it is surely Vanuatu. Ranked at the top of the 111 countries in the Commonwealth Secretariat index of vulnerability (Atkins *et al.* 2000),[2] it is three hours' flight from its nearest major market, Australia and has a population of only around 210,000.[3]

Since independence in 1980 Vanuatu has been designated a Least-Developed Country (LDC) by the United Nations (UNCTAD 2004). It is unlikely to lose its LDC ranking until at least 2013 owing to its inability to show improvement in two of the three categories by which LDC status is assessed – economic vulnerability and the development of human resources. Official GDP statistics are unreliable, but per capita

GDP appears relatively high for an LDC, at US$1,360 in 2005.[4] GDP growth is recorded at an average of 3.5 per cent between 1980 and 2000 but has slowed in recent years (ADB 1996; Vanuatu 2004).

A number of peculiar social and geographic features have influenced Vanuatu's recent economic experience. It is an archipelago of 83 islands, mostly inhabited, and spread across an exclusive economic zone of 530,162 km^2 – an area roughly the size of France. This economic fragmentation has hindered internal trade. The country's remote location in Melanesia in the southwest Pacific puts it far removed from major shipping and telecommunications links. A combination of smallness and fragmentation has hampered the achievement economies of scale and competition, and has rendered the economy naturally open. Tropical cyclones and earthquakes are regular.

Vanuatu's history after 1907 as a joint British and French condominium administration (known as the New Hebrides) has had further economic implications. Most inhabitants speak French or English as well as Bislama, the national Pidjin, and their own vernacular. Vanuatu has among the highest number of languages per capita of any country, at approximately one per 1,000 people. The linguistic diversity has inhibited communication and therefore internal trade and investment. A combination of French and British civil services and legal codes creates significant bureaucracy.

The centrist approach of the colonial administration meant that many of the outlying islands, away from the main islands of Espirito Santo and Efate, received little 'development' and instead were used as pools of cheap labour and resources. Considerable resentment still lingers over the late nineteenth- and early twentieth-century practice of blackbirding whereby people were tricked or taken by force to work as indentured labour on Queensland plantations and elsewhere.[5] As a result of the concentration of economic activity on two islands, only around a quarter of the population can be considered part of the cash economy. The rest of the population are mostly subsistence farmers who occasionally gather copra to pay for school fees or to serve temporary cash needs.

Another important residue of colonialism was that Vanuatu became the main tax haven among the Pacific islands. In the run-up to their swift departure after 1980, and realising that the economy was highly undiversified, UK administrators hoped to make the country a focus for foreign capital flows. The government's reliance on border taxes for revenue has had implications for the country's recent economic experience, as will be seen later.

Section 6.2 corresponds with the first point of the taxonomy – an examination of the importance of external values and norms. This section focuses on the ways in which Vanuatu was influenced by accepted economic wisdom, or Washington Consensus-type advice, as it was realised in practice. The idea is not primarily to assess the structural adjustment experience, which has been done elsewhere (Gay 2004), but to analyse the modernism inherent in the reforms. The identification of problems was done in a standard way, and it was not clear whether the plan for the CRP took account of local values or norms.

Section 6.3 corresponds with point two of the taxonomy, exploring the extent to which local context was important and highlighting features peculiar to the Vanuatu economy which influenced economic development. Social and contextual influences affected the way outside economists and policymakers designed the CRP. It is suggested that they brought in particular values to the project without appropriate consultation of local politicians, civil servants and members of the public.

Section 6.4 shows how certain economic tools, concepts and policies undermined themselves, even though they were designed for greater control. As a result of the confrontation between foreign values and local demands, a number of policies fell short of their objectives. Not only did the CRP fall short of local expectations but it failed on its own terms, undermining the very results which it aimed to achieve. The CRP produced a reflexive process whereby economic tools and concepts employed with specific goals in mind ended up directly hampering the achievement of those goals. This was not just bad policy; it was the specific result of a lack of attention to local nuance.

Section 6.5 examines the CRP in light of point four of the taxonomy, suggesting that Vanuatu's reforms might have been more successful had there been an allowance for the thinking behind the reforms to be revised as circumstances changed, or if the reforms proved inadequate.

The final section ties together the points raised throughout the chapter and draws some conclusions.

6.2 The influence of external values and norms

6.2.1 The need for reform

There was little doubt that, by the mid-1990s, the Vanuatu economy was in need of structural reform.[6] One of the prominent features of the economy following independence was the chronic visible trade deficit. As table 6.1 shows, the deficit ranged from 7 per cent to 38 per cent

Table 6.1 Vanuatu trade trends, million vatu, 1983–2005

Year	Exports	Imports	Trade deficit as % of GDP
1983	2,583	4,338	16
1984	3,939	4,826	7
1985	2,753	5,257	19
1986	1,806	4,849	24
1987	1,937	6,157	29
1988	1,559	5,883	28
1989	1,609	6,727	31
1990	1,783	8,854	38
1991	1,600	7,128	26
1992	2,027	7,131	23
1993	2,140	7,406	23
1994	2,402	8,203	23
1995	2,552	8,507	23
1996	2,708	8,647	22
1997	3,565	8,613	17
1998	4,323	11,257	21
1999	3,327	12,451	28
2000	3,622	12,315	26
2001	2,895	13,118	30
2002	2,590	12,433	30
2003	3,252	12,703	28
2004	4,167	14,306	29
2005	4,126	16,315	33

Sources: Vanuatu Department of Statistics; author's calculations
NB. Imports cleared for home consumption; Merchandise exports;
figures in million vatu

of GDP between 1983 and 2005.[7] Almost all processed products were imported. Exports were generally very low due to a limited market size, a small, fragmented production base and dependence on a narrow range of volatile commodities such as copra. Exports by the start of the CRP in 1997 were worth 13 per cent of GDP and have generally been lower as a proportion of output than in other Melanesian economies. In 1997 the trade deficit was worth 17 per cent of GDP.

Within the current account, the visible trade deficit was compensated partly by a surplus in services, around half of which was tourism-related. Remittances from overseas have been negligible, although they may increase with the possibility of guest-worker schemes in Australia and New Zealand. In the capital account, in 1997 as now, aid flows dominated capital transfers, with roughly half of aid payments

Table 6.2   Vanuatu Balance of Payments 2004–5, VT million

Item	2004	2005
Current account	−2702	−3963
Balance on merchandise trade	−8291	−10,094
Balance on services trade	5,746	6,515
Balance on investment income	1,764	2,475
Net current transfers	1,607	2,091
Capital account	−351	−177
Financial account	2,526	4617
Net errors and omissions	527	−477
Gross official reserves	6,615	7,596

Source: Reserve Bank of Vanuatu

distributed to government and half going to other sectors. The main donors were Australia, New Zealand, the European Union, France, Japan and China. Net private investment flows were strongly negative. Inward foreign direct investment during 2001 was only around US$9 million, but increased to around US$20 million in 2004.

Vanuatu has, and in 1997 had, a balance of payments problem. Although figures for 1997 are unavailable, a deficit in merchandise trade worth VT10.1 billion (US$92 million) by 2005 is typical of the previous decade. It might be pointed out that many countries, most notably the United States from the 1990s to 2007, enjoy long periods of economic success with a current-account deficit. However the Vanuatu government has long declared economic self-reliance as its principal policy objective – and it can hardly be included in the same category as the United States, which was able to attract capital at unprecedented levels to fund its current-account deficit.[8] Whilst aid in Vanuatu (which is the largest part of net current transfers above) temporarily compensates for the trade deficit, dependence on foreign donors was undesirable over the long term, not least because it has contributed to the existence of the economic schism between the capital, where most aid is spent, and the cash-poor outer islands. To paraphrase one of the IMF's key principles, Vanuatu did not have non-aid net capital inflows compatible with its development and growth prospects that were sufficient to sustainably finance the current-account deficit (Guitian 1981: 4).

Political volatility resulted in policy paralysis, further supporting the case for economic and political reform.[9] Instability was a product of the considerable constitutional power vested in the executive and the possibility of forming a new government without holding elections. The result was an administration in constant flux, since back-benchers had nothing to lose by trying to form a new coalition. Ministers had no incentive to implement long-term policies because they knew they were only in office for a matter of months.

Many arms of government simply performed badly. At the first CRP training seminar for parliamentarians on 2 June 1997 then Prime Minister Rialuth Serge Vohor, probably Vanuatu's most prominent politician from the mid-1990s onwards, said: 'The continuous poor performance of institutions of government has had a destabilising effect on the economy and the community. It is a major impediment to reform and growth...' (CRP 1997: 15).

By the middle of 1997 several extra-budgetary provisions threatened a cash-flow problem. Corruption was also growing, building up to protests during 1998 when a politician tried to steal assets from the Vanuatu National Provident Fund. Later in the same year there was a botched attempt to devalue the vatu.

This culmination of events partly explains the rush to enact the programme and may also give some clues as to why the reforms used such a generic template. Some domestic civil servants may have been led to believe that a crisis was imminent, while foreign consultants were probably unfamiliar with the volatile nature of Melanesian politics and believed that action needed to be taken rapidly.[10]

Unlike some other structural adjustment programmes which aimed at rapid change, the CRP 'big bang' was followed by a programme lasting many years. Phase 1, entailing a spate of public-sector reforms, began in July 1997 and ended in December 1998. Phase 2, dealing more with economic policy, lasted until the end of 2000. Phase 3 was still in progress by 2006. Annual summits take stock of the CRP's progress and aim to prioritise issues for the coming year.

6.2.2   The universals of development practice

The original CRP (1997) document details five main objectives which can be found in identical ADB reform programmes in the Cook Islands, the Federated States of Micronesia, the Republic of the Northern Mariana Islands, Samoa and the Solomon Islands: (Knapman and Saldahna 1999: 177–84)

1. Renewing the institutions of governance
2. Redefining the role of the public sector
3. Improving public sector efficiency

4. Encouraging the private sector to lead growth
5. Improving social equity.

These objectives were split into a further 25 specific aims complete with actions to be carried out by particular ministries and departments. The universal and generic nature of the reforms held selected benefits. Objectives 1 to 3 resulted in discernible improvements. Because the ADB had implemented the reforms elsewhere, it carried them out quickly and, presumably, more cheaply than it otherwise would have done. Government and civil service decision-making became more transparent. For example before the CRP the Minister for Immigration could issue a 'green letter' to expel foreign residents without reason or redress. Now such decisions can only be made through court.

The emphasis on good governance, common in foreign donor programmes around the world in recent years, has borne some fruit. The public sector has become more modern and accountable although there are problems in this area, as will be seen below (Huffer and Molisa 1999). A new public service code has reduced nepotism. The free press, an important watchdog on government, has developed under the era of more open government. It is unlikely that Transparency International would have been able to operate freely before 1997.

Prior to the CRP the Minister of Finance vetted investment proposals. This created opportunities for bribes and could be time-consuming and arbitrary. The Vanuatu Investment Promotion Authority, created under the CRP, has a mandate to approve and process investment applications quickly and consistently. This move was in line with the World Trade Organisation's emphasis on more easily facilitating foreign investment.

Financial management has become more consistent and professional, with a long-term AusAID project in place to build capacity. A strict payments system is now in place and proper accountancy procedures support ministerial budgetary decisions. Consultants have achieved some success in training their local counterparts. (The process of financial management is different to the magnitude of government finances, an issue which will be discussed below.)

The CRP aimed to improve the quality of statistics, partly because international agencies demanded a standardised, apparently non-subjective way of analysing policy and the economy. Some success was achieved. Data series before 1997 suffer major gaps, and basic data such as consumer-price indices are unavailable or clearly unreliable. Following the CRP, trade data became more reliable because it used the UN Automated System for Customs Database (ASYCUDA), whereby

Customs officers log entries into a database at the border. In recent years, however, the system has failed to work properly because it requires particular IT skills and because a system of self-declaration has been used. Several importers are suspected of mis-classifying their purchases in order to pay lower duties.

Debt data are reasonably reliable, in large part because they are monitored by the external agencies who are owed money (an amount which has increased as a result of the CRP). Finally, GDP data improved but are still essentially the result of a group of civil servants using basic models quarterly to estimate growth in expenditure by demand component. Collection of primary expenditure data remains weak.

A more general advantage of the externally imposed nature of the CRP was that, like other structural adjustment programmes, it allowed local policymakers to begin rapid and radical change without suffering the blame for painful decisions. Without the intervention of an external agency reform would probably have been piecemeal and fragmented, and hence might have been less effective: 'The most important point is that reform must be comprehensive.' (CRP 1997: 11)

Local knowledge was in short supply – few local civil servants could have produced the small improvements to transparency, the investment procedure, financial management and statistics mentioned above. Those local officials who may have possessed the skills were mostly recent economics or business-studies graduates on the lower rungs of the public service. It was also clear that a fresh outside perspective could identify policy failures, free from the subjective constraints of everyday work. Useful lessons should have been available from other countries in which the ADB had initiated reforms.

6.2.3 Could Vanuatu follow its own path?

Unfortunately the lessons learnt did not extend beyond the general level. As mentioned earlier, the ADB had recently, or was simultaneously, conducting reforms in five other Pacific island countries. Rather than moulding reforms to suit individual circumstances, the specific aims of all the programmes were almost identical. Little attempt was made to assess Vanuatu's individual case. From the ADB's own assessment report on the regional reforms it can be seen that every country was told to reduce the size of its public service, improve 'governance' and corporatise and privatise state-owned businesses (Knapman and Saldahna 1999: 177–84). Every country received a small grant and a large loan, the payments of which were conditional on the successful achievement of the stated objectives. Trade liberalisation was a standard goal. Unlike Kalecki, who would emphasise the need to develop productive capacity via the development of agriculture, proponents of reform in Vanuatu imagined that international demand-side measures would lead to an automatic domestic supply response. In truth, the export sector did not respond to increased market access overseas. As shown in Appendix 1, this type of programme intentionally followed the neoliberal Washington Consensus applied throughout the developing world in the past 25 years.

Major ethnic, historical, economic and geographical factors differentiate the Pacific islands, and to apply an identical template everywhere was fraught with difficulties. For instance relatively dynamic Samoa, in Polynesia, is often compared with Vanuatu (usually to the detriment of Vanuatu policymaking) because it is an LDC and its population is roughly the same.[11] However Samoa's economy has the benefit of overseas remittances worth up to a half of GNP; it does not suffer the disadvantage of geographic fragmentation because it comprises two main islands; and it has a supportive and nearby former colonial power in New Zealand. Further, it is a more mature nation, having achieved independence in 1962. As will be shown in Section 6.3, additional economic differences set Vanuatu apart from the other Pacific islands. It is doubtful whether generic reforms from other parts of the globe were in their entirety relevant to the Pacific.

Underlying the CRP was the implicit belief, inherent in all neoliberal structural adjustment programmes, that markets alone would solve the development problems facing Vanuatu. All that was required was to build up selected institutions and to improve governance. Of the five main CRP objectives stated above, only two are 'macroeconomic', and these were half-hearted and unsuccessful; indeed there seems to have been a suspicion about the effectiveness of *any* economic policy. The classical belief in the benevolence of free markets was left implicit, but plainly here was a case of a laissez-faire doctrine that a reduction in the role of government would return the economy to full employment in the long term, with no question of deficiency in demand. Perhaps a quote from Keynes on Ricardo is applicable here: '[He] offered us the supreme intellectual achievement, unattainable by weaker spirits, of adopting a hypothetical world remote from experience as though it was the world of experience and then living in it consistently' (Keynes 1936: 192).

Whilst Vanuatu cannot yet be said to have reached the 'long term', the signs during the following seven years were not promising, with GDP

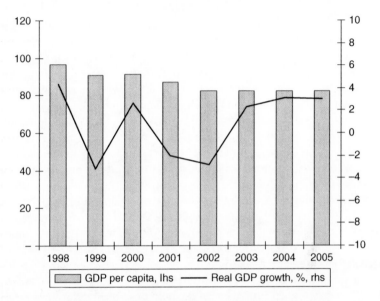

Figure 6.1 Vanuatu real GDP growth and per capita GDP, 1997–2005
Sources: Vanuatu Department of Finance and Economic Management
Figures on left-hand scale in thousand vatu; Data for 2004–5 are estimates

suffering its worst period of growth since independence (see figure 6.1) and unemployment – as far as such a category is relevant to a largely subsistence economy – just as high as it was in 1997.[12] It will be shown later that some of the reforms actually slowed economic growth. Furthermore, applying a model with purely material objectives may not have been suitable for Vanuatu.

The CRP document tried to compare Vanuatu with East Asia, while the ADB, using a modernist and generic approach, adopted the same model that it had promoted there. According to the original 1997 CRP plan: 'The country has experienced such low economic growth that, on average, people are little better off now than they were ten years ago. This is in sharp contrast to most other countries, especially the dynamic economies on the Pacific rim' (CRP 1997: 8). The CRP document further claims that studies of fast-growing economies, particularly in East Asia, indicate that economic growth is best promoted by a 'high degree of openness to the global economy' (ibid.: 11).

This statement is misleading. As a number of studies have suggested, the rest of the world was open to the East Asian tigers, but the tigers were not necessarily open to the rest of the world (World Bank 1993; Chang 2007). Many were selective about foreign investment, employed fixed exchange rates and capital controls and used significant protective barriers to nurture their infant export industries. Such recognitions form the basis of important theoretical trade papers such as Brander and Spencer (1985) and Krugman (1984). The lessons from the various models employed by industrial powerhouses like South Korea and Singapore are limited for least-developed Vanuatu, a young, fragmented, tiny and isolated country. Liberalisation should perhaps be even more cautious in a country with a persistent trade deficit where government revenue depends on import duties.

The CRP reinforced the impression that Vanuatu could emulate the East Asian boom by predicting that: 'In the second period [of the reform programme] between 2000 and 2005 the fruits of reform really begin to "kick in" and GDP growth accelerates to an average rate of 5.8 per cent' (Asian Development Bank 1996: xv). It is unclear how such a precise figure was generated, particularly as data were weak. As figure 6.1 shows, GDP in fact shrank during three of the next five years, performing worse than at any time since independence. The higher rates of growth in 1998 and 2000 are a result of CRP loan spending. Per capita GDP fell gradually from 1997 to 2004. On the most basic measure of economic development, the CRP had failed.

The CRP, following most other structural adjustment programmes, advocated joining regional trade blocs and the World Trade Organisation, moves which were presumed to lead towards current-account liberalisation (CRP, op. cit.: 35).[13] This is further evidence of the one-size-fits-all nature of the reforms – it was easier to insert Vanuatu into a regional and global system of liberalisation than to design an integrated programme with which Vanuatu could cope. Unfortunately, this meant subjecting inexperienced civil servants to the negotiating muscle of the United States, resulting in the suspension of accession in 2001 (Grynberg and Joy 2000; Gay 2005).

Ironically WTO accession negotiations did not result in a proposal to lower import tariffs, since all negotiated upper limits for duties (known as 'bound rates' in WTO parlance) were higher than applied rates.[14] The government wanted to maintain high tariffs because it depended on them for revenue. Vanuatu would have been the first LDC in the world to join the WTO. Therefore its accession required particular and detailed study and should have been incorporated carefully into any reform programme instead of simply being set into motion and left to operate as an autonomous process.

The World Bank (2002) and others, such as Narsey (2004) have argued the standard case for unilateral tariff reduction in the Pacific region, which is that it would reduce the 'deadweight loss', resulting in a more efficient allocation of resources and an increase in consumer surplus. In other words, Vanuatu should not adopt a mercantilist attitude to trade liberalisation. Such issues require more detailed discussion, but it is worth pointing out that the retail and wholesale sectors, like in many small economies, suffer highly imperfect competition, so any price reduction due to lower tariffs is unlikely to be passed on to consumers. Instead it would probably be appropriated by the only major import company. Unless government or consumers can capture a large part of the welfare improvement resulting from tax reform, rapid trade liberalisation is likely to severely drain government finances, in turn further weakening its capacity.

There are reasons for believing that trade policy should be flexible in small, exposed economies that need adaptability in times of hardship. A number of commentators on trade policy, such as Grynberg and Remy (2004) and Bernal (2001), argue that within the context of the global trading regime, 'Small developing economies have structural and institutional characteristics, which affect the process of economic growth, constrain their ability to compete, increase their vulnerability to external events and limit their capacity for adjustment' (Bernal, op. cit.: 1). As part of its WTO accession Vanuatu was required by members of the Cairns group of agricultural exporters to prohibit the subsidies that it occasionally distributed to coconut farmers when prices were low or when a cyclone destroyed their crops (Grynberg and Joy 2000; WTO 2001a).

This was a particularly inappropriate restriction on policy. Not only had it the potential to render the economy vulnerable to international price shocks, but it would leave farmers with no source of cash income. The prohibition ignored two of the most notable features of the economy: its reliance on a single commodity and its susceptibility to natural disasters.

Whilst WTO accession left room for flexibility in import tariffs, the CRP's emphasis on trade liberalisation via regional trade blocs did not. The narrowness of the tax base and difficulty of collecting revenue require some room to change import tariff rates outside the strictures of international trade negotiations.[15] The government evidently also sees tariff rate flexibility as a priority for protective reasons because it raised duties to 35 per cent on 6 manufactured products during October 2002. Ministers have made repeated demands for more adaptability in regional trade agreements, often using the argument that they are uncertain about the future so they would prefer to keep tariff policy under their own control.[16]

A computable general equilibrium (CGE) study of regional trade liberalisation was completed in 1998 (Scollay 1998). Unsurprisingly considering the author's neoclassical theoretical perspective, the results showed that non-preferential trade liberalisation yielded the greatest welfare gains for regional economies. Its findings were questioned by the Vanuatu Department of Trade partly because officials did not understand it, but also because the statistics on which it was based were unreliable. Its assumptions were unrealistic in a way that limited its applicability – including the belief that import taxes could easily be replaced by income tax or VAT – and the results so precise as to be questionable in such a volatile and poorly measured economic environment. Quite apart from the criticisms of Arrow–Debreu general equilibrium levelled by advocates of open-systems ontology, some commentators have specifically argued against using CGE to analyse trade in developing countries:

> The data needed are generally beyond what is available and reliable in developing countries. More problematic are the unrealistic assumptions that must be made to conform to the theoretical demands of the model, in particular the assumptions of full employment of resources, perfect competition, perfect information available to all actors, the absence of risk, and efficiently functioning markets. Most crippling of all is the expectation that the supply-side will take care of itself without the need for targeted interventions.
>
> (Brewster 2003: 3)

A desire to retain national influence over economic policy underlay Vanuatu's decision to shelve WTO accession in 2001 after a package had almost been finalised. In the final schedule of commitments on services, Vanuatu was asked to liberalise 10 general areas out of a possible 11, with 50 specific commitments (WTO 2001b). This is higher than most neighbouring economies and above the average for WTO members. The Solomon Islands included nine general services areas and Fiji only two. In its revised offer to the United States during 2004, Vanuatu requested the exclusion of six key areas, arguing that it wanted to reserve the option of safeguarding health, environmental and social services against foreign ownership and that it would be too costly to provide national treatment in these areas.[17]

Confirming its Washington Consensus credentials, the CRP advocated the sale of a number of public assets. The stated aim was to make companies more efficient and to encourage the government to concentrate on providing an improved environment for enterprise. The resulting outcome, however, had a number of shortcomings. Most corporatised and privatised entities simply moved out of government jurisdiction and became private monopolies. Limited technical capacity and scant government resources – particularly at a time of budget cuts – meant that effective regulation was always unlikely. Although the lack of competition and high costs were mentioned in the CRP documentation, the relevant institutional improvements were not given the central importance that they should have received.[18] The absence of antitrust legislation or meaningful competition has meant that prices for many crucial services, such as water, electricity, telecommunications and transport, remained high for many years after reform. The one clear success was the privatisation of the post office, which is now run by New Zealand Post.

During the subsequent seven years no attempts were made to improve competition, while some political appointees retained major corporate influence. With 29 members, Air Vanuatu has the biggest board of any airline in the world. Many members are politically affiliated and yet the government has little influence over the airline's operations.

The corporatisation programme was so fast and assets were sold so cheaply that it quickly depleted government revenues by removing the benefit of profits and dividends. According to a 2002 UN assessment report the 'wrong sequencing of privatisation and corporatisation has deprived the Vanuatu government [of] over 3.5 billion Vt. [about US$35 million] in gross revenue' (UNESCAP 2002: 18). This sum is the equivalent of about 62 per cent of 1997 government expenditure.[19]

The CRP displayed an emphasis on cutting government expenditure typical of Washington Consensus-inspired structural adjustment programmes. The belief was that the smaller was the size of government, the bigger would be the role of markets and the more efficient the allocation of resources. Market equilibriation would automatically bring about efficient outcomes. Again this seemed to ignore Vanuatu's specific situation. Government was never big, with public expenditure averaging only 27 per cent of GDP during the 1990s. This is about the same as the median level for all developing countries over the same period.[20] On average the budget was exactly in balance from 1990 until 1997.[21] The ADB itself points out that in 1990 Vanuatu had one of the lowest ratios of government employees per capita among Pacific island economies, at three per one hundred country inhabitants. This compared with the Cook islands at 18.2, Tuvalu at eight and Fiji with six (ADB 1996: 103).

Vanuatu's tax-haven status meant there is no income tax, capital gains tax, value-added or land tax. Around 35 per cent of government revenue now comes from value-added tax, which was introduced in 1998 with New Zealand funding. VAT revenues, however, are declining because of the difficulty of enforcing payment. Companies are legally liable for VAT only if they have a turnover exceeding around US$40,000 and most declare an amount just below this level.

The subsistence nature of most of the economy, and therefore the non-cash basis of much economic activity, renders the tax base particularly narrow. One large company, the supermarket Au Bon Marché, contributes almost all of VAT. The government does not have the technical capacity to introduce and enforce new taxes, while the idea of income tax is controversial. Import duties comprise the biggest single source of revenue because they have an established history and are easier to collect. The tax haven thus renders the government even more vulnerable to the problem of revenue collection common in developing countries.[22]

One of the most harmful effects of the misplaced emphasis on fiscal austerity was that bigger cuts were made to overheads than staff, because it was always easier to reduce the stationery bill than it was to make an employee redundant. As a result, salaries rose to 60 per cent of recurrent government expenditure by 2003 from 50 per cent in 1997. Redundancies were made generally, rather than according to merit. Departments find it increasingly difficult to function properly without sufficient funds for overheads. These results are consistent with the findings of Killick (1995), quoted in Toye (2000), which suggest that developing-country governments tend to cut economic services first in an attempt to avoid a reduction in the size of the civil service. In Vanuatu it is difficult to understand why so much effort was devoted to curbing public spending when government extravagance was not a problem. Moreover, domestic credit creation was not rising quickly and neither was inflation. In a small open economy dependent on foreign prices and interest rates there was little likelihood of inflation running out of control.

Worsening the fiscal situation, during 1998 and 1999 the government was required to match ADB loans with about US$14 million of its own money for financial restructuring, and a further US$0.6 million between 2000 and 2001.[23]

Table 6.3 Asian Development Bank loans to Vanuatu, US$ million

Purpose	First tranche		Second tranche	Total
	Release one	Release two		
	Public sector cuts and restructuring	4	1	2
7 Financial restructuring	3	3	2	8
Fiscal stabilisation	3	1	1	5
Total	10	5	5	20

Source: United Nations Economic and Social Commission for Asia and the Pacific (2002)

To assist restructuring and 'fiscal stabilisation', the ADB lent US$20 million in two tranches during phases one and two (shown in table 6.3) – equivalent to half of annual government expenditure during those years and 8.3 per cent of 1997 GDP. The incentive of a large loan at below-market rates, together with small grants, undoubtedly helped the ADB gain acceptance of its plan. Other bilateral donors were also involved, led by Australia. Part of the loan was used to employ 42 international consultants who were to carry out the first stages of the programme. The loan disbursement was front-loaded, with the biggest source coming in the first tranche, including a total of US$6 million for financial restructuring. A total of US$10 million, or half of the total, was released in one payment.

Paradoxically, rather than improving economic growth and therefore the fiscal situation, the CRP loans lumbered the government with a worse external borrowing position. A significant proportion of the initial lending was used to pay for the consultants. When they departed, there were few lasting results and yet the government was still paying off the loans used for their salaries. The remainder of the loan funds were used mostly for near-term consumption-orientated programmes, artificially boosting the economy in the short run and establishing a pro-cyclical spending pattern which was worse than if nothing had been done. Exacerbating this problem, forecasts of revenue and expenditure were based on the artificially high GDP figures mentioned earlier.

Figure 6.2 shows that the external debt stock, mostly ADB foreign-currency loans, rose sharply in 1997, doubling by 2004. It reached 40 per cent of GDP by 2003 compared with 15.6 per cent of GDP in 1990.

More worrying from a financial management point of view is that debt servicing costs were expected to rise sharply from 2007 onwards as

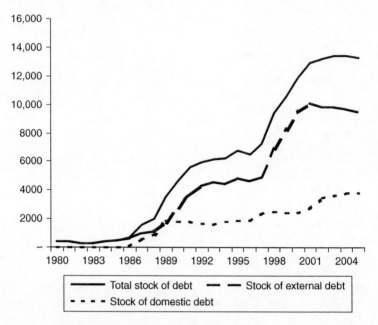

Figure 6.2   Vanuatu public debt, million vatu, 1980–2005
Source: Vanuatu Department of Finance and Economic Management[24]

the principal on a number of loans comes due, as shown by figure 6.3. The Department of Finance and Economic Management predicted that total interest payments would rise to 8 per cent of domestic revenue by 2007 from 7 per cent in 2003. This will cut into vital development expenditure on health, education and other areas. As a result of the debt problem the government adopted a limit on foreign lending.

To summarise, the CRP contained a certain number of basic universals that helped ameliorate the consequences of a deteriorating economic and governmental situation, such as the improvement of statistics and the influence of an outside agency on which painful decisions could be blamed. However external values and norms played a strong influence, and in fact the government was deprived of the opportunity to assess the extent to which it accepted these outside universals, and to what extent it wished to focus policy around national economic context. The consequence of this surrendering of policy autonomy and the over-influence of external values and norms was a recession, and the country was burdened with a substantial amount of debt which will restrict development expenditure in years to come.

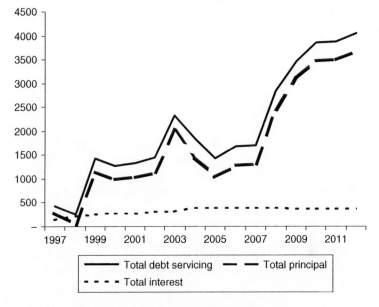

Figure 6.3   Vanuatu debt servicing, million vatu, 1997–2012
Source: Vanuatu Department of Finance and Economic Management

6.3   The importance of local context

The previous section showed how the CRP involved certain universal tendencies, many of which were inappropriate to Vanuatu's particular circumstances. Every economy has unique features, but some are more important than others, and perhaps the more unique the economy, the more economic policy must be more tailored. This section highlights additional qualities pivotal to Vanuatu's economic future which the reform programme might have taken positive steps to address. The reform programme sought its own goals, desired by donors, but to what extent did the CRP reflect local objectives?

6.3.1   Differences in institutions

The relation of people to their island and birthplace defines many social and cultural relations in Vanuatu. The transition to independence revolved around this issue, while throughout Vanuatu's colonial history there was a conflict between traditional ideas about land and European notions of ownership (Van Trease 1987). The Constitution states

that: 'All land in the Republic of Vanuatu belongs to the indigenous cus-
tom owners and their descendants.' Most ni-Vanuatu people feel a sense
of belonging to a particular island or community before they consider
themselves nationals of Vanuatu (meaning 'our land'), itself a name
which only dates to 1980. Although relationships to the land vary across
time and between islands, almost every family has inherited at least a
small plot of land on which they grow fruit and vegetables and which
serves as a social safety net. They do not 'own' land as private property
in the capitalist sense; it is more a case of temporary stewardship.

According to anthropologist Knut Rio (2003):

> it is a fundamental idea on Ambrym [island] that even if people see
> themselves as the 'owner' of something or the beholder of the 'right'
> to something, it also has to be acknowledged that the thing owned or
> claimed possibly came from somewhere else...There is both a focus
> on the finality of transactions in the here-and-now and on the infin-
> ity of the road of the things and people transacted...Therefore there
> is no property here that is not also the property of someone else.

The alien nature of private property in the Western sense has resulted
in the prohibition of the freehold ownership of land. Leasehold lasting 75 years is allowed in some, mostly urban areas. Yet during WTO
accession the United States made the standard demand made of most
acceding countries: that land laws be revised to permit freehold ownership (WTO 2001a; Grynberg and Joy, op. cit.). This would have been
politically suicidal and culturally unacceptable, so Vanuatu negotiators
could not compromise. As a result, significant concessions had to be
made in other areas.

6.3.2   Differences in values

In Vanuatu the objectives of the CRP were incompatible with traditional
vales. The tacit model of the CRP was methodologically individualist and assumed that people would be motivated largely by material
gains. A number of prominent cultural features lead to the suspicion
that, had they been properly consulted, ni-Vanuatu people would have
chosen a more inclusive reform programme which was based on traditional values. Although traditions change and there are dangers in
identifying fixity in cultural values, themes of both community and
non-materialism have featured throughout Vanuatu's recent history.

The desire to accumulate material goods has been muted. When European traders first arrived on the island of Erromango to buy sandalwood

in 1820, inhabitants showed little interest in the objects proffered for exchange (MacClancy 1981: 40; Van Trease 1987: 12). The linguistic diversity of the islands and the division into self-contained villages suggest that trade was limited, while there was little point in exchange with neighbours when everything necessary for subsistence could be found locally.

Strong community bonds still mean that there are few incentives to build up personal wealth. Throughout Melanesia, family members are commonly required to provide financial help to relatives in times of hardship. There is, as a result, little personal benefit from saving, and indeed many people do not think in such individualistic terms.

The role of tradition, or kastom, was considered by many to be so important that it combined with Christianity to evolve into a powerful political force, as shown by Miles (1998). The nationalist movement headed by Father Walter Lini, prime minister for the first decade after independence, proposed a 'version of liberation theology that linked spiritual freedom to political independence for the oppressed' (Miles 1998: 20). This ideology developed the idea that: 'In pre-contact times, land was vested in groups which were based on common descent, residence in a particular area and participation in various activities. The group was the land – its ancestors were buried in it' (Van Trease, op. cit.: 3).

Lini's 'Melanesian Socialism' (Premdas 1987), drawing on other colonial liberation movements, promoted economic independence from former colonial powers as well as Australia and New Zealand, and it was during this period that a policy of import-substitution was adopted, although unsuccessfully. Membership of the Non-Aligned Movement, close links with Gaddafi's Libya in the 1980s and opposition to nuclear testing in the French Polynesian Atoll of Mururoa confirmed that Vanuatu saw little in common with the international agenda of neighbouring and former colonialist countries.

It can be seen that the importance of community, a refuge in spirituality rather than materialism, and the need for self-determination have figured strongly in Vanuatu's recent history. The assumption of the structural adjustment programme that material gain would be the prime motivator of individual action appears misplaced.

6.3.3 Differences in behaviour

Behaviour regarding money took an unusual form in Vanuatu, and this had implications for economic development. Traditional money took the form of woven mats, pig tusks and shells. Certain foodstuffs also worked as a kind of currency since they were passed around as gifts at frequent social gatherings. Again, money was not used in the Western way. It could not be considered according to the textbook definition as only a medium of exchange, a unit of account or a store of value. It also performed a more social role, binding communities together by ensuring that people were continually obliged to one another (Rio, op. cit.). There was little point in hoarding money with the purpose of buying material items as few problems of scarcity existed. Most people had enough to eat and devoted considerable time for activities not related to material production.

The behaviour behind this traditional use of money has affected its use in modern urban society. Savings rates are very low and generosity high, with a significant amount of gift-giving. Micro-finance programmes have displayed a poor record because traditional lending and borrowing were not quantified precisely, and many people do not fully understand the concepts of loans and interest. In addition, the continued absence of serious scarcity for subsistence farmers has meant people remain ambivalent towards the cash economy. Those who have no experience of the market economy and do not value material accumulation do not appear to be motivated by income.[25] A man on the island of Tanna expressed an idea which I have heard many times: 'Long Vila, mi mas pem long kaikai. Hemi wan rabis ting-ting.' (In Port Vila, the capital, I have to pay for food. This is a silly idea.)

The particular role of money has meant that it is unrealistic to assume that a reduction in the size of government would automatically lead to a flourishing of market forces. A general paucity of business experience, which springs from an absence of desire for cash accumulation and lack of access to finance, means that it is difficult to talk of government 'crowding out' private investment. There is a cash economy but it appears unlikely to expand quickly. Government, although it is not large, acts as an essential provider of basic services not supplied elsewhere.

6.4   How economic tools, concepts and policies affected themselves

The CRP fell short of is own expectations, as shown in Section 6.2. Further, the programme did not fit with subjective national goals. The suggestion in Section 6.3 was that local people would probably have targeted a different set of priorities had they been properly involved. These two questions overlap. In attempting to achieve standardised economic objectives the CRP actually undermined national values. By promoting the same kind of programme that Washington-based policymakers have advocated globally over recent decades, a set of principles was imposed on Vanuatu that conflicted with local priorities. Not only did the CRP reduce policy autonomy, but the intrusion of individualist and materialist ideas actually made it harder for local people to achieve the kind of economic system that they wanted.

This point will be developed in the current section, which aims to show how the tools and concepts employed during structural adjustment are 'biting back' with unintended consequences. A rupture between desired policy and practical outcomes meant that policies designed with the intention of greater control had the opposite effect. A reflexive feedback mechanism resulted in apparent policy solutions worsening the very problems that were identified in the first place.

The possibility of reflexivity presupposes three of the critiques of modernism highlighted in Chapter 2; those of foundationalism, scientism and determinism. Modernist economic method as used in the CRP was foundationalist in that it perceived there to be only one basis to knowledge irrespective of how it is expressed. However thinkers as diverse as Marx (op. cit.), Foucault (op. cit.), Lawson (op. cit.) and Woolgar (op. cit.) have shown that knowledge is situated in a social context – it is produced, rather than pre-existing discussion. The CRP's unstated belief in the validity of only one way of looking at knowledge – its own – had undesirable outcomes. If reformers were to have been sceptical about foundationalism in knowledge, they would have sought the views of nationals and indeed could have delegated aspects of the design and execution of the programme to local policymakers in order to include their types of knowledge.

The CRP was imbued with a modernist conception of science. In effect the ADB used the mainstream economics and Washington Consensus version of science and proceeded to conduct analysis exclusively using methods considered to meet scientific standards. These included establishing statistical series to calculate precise growth forecasts; generating computable general equilibrium models; and fitting Vanuatu's experience into official development categories that could be objectively assessed. Whilst it is going too far to assign equal validity to *kastom* 'science' and so-called Western science, as some have advocated,[26] using local methods of attaining knowledge would have at least been more likely to have allowed effective communication with local people.

Perhaps most important for the aspect of reflexivity discussed here is the postmodern critique of determinism. By assuming that specific policy tools would predictably produce stated economic objectives, based on stochastic CGE models, the CRP failed to take account of the role of chance, the mutability of the relation between causes and effects and the possibility of worse consequences than had nothing been done at all (Cullenberg *et al.* op cit.: 31). In reality, the absence of a deterministic relation between cause and effect and an inadequate explanation of real causal mechanisms at work in Vanuatu removed the outcomes of the CRP from what was intended. Seeing the economy as an open system in a manner suggested by Keynes or critical realists might have mitigated the more damaging outcomes.

6.4.1 The Public Service Commission

The implicit model of the CRP was that reducing the size of government would leave a bigger role for market forces and reduce the crowding-out of investment. It was believed that improving governance and promoting greater public-service efficiency would correct the role of government and allow it to play its proper role, which was stated to be that of creating a fertile economic environment. Of the total US$20 million in loans, US$7 million was devoted to public-sector cuts and restructuring along with substantial obligatory government spending, although unbalanced between labour and non-labour inputs. It has already been shown that the CRP worsened the government fiscal situation despite attempting the opposite.

In a further paradox, attempts to make the public sector more efficient actually reduced efficiency. It has already been shown that across-the-board shrinkage in government spending resulted in inadequate departmental budgets and lowered productivity. Building up the Public Service Commission, including the publishing of a rigorous public service code, ironically increased the number of officials in this area, created more bureaucracy and increased litigation.

The public service model, borrowed from larger countries like New Zealand and Australia where the consultants involved in its execution came from, was simply too big and complicated for Vanuatu. Before the CRP, staff issues were dealt with relatively informally by communal decision-making. Often matters would be settled out of office hours. After 1997, however, the increase in officialdom connected with salary issues and hiring and firing began to erode the time available for normal duties. The bureaucratisation of the public service has influenced the way in which officials work, with an increasing number believing that a large part of their job should be devoted to form-filling and letter-writing.

Jean-Alain Mahé, the former Minister of Trade and a member of the Francophone Union of Moderate Parties, was appointed head of the Public Service Commission in 2004. Mahé was considered proactive and senior enough to make decisions which were seen as legitimate, but the move fell foul of the political and personal rivalry that is unavoidable in such a small country. Mahé immediately sacked the Director of Tourism because the two had conflicted during his term in office, while he ignored endemic and open corruption in the Department of Lands, partly because the perpetrators were sympathetic to his party. In creating a powerful position which could impose decisions that were difficult to oppose, the public service reforms had worsened and institutionalised the very problems of political interference that they had set out to solve.

6.4.2 The quantification of the economy

Quantifying standard economic indicators was intended to improve understanding and to help policy design. The enhancement of data helped with the description of the economy and enabled a better general comparison with the same data in other countries. As suggested earlier, this had certain advantages. However the increasing use of technical concepts began to supplant customary ways of thinking about the economy. For example the government's focus shifted from anecdotal and subjective knowledge of seasonal agricultural output, with which many people are familiar, towards constructing the quarterly consumer price index. Such terminology was alien to most people in government. As part of my work for the government I collected fruit and vegetable price data directly from the main market every month for a year, and it conflicted strongly with the official CPI data. Further confirming the impression that it was fabricated, most of the CPI data did not vary in nominal terms over a five-year period, contradicting other measures which suggested consumer price inflation.

The increased amount of statistical information produced outcomes which were contrary to the spirit of the CRP, such as the emergence of a 'price control unit' which imagined it could collect data and set prices for important consumer goods. This approach faced all the problems associated with central planning, such as the undersupply of goods priced too cheaply and the inadequacy of information about individual consumer behaviour as highlighted by Hayek (1945). In the end much effort was expended with few results.

But the most perverse effect of the quantification of economic management was that it created an arena of expert knowledge that most civil servants could not understand. It actually perpetuated reliance on foreign technical assistants because they were among the few who could use the data for policy design. Of course, local graduates who are sufficiently trained in statistics and economics did exist, but they were only around a dozen in number and were mostly quite junior. The overall result was a reduction in capacity and an increase in confusion about policy design.

6.4.3 Trust in outside agencies

Another way in which the CRP undermined itself was in its erosion of trust in outside agencies. When it became obvious that the CRP was failing, many local people and civil servants began to show suspicion of any foreign initiative, including important development projects. This is also a reason behind the erosion of support for WTO accession: members of the public, civil servants and politicians lost confidence simply because the organisation was located abroad. As mentioned earlier, the government decided to adopt a general policy of accepting no more foreign loans even if they might have had a positive rate of return.

During 2004 relations with Australia, the main aid donor, reached such a low that the Prime Minister expelled five consultants and threatened to close down the High Commission. There was an overt attempt to replace Australian aid with funding from other countries. As a result of the difficult early experience with foreign consultants, most new development or aid workers have found it more challenging to establish legitimacy. This worsened the delivery of vital health and education services – social objectives with which the CRP was supposed to help.

6.4.4 GDP as an end of policy

Sen (2000) has argued that development should not focus solely on wealth generation but should aim at the improvement of freedoms and capabilities. Stiglitz (1998b) has suggested that the notion of development as a transformation of society should supersede a purely material perspective. Because the CRP involved the old, growth-orientated version of development thinking, it ended up undercutting its own economic aims. GDP stagnated and per capita GDP declined.

Simultaneously the CRP ended up shifting the emphasis of national policy away from local values. For example following independence the constitution created a second chamber of parliament with limited powers. The Malvatumauri, or Council of Chiefs, could debate political decisions and recommend alterations. It was less powerful than a Westminster-style upper house, but it had influence on cultural matters. The CRP, however, with its emphasis on material economic growth, relegated the house to little more than a rubber-stamping operation. Issues of tradition were shifted aside to make way for the 'more important' concern of making the economy grow.

This decision has backfired, with the Council of Chiefs becoming more vocal and a number of chiefs advocating a return to what they perceive as a pre-Western organisation of society. The leader of the Malvatumauri suggested during presidential elections that it would have been inappropriate to elect a woman. One island, with a population of around 10,000, has developed a strong independence movement which advocates a return to traditional hierarchical society. Of course all versions of Vanuatu's history, be they local or foreign, are seen through the lenses of the present. Trying to hark back to a 'traditional' past inevitably involves invention, and indeed there is strong evidence to suggest that tradition evolved, varied between different islands and that some communities were organised along matriarchal lines. Ultimately the ideas expressed by the Malvatumauri are anti-development by any definition.

In sum, it can be seen that, partly as a result of its foundationalism, scientism and determinism, the CRP invoked a reflexive feedback mechanism which meant that policies actually weakened their intended outcomes. Four examples have been presented: efforts to build the Public Service Commission ended up making the public service less efficient. Trying to quantify parts of the economy, although not without selected benefits, reduced the ability of local officials to design policy. The foreign nature of the CRP made future intervention more difficult. Aiming primarily at the accumulation of material wealth resulted in a decline in per capita GDP and prompted certain figures to try and undo many of the benefits of development.

6.5 The revision of theory as circumstances changed

The CRP undermined the ability of government to revise theory if it proved inadequate, or as circumstances changed. While the government is attempting to retain its capacity to change the theoretical backdrop to policy, structural adjustment reduced government autonomy in three ways. First, by forcing the government to engage in one-off spending worth a tenth of 1997 GDP, the Asian Development Bank worsened Vanuatu's indebtedness, as shown in figure 6.2. The doubling of dollar-denominated loans over six years raised the cost of policies such as currency devaluation. This might have been an option to tackle the trade deficit. The debt also gives the ADB leverage over national policy. The ADB provides an assessment of Vanuatu's investment grade, and Ministry of Finance officials feel that they must stay in line if they are to attract investment. In effect the advice of the major lender must now be acknowledged irrespective of whether it fits with national priorities.

A second way in which the government's theoretical and policy autonomy was curtailed was via the reduction in discretionary spending, which made it harder for government officials to do their jobs. A typical example is that of the Department of Trade, Industry and Investment, where the budget had fallen to US$143,000 in 2004. Around three-fifths of this was spent on the five professional staff and one secretary. The department simply could not function properly– there were no funds for research or travel and working conditions were inadequate. The department experienced 18 months without Internet access between 2003 and 2004, had its electricity turned off, enjoyed infrequent telephone access and possessed insufficient funds to repair the air-conditioning. It is precisely such critical details that are ignored by the universal policy prescription of general budget cuts.

Third, the policy of placing a large number of overseas consultants in senior civil service positions further restricted the government's ability to change theory and policy. In addition to the hiring of 42 short-term consultants, during the latter stages of the CRP there were moves to install a foreign national as head of the Department of Customs, while three legal advisers operated in the State Law Office. The long-term nature of these postings and the understandable tendency of the staff to promote the programme under which they were operating meant that government was less free to pursue the policies that it wanted.

Thomas Friedman's (1999) 'Golden Straitjacket' argument (outlined in Chapter 4) suggests that this kind of reduction in policy autonomy should be an advantage. However this is far from what happened in reality. Political stability might have been beneficial for Vanuatu in that it would have improved certainty about economic policy, but this is a long way from arguing that the country ought to put on a 'Golden Straitjacket'. For the reasons stated above it would seem beneficial for the government to decide its own policy mix rather than have it dictated from outside. The economy began to stagnate when policy autonomy was reduced.

Seen from a Bourdieuean standpoint, the reform programme shifted too far to the extreme of objectivism, without taking into account subjective experience. In order to fully align the programme with economic reality, instead of the programme being designed from above, by foreign economists whose experience was largely elsewhere and whose methods were mostly formal, better results might have been achieved by a programme which used the subjective knowledge of local culture and mores.

To achieve useful reforms it would be necessary to cede greater control of the programme to Vanuatu nationals rather than enacting it on their behalf. Foreign policymakers, bringing with them the advantages of an outside perspective, might have brought local voices to the fore. The programme could subsequently have been designed by both Vanuatu and foreign policymakers. This may sound idealistic, but it was perhaps more unrealistic to expect the actual design of the CRP to work, with its lack of consultation of local civil servants and the public.

In the document which sets out the original CRP there is a distinct absence of local voices. Only once is a Vanuatu member of parliament quoted, and then to give assent, and no opinions of members of the public are given. The document is translated into French but not Bislama, the only common tongue and the language of everyday life. The vocabulary is foreign, and reference is made throughout to modernist terms like 'Renewing the Institutions of Governance' and 'The Role of a Modern Government' (CRP 1997). Such language had limited meaning in Vanuatu.

A lack of consultation meant that the programme did not belong to Vanuatu people. The ADB assessment of the reforms, written by Knapman and Saldana (1999), acknowledges that: 'The most significant success factor of Bank assistance for reforms in the Pacific is also the most obvious: political commitment to and ownership of the reform program is essential. Externally imposed reform measures (conditionalities) that have little government ownership are doomed to certain failure' (Knapman and Saldanha 1999: 169). It might be added that ownership beyond parliament, amongst ordinary people, should have been given equal importance.

After the early stages of the CRP most of the foreign consultants left Vanuatu, while in 1999 and 2001 successful motions of no-confidence resulted in changes of government, meaning that few of the original initiators of the CRP were in office or in-country. Civil servants felt that the CRP burdened them with a new set of problems – the economy was performing worse and the foreign loan stock had increased, while a host of new legislation was on the books. They felt neither ownership nor a desire to promote awareness amongst the public. It is unlikely that many officials or ordinary people fully understood the aims or logic of the programme.

It is difficult to find an official or politician who speaks favourably of the consultative process. Almost all appear to believe that the programme was driven through too fast and with inadequate discussion. A few have become pessimistic after seeing the results. Serge Vohor, Prime Minister in 1997 and again in 2004, is quoted in the newspaper thus: '...the CRP is a failed initiative because it was driven towards the interest of foreigners. He would have liked the CRP to be founded on traditional and cultural principles.'[27]

By 2004 civil servants expressed widespread scepticism. For example Roy Mickey Joy, the Director of Trade, Industry and Investment said that: 'The CRP was a complete waste of time. It paid for the salaries of a few consultants and did nothing for the country' (Pers. comm. 2004). The head of the Department of Comprehensive Reform Bethuel Solomon, charged with implementing what is left of the CRP, believed that the ADB pushed reforms without asking local partners what they expected (Pers. comm. 2004).

The 2002 UNESCAP assessment of the CRP makes a related point: 'Most of the consultants came from developed countries...They...ploughed through the change process at speeds which local counterpart staff could not keep pace with. The cultural shock...left the local counterpart staff somewhat baffled...' (ESCAP 2002: 14).

A local commentator who was present at the June 1997 national summit when the CRP was adopted also believed that reform was too fast.

> By June 1997 the blueprint for economic and public sector reforms had been drawn up. A year later, the legislative requirements for the ADB loan to implement the CRP were being debated in parliament at a speed uncharacteristic of the usual prolonged ni-Vanuatu processes. This accelerated process leads one to question whether the CRP is a home grown product.
>
> (Salong 1998: 17)

Knapman and Saldanha agree: 'The speed of formal rule-making has made it difficult to adequately explain to the population the key aspects of the reform...' (Knapman and Saldanha, op. cit.: 160).

Although outside consultants may feel that they sought opinions, many local people feel they did not take account of traditional decision-making. According to people who were there at the time, workshops were not conducted in Bislama. Traditional ni-Vanuatu decision-making takes a long time and is usually non-confrontational. A succession of newly arrived consultants has been wrong-footed by consultants' assumption that silence means acquiescence. People often appear to be agreeing with proposals when in reality they will go away and think about the issues, later arriving at a firm conclusion. This makes the public workshop a particularly poor environment for discussion.

By emphasising public-sector reform and basing the reforms on governance, the CRP appeared to shift blame on to Vanuatu legislators rather than structural macroeconomic factors. This further undermined ownership. It is also questionable whether short-term outside consultants knew more than some local civil servants about the productive sectors. As Knapman and Saldanha sum up, 'the results [of using consultants and external advisers] are far from encouraging' (ibid.: 174).

WTO membership represents an example in which there was a similar lack of consultation. Part of the reason for the shelving of accession was that several important officials were simply excluded from the discussions. The leader of the negotiating team, Director of Trade Roy Mickey Joy, admits that:

> Firstly, and importantly, there was minimal consultation with or information provided to civil society, government and non-government organisations. The capacity available locally was insufficient. The suspension of accession was timely. It gave us an opportunity to do more work, and to realise the pros and cons and costs and benefits. We have held more seminars, forums and consultations since the suspension of accession.
>
> (pers. comm. 2004)

Officials at the Chamber of Commerce, although in favour of WTO entry, believe they should have been consulted more closely:

> People weren't sure what the WTO was. They didn't know what the benefits were for Vanuatu... The private sector and NGOs were not consulted on the process. That's why there wasn't any support from

the stakeholders. There wasn't enough awareness on the WTO as a whole.[28]

A former official from the Department of Customs and Inland Revenue says that the WTO secretariat, which is supposed to act neutrally, tried to force through a highly liberal accession package without allowing Vanuatu negotiators the opportunity for input. Under the remit of providing 'technical assistance', the WTO secretariat appears to have believed that, without consultation, it could write Vanuatu's schedule of commitments on services. Demands typical of the United States were included, such as the liberalisation of the wholesale and retail sectors and the opening of the telecoms and audiovisual sectors. It was only after the Minister of Trade belatedly understood what was in the package that accession was put on hold.

> The WTO was, in my view, representing the US when it came here view, representing the US when he came here. There was no face-to-face bilateral; we were only exchanging correspondence... The WTO Secretariat appeared not to be acting independently – it was pushing on behalf of the US.[29]

The WTO deputy director of accessions has painted a different picture to me, but the balance of evidence suggests that the WTO secretariat and members of the Vanuatu working party wanted to bring negotiations to a swift conclusion. To enhance the development credentials of the WTO following the failure of the Seattle Ministerial meeting in 1999, it appeared that WTO officials as well as prominent members wanted countries from the three recognised levels of development to join at the Doha Ministerial in 2001: Taiwan, a newly industrialised country, China, a developing country and least-developed Vanuatu. In the end, only China and Taiwan joined.

WTO rules require opening up to foreign investment from one country on a basis 'no less favourable' than another and to offer foreign and local companies similar terms.[30] This usually requires liberalising investment rules and could mean that the government lost some of its ability to veto investment projects. In other words government may lose its ability to vet foreign investors. However Vanuatu has been reluctant to do this, as its tax-haven status tends to attract disreputable businesses. Unscrupulous investors often try to take advantage of the lack of regulatory capacity. For example in the late 1990s an Indian fraudster bribed the Finance Minister to underwrite bonds worth several million dollars with a fake ruby. In 2003 a Vanuatu banker was arrested by the FBI for allegedly laundering money from a global lottery scam. In 2004 a US investor paid a deposit for a holiday resort, stripped it of most moveable assets and left the country.

The experiences of WTO membership and structural adjustment have to be seen against the backdrop of recent memories of colonialism. Many people were suspicious that Vanuatu was re-selling its country to foreign interests. Prominent civil society and NGO members have expressed fears of 're-colonisation'. (Salong 1998). 'What are the chances of the ni-Vanuatu taking on businesses and becoming capitalists themselves,' asked one official at a non-government organisation. 'They will remain labourers.' [31]

6.6 Conclusion

By the mid-1990s economic change was imperative. The economy and political institutions were delivering neither economic growth nor development in line with local values. The current account was in chronic deficit, whilst large annual aid payments were the only means of partially funding the visible trade deficit. The culmination of a series of political setbacks was perhaps the 'tipping point' that sent Vanuatu down the path of structural adjustment.

The adaptation in economic structure promoted by the CRP followed the modernist Washington Consensus that had been enacted around the world in the previous two decades. This universalism had a number of benefits, the most important of which were that useful lessons could be drawn from other countries and that the reforms could reduce the culpability of local officials or politicians whilst remaining all-encompassing.

The universals of the CRP, however, presented major problems. As Rodrik (2002a: 7) says, 'transitions to high growth are rarely sparked by blueprints from abroad.' The CRP's laissez-faire stance wrongly assumed that a reduction in the role of the state would automatically improve economic fortunes. In fact the economy stagnated during the seven years after 1997, while wealth per person shrank. The role of the state remains open for debate, and there are strong reasons for thinking that in small, vulnerable economies – and others – fiscal policy and government intervention still have an important role.

A number of misleading comparisons with East Asian economies further confirmed the problems resulting from the 'one-size-fits-all' character of the reform package. It was inappropriate to liberalise trade without thinking carefully about Vanuatu's particular situation. Corporatisation, privatisation and fiscal tightening were all enacted without attention to local detail. Arguably the biggest criticism of the CRP is that it lumbered the country with a growing external debt problem: Vanuatu was obliged to pay for foreign consultants out of its own revenues, a fiscal drain that still persists.

The CRP ignored specific economic characteristics, including the role of money, the role of land and the unusual tax structure, which should have necessitated careful attention to trade policy. As it was, the model of trade policy applied to Vanuatu was rigid and inflexible. It forced national policymakers to carry out standard policies which were contrary to the country's own interests. A more suitable set of reforms would have recognised the need for officials to retain control of policy, which in turn would have enabled them to accommodate the features peculiar to the economy and social situation.

It is hardly to be expected that all development practitioners should indulge in epistemology, but on the other hand the application of economics usually does involve an unspoken way of using knowledge. Chapters 3 and 4 showed that mainstream economics employs a modernist epistemology, and that the kind of economic development policy advocated under the Washington Consensus is no exception. This chapter has tried to show that raising methodological questions is useful when designing policy. Making the underlying perspective and methods explicit can help tailor policy towards practical outcomes, in line with development goals.

The CRP conceived of the economy as a closed system. The thinking behind the programme was non-reflexive, meaning that it was not grounded in the social situation in which it was to be applied and that its executors did not perform self-enquiry, turning the techniques of their analysis on themselves. Rather, the programme had an objectivist stance which precluded full input by Vanuatu nationals. Had the programme been reflexive, and largely nationally owned, it would have been more likely to meet traditional demands and would have led to better policy. For example if local people had fully understood and owned the reform package they would probably not have agreed to pay for foreign consultants' salaries with a dollar-denominated loan worth a tenth of annual economic output.

The modernist credentials of the CRP were most evident in its foundationalist view of knowledge, its implicit appropriation of the label 'science' and its determinism. Problems here caused certain policies to react back on themselves in a feedback loop which undermined the very objectives being sought. Investment in the Public Service Commission weakened the efficiency of the public service. Quantifying the economy led to worse policymaking. Outside intervention in the economy made the task of future intervention harder. Finally, focusing on GDP as an end in itself worsened economic performance and threatened the attainment of national goals.

It is tempting to suggest that Vanuatu's economy is beyond development; that the country faces such immense difficulties of size, vulnerability, distance from markets and capacity that perhaps it should be left to pursue its own traditional values without materialistic 'Western' intervention. The argument here, although in favour of particularism and attention to context where helpful, does not advocate such relativism. A reflexive view of economic policymaking suggests that there are benefits from engagement with the outside world and that developed countries have a responsibility towards less-advantaged nations. What distinguishes reflexivity from reflection is that there is a *two-way* inter-relation between subject and object rather than a one-way causality. The objectivism associated with modernist policy intervention should complement subjective local experience, with the two poles interacting to produce appropriate policy solutions. Economic development practice may have swung too far towards modernist universalism, but this does not require a resulting shift to the other side, where economics abandons struggling states to their own fate.

Certain universals would probably be included in any economic reform programme and endorsed by national policymakers, such as grants for improved education and health. Helping country inhabitants to change the economic structure in order to achieve local goals can result in better policy. Foreign staff can be used by national politicians and officials to avoid the blame for painful reforms. In Vanuatu there is a role for qualified, long-term technical consultants in bolstering government capacity, which suffers mostly as a result of the small population size and insufficient standards of education. As mentioned at the beginning, one of the main benefits of outside involvement is that overseas development personnel can help facilitate the process of learning from other countries. The various global development experiences, including certain specific features of the various successful East Asian countries, all hold grains of truth for Vanuatu.

Structural adjustment in Vanuatu actively reduced economic policy autonomy. Abandoning Vanuatu to fend for itself, however, would have resulted in a similar outcome – the kind of economic conservatism propagated by accepted wisdom, which suggests that globalisation inevitably forces small and less-developed countries to accept a smaller role for the state and to submit to the diktats of international capital.

An implication of the argument in this chapter is that the economy is not different to other spheres of social reality in somehow being beyond human agency. Indeed failing to realise the existence of agency can itself close down policy options. Economic interventions do make a difference, but it is up to the institutions and officials involved to decide in which direction policy should proceed and how much autonomy is subsequently available. The spectre of the straitjacket may seem inevitable, but this does not need to be so. Recognising the existence of reflexivity will lead to economic policies that mirror local needs and that maximise the benefits from engagement with the international economy.

The next chapter examines the taxonomy in the case of Singapore, which experienced a much more successful development process, and which retained an increasing degree of autonomy from the international development institutions.

Appendix 1: Summary of how the Comprehensive Reform Programme (CRP) in Vanuatu related to the 10 points of the Washington Consensus

Washington Consensus (Williamson 2004–5: 196)	Vanuatu's CRP
1. 'Budget deficits should be small enough to be financed without recourse to the inflation tax.'	Government expenditure averaged only 27 per cent of GDP during the 1990s. This is about the same as the median level for all developing countries over the same period. On average the budget was exactly in balance from 1990 until 1997. In 1990 Vanuatu had one of the lowest ratios of government employees per capita among Pacific island economies, at three per one hundred country inhabitants. This compared with the Cook islands at 18.2, Tuvalu at eight and Fiji with six (ADB 1996: 103). The ADB urged Vanuatu to cut public spending further, although in practice this did not happen.
2. 'Public expenditure should be redirected from politically sensitive areas that	Four of the original five objectives of the CRP related to this point. These were: redefining the role of the public sector; improving public sector efficiency; encouraging the

receive more resources than their economic return can justify... toward neglected fields with high economic returns and the potential to improve income distribution...'[32]

private sector to lead growth; and improving social equity (Knapman and Saldahna, op. cit.: 177–84). Although these were the stated objectives, the results were less than satisfactory, as argued in Chapter 6.

3. 'Tax reform... so as to broaden the tax base and cut marginal tax rates.'

Value-added tax was introduced under the CRP, with the explicit aim of broadening the tax base. It was also assumed that import duties would fall under regional trade agreements and World Trade Organisation (WTO) membership. Marginal tax rates did not fall, however. Given that the CRP (and the Washington Consensus) stated that its aim was to improve income distribution, it might have considered the introduction of income tax.

4. 'Financial liberalisation, involving an ultimate objective of market-determined interest rates.'

Vanuatu, as a tax haven, was already financially liberal. Interest rates are in theory determined by the market, although the tiny size of the economy and the small number of banks, many of which are orientated almost exclusively towards the offshore sector, means that financial markets tend to be highly illiquid and dominated by the operations of the government and the Reserve Bank of Vanuatu.

5. 'A unified exchange rate at a level sufficiently competitive to induce a rapid growth in nontraditional exports.'

The CRP did not induce any change in the exchange rate regime, nor did it advocate devaluation of the vatu. It did imply the possibility of growth in nontraditional exports, but without suggesting concrete policy measures to achieve this aim.

6. 'Quantitative trade restrictions to be rapidly replaced by

This was a key aim of the CRP, although as shown in Chapter 6, actual tariff reform was not strictly part of the CRP. Instead, regional

144

(Continued)

Washington Consensus (Williamson 2004–5: 196)	Vanuatu's CRP
tariffs, which would be progressively reduced until a uniform low rate in the range of 10 to 20 per cent was achieved.'	trade agreements and WTO membership were eventually to lower most tariffs to around this range.
7. 'Abolition of barriers impeding the entry of FDI'	The Vanuatu Investment Promotion Agency was established in 1998 and certain regulations impeding the entry of FDI, such as the 'green letter' under which the Minister for Immigration could expel foreigners, were abolished. The Minister of Finance was no longer responsible for vetting investment proposals.
8. 'Privatisation of state enterprises'	A number of key businesses were corporatised or privatised, including the post office and airline. The gains from privatisation and corporatisation, however, were limited, since in such a small market most of the newly privatised entities faced little competition, whilst regulation was near-absent.
9. 'Abolition of regulations that impede the entry of new firms or restrict competition'	The CRP aimed to reduce the number of companies on the 'reserved list' of investments, which named certain areas in which foreign companies were prohibited from involvement. As shown in Chapter 6, WTO membership was to have been directed towards the abolition of regulations impeding the entry of new firms. In particular, the schedule indicating Vanuatu's commitments on services included opening up almost all sectors with few restrictions.

10. 'The provision of secure property rights, especially to the informal sector.'	This was the one major area in which the CRP did not follow the Washington Consensus, although the issue of land ownership was discussed. Politicians considered land to be an area too sensitive for policy to changed, and freehold ownership is still prohibited.

Summary

The CRP followed seven out of the 10 points of the Washington Consensus. In the main areas – current-account liberalisation, government expenditure and privatisation – the programme was a classical case of old-style structural adjustment. The key objectives were to reduce the role of government in the economy; to allow a bigger role for markets; and to increase international openness.

In three areas the CRP did not strictly follow the Washington Consensus, although this was partly because policy was already in line with what was demanded. On point 4, as a tax haven Vanuatu's financial markets were already somewhat liberal, although this is not to suggest that they were highly developed or functional. Regarding point 5, the CRP did not change the exchange rate regime or suggest devaluation. The area in which the CRP directly contradicted the Washington Consensus was land ownership, which was so culturally sensitive that it constituted a bottom line beyond which politicians could not proceed. An area not mentioned in Williamson's list is the speed of reform. The case of Vanuatu differed from many other structural adjustment packages in that it was slower. Instead of a 'big bang' the reform package lasted many years.

Chapter 6 argued that many of the measures of the CRP were inappropriate to Vanuatu's specific situation, and that the CRP did not meet its own objectives. In particular government expenditure did not fall in the years after the CRP (partly because of the residual amount of spending necessary for running the civil service, as well as the significant additional debt burden); privatisation did not generate significant efficiency improvements; and a more liberal environment for FDI did not lead to an immediate upturn in incoming investment. As time goes on, the influence of the CRP appears to be waning, and the government is reverting to policies that more directly meet its requirements.

7
Singapore: The Lionized City

7.1 Introduction

Singapore (from the Malay words Singa Pura, meaning Lion City) is one of the most successful economic growth stories in history. GDP expanded at an annual average of 8 per cent between 1960 and 2004, contracting in only four of those years and at times averaging double-digit levels for half a decade (Peebles and Wilson 1996: 43; Ministry of Trade and Industry 1998–2005). Growth in per capita income, shown in Figure 7.1, placed Singapore among the top five developing countries during the two decades after it separated from the United Kingdom in 1959. By 2004 GDP per capita was US$25,191, among the richest 30 countries, having expanded tenfold in real terms since independence. Unemployment and inflation have been low and stable since the 1970s. Economic growth was so great that Lee Kuan Yew, Singapore's autocratic prime minister for the first 25 years and now 'Minister Mentor', titled the second volume of his memoirs 'From Third World to First' (Lee 2000).

Yet there is more to the story than numbers. The very fact that Singapore could retain the same prime minister for a quarter-century betrays the social and political dimensions of economic success. Several authors have argued that it is impossible to examine Singapore's economic growth without addressing the political and social situation. Castells (1988: 73) says that: 'Singapore's development is, above anything else, a political process, decided upon and guided by a strong government determined to overcome its underdeveloped status in the international economy.' Alten (1995: 230) and Peebles and Wilson (2002) echo this statement. Tremewan highlights the social control exercised by an authoritarian regime, writing that he is 'critical of the dominant view

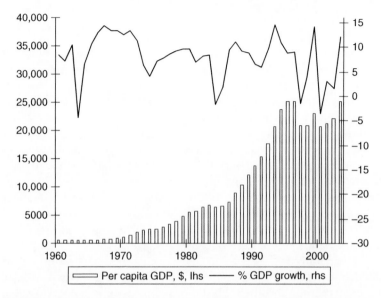

Figure 7.1 Singapore GDP growth rate and US$ per capita GDP, 1960–2004
Sources: Peebles and Wilson (1996): 43; Ministry of Trade and Industry 1998–2005,
http://www.singstat.gov.sg

of Singapore which abstracts the economy from the reality of concrete social relations' (Tremewan 1994: 1).

The current chapter will, as in the previous chapter, and suggested by the taxonomy proposed in Chapter 4, try to examine the social and political context of the economy. The chapter will examine how the taxonomy fits with Singapore's economic development process, and whether the Singapore government generally followed the kind of approach suggested by the taxonomy. I will consider a much longer period of development than in Vanuatu: from separation from the United Kingdom in 1959 until 2004. The reasons are twofold. Firstly, I did not work in the Singapore government, which meant that I gained a less detailed knowledge of how government worked, although I spent three years based in the country writing about business and economics from 1999 to 2001 (for example, see AsiaWise 2001a; 2001b; Asiaweek 2001). Secondly, the postcolonial era forms a natural period for the study of the development narrative, enabling a better comparison with the structural adjustment years in Vanuatu.

A secondary objective is to use the taxonomy to assess the Washington Consensus as a model for economic development. The previous chapter argued that Washington Consensus-type policies were applied unsuccessfully in Vanuatu. Here, I address the issue of whether Singapore followed Washington Consensus-style advice. If at all, how did Singapore move beyond the universalism offered by Washington and the particularism advocated by postmodern-type policies?

Debate over Singapore's economic success revolves around two general explanations: geography and policy. Some argue that the city-state's location on one of the world's busiest shipping lanes at the gateway to East Asia and the lack of dependence on agriculture made rapid economic growth likely (Huff 1997). These kind of explanations can generally be labelled objectivist or related to structure. Other commentators, above all government ministers (Goh 1995a, 1995b; Lee 2000) concentrate more on the role played by proactive economic policymaking. These sort of explanations can be considered largely subjectivist in the sense defined in Chapter 4, focusing on agency.

The structure of the current chapter will follow the taxonomy in Chapter 4 and therefore the same general outline as Chapter 6 on Vanuatu. This should shed light on the relationship between the objective and the subjective, and in turn geography and policy. First is a discussion of how the Singapore government examined the influence of external values and norms. The government explicitly assessed the extent of outside influence, ensuring that it was never in a financial situation which forced it to accept undesirable conditionalities. Section 7.3 shows how the government assessed the importance of local context. Singaporean leaders have emphasised the differences between what they term the 'Western' model and what they perceive as Singaporean values, institutions and behaviour. Section 7.4 examines the ways in which tools, concepts and policies affected themselves. The final section shows that there was an allowance for theory to be revised if it proved inadequate or as circumstances changed. Schumpeterian ideas, and a response to the new growth theory, are replacing the developmentalist theoretical perspective.

7.2   The influence of external values and norms

7.2.1   The need for reform

Singapore became a self-governing province in 1959 following 140 years of British rule. Membership of the Malaysian Federation in 1963 ended two years later amid political tensions, bringing about full independence. At the time many thought that the tiny state was unviable, above all the Prime Minister (Lee 2000: 25), who famously cried in public after the breakdown of relations with Kuala Lumpur. In 1965 the island had a per capita income of only US$1,500 and a population of 1.9 million (Singapore Department of Statistics 1974: 1). Before land reclamation the main island and small surrounding ones had a land area of only about 600 km^2, slightly smaller than East Lothian in Scotland. Industrialisation was in its infancy and agriculture undeveloped. Singapore depended heavily on its status as an entrepôt and staple port for the trans-shipment of goods such as tin and rubber from neighbouring Malaysia. Unemployment was almost 14 per cent, while labour unrest was frequent. The British defence presence comprised almost a fifth of economic output, and plans to pull back the military 'East of Suez' threatened not only to deprive the once-important East Asian colonial stronghold of vital income, but to leave it vulnerable to attack from hostile neighbours. Reform therefore seemed imperative to ensure survival.

Yet it is possible to overplay Singapore's economic vulnerability at this time and therefore to imagine that reform was more pressing that it truly was. While Lee talks of the limitations of having no hinterland, Sachs (2005) has highlighted the adaptability that comes of having no 'resource burden'. The near-absence of natural resources meant that the composition of exports was more easily influenced by government strategy. The economy of neighbouring Malaysia grew more slowly, partly because it is bigger and burdened with large rubber and palm oil sectors, which add less value than technologically orientated industries.

Huff (1997) emphasises the continuity between Singapore's 140-year history as an entrepôt staple port and contemporary export-orientated growth. Singapore thrived on trade since its establishment as a colony by Sir Stamford Raffles in 1819. It lies southeast of the Malacca Straits through which any ship must pass on its journey east unless going through the Sunda Strait. The port was a convenient stopping point for the large markets of Indonesia, Malaysia and even Indochina. At independence trade was worth 230 per cent of GDP, similar to the current proportion, and Sachs and Warner (1995) point out that Singapore is one of only eight developing countries to have been open to trade since independence. A boom in imports and exports over the subsequent decade would widen the trade deficit as Singapore imported the machinery, technology and raw materials necessary for development. Table 7.1 shows that in 1965 the balance of payments was sustainable for an economy of US$3.0 billion (US$500 million at the time).

Table 7.1   Balance of payments, 1965–95, million Singapore dollars

Item	1965	1975	1985	1995
A. Goods and services (net)	−101.2	−1,677.0	461.2	21,709.7
Balance of merchandise trade	−759.8	−5,897.6	−6,223.5	−1,855.2
Balance on services trade (net)	658.9	4,220.6	6,684.7	23,564.9
B. Transfer payments (net)	−48.9	−99.4	−469.0	−1,261.4
C. Capital account (net)	104.3	1,386.9	1,536.9	−3,465.9
D. Balancing item	31.6	1,361.4	1,412.6	−4,808.5
E. Overall balance (A+B+C+D)	−11.8	971.9	2,941.7	12,173.9
F. Reserves (net)*	11.8	−971.9	−2,941.7	−12,173.9

* An increase in assets is indicated by a minus sign
Source: Singapore Department of Statistics, 1974–96

A goods trade deficit in 1965 worth 23 per cent of GDP was largely balanced by a surplus on services trade. The overall current-account deficit (A+B) was funded by net inflows to the banking sector (C), which was as yet undeveloped, dealing mainly with trade finance. Aid flows were insignificant. The only two years in which there was an overall balance of payments deficit were 1964 and 1965, except during the recession of 1986, reflecting the trade-orientated structure of the economy and the subsequent build-up of reserves. Although the absolute sums grew much larger in subsequent years, and the economy became much richer, the trade and capital-account deficits in 1965 were not historically the highest. The development of the financial sector by the mid-nineties resulted in a large net outflow of capital. One of the most notable features of Table 7.1 is the US$23.5 billion balance on services trade by 1995. This is a result of the development of Singapore as services-orientated rather than a goods producer, and reflects the advantage of having no 'resource burden'. It can be seen, in sum, that Singapore's reasonably healthy balance of payments situation perhaps suggests that reform was less pressing than in other comparable nations at the time.

Another distinctive advantage of the Singaporean economy at independence was the high level of education amongst local administrators. The largely English-educated People's Action Party (PAP) consisted mostly of moderate professionals who had hit a glass ceiling under colonialism. Lee, who studied Law at Cambridge University, and whom Margaret Thatcher liked to refer by his nickname 'Harry', had to learn Mandarin Chinese to talk to his constituents. A capable, technocratic administration, fluent in English, could deal with an international audience.

Singapore's strategic importance to Britain and proximity to Malaya had meant that at independence it was well-run and prosperous relative to other newly decolonised East Asian nations. Unlike elsewhere, there was little hurry or animosity during the handover. Britain only shut down its military bases in 1973. Although major obstacles had to be overcome, the economy was in a reasonable initial position, which would help the task of development. Reform was therefore not as pressing as in some other newly independent countries.

7.2.2   The universals of development practice

From the start Singaporean administrators were keen to learn lessons from overseas. The role of the United Nations Development Programme (UNDP) is often overlooked. Singapore received US$27.2 million in technical assistance support from 1950, when UNDP assistance began, until 1985. Regular UN aid over the same period was US$2.9 million, while the government contributed a total of US$3.23 million (Chow *et al.* 1997: 15, 131). While these sums are not particularly large relative to the size of the economy, the co-operation programme included the services of 744 technical assistants and 2,029 fellowships, reflecting considerable training and knowledge transfer. The United Kingdom was the main source of funds. Other donors included Japan, Australia, Canada, New Zealand, Germany and France.

In 1960 a visiting UNDP team led by Dutchman Dr Albert Winsemius, who became a trusted adviser to Lee Kuan Yew until the 1980s, wrote a report entitled 'A proposed industrialisation programme for the State of Singapore' (United Nations 1961). This document formed the basis of early development strategy. Lee (2000: 67) says that he could not understand why Winsemius suggested keeping the statue of Raffles and defeating the then-popular Communist party. He would later realise that these moves were aimed at reinforcing international confidence in what was then an untested socialist government.

The UNDP urged Singapore to make foreign direct investment (FDI) a central plank of development, and it did indeed play a prominent role after the 1960s. Lee wanted to 'create a First World oasis in a Third World region' (ibid.: 76) and to try to 'leapfrog' other nations by attracting investment in new technologies. He says that he learnt about foreign business values during a sabbatical at Harvard University in 1968, when he had the opportunity to meet foreign business people potentially interested in investing in East Asia (ibid.: 73). From then on, FDI became a priority. Foreign investment boomed from the late 1960s, when GDP growth was at its highest. Singapore gained 11.8 per cent of total FDI to developing countries between 1980 and 1984, the highest of any East Asian country. FDI averaged a quarter of gross fixed capital formation between 1980 and 2000, again higher than any other East Asian nation (Peebles and Wilson 2002: 171). Foreign corporations were estimated to contribute up to a third of GDP by 2004, around double that of local companies. But importantly attracting investment did not mean further liberalisation. It meant giving tax incentives and expanding public investment in the economy rather than shrinking it (Rodrik 2007: 39).

Singaporean government ministers have suggested that they had no new formula for economic success. Goh Keng Swee, the first Finance Minister writes:

> our policies were not novel, innovative *or* path-breaking... The general policy line follows what had already been attempted in many developing countries. What was different was that perhaps our policies produced results. This could be because they were implemented more thoroughly, and with a high standard of integrity.
>
> (Goh 1995b: 101)

One of his successors, Hon Sui Sen said in his 1978 budget statement:

> In retrospect, I can fairly describe Singapore's evolution since 1960, when the UN team on Economic Development led by Dr Winsemius first studied us, as the prototype of economic development promoted by international institutions such as the World Bank, IMF and GATT. We have followed policies which developed countries have urged all developing countries to pursue, that is, to start with simple manufactures (which the developed countries helped by opening markets via GSP [Generalised system of preferences]) and then to upgrade our economic skills and go on to more skill intensive manufacture.
>
> (Cited in Chow *et al.* 1997: 19)[1]

The role played by universal policy advice carried a number of advantages. Lee Kuan Yew believed that international confidence was central to economic success (Lee 2000: 87). He was keen to avoid the corruption that afflicted neighbouring countries, and paid high government salaries.[2] By accepting foreign advice, Lee could show that his was an internationalist administration committed to attracting investment unlike nationalistic and more inwardly focused, newly independent neighbours such as Malaysia and Indonesia. International confidence was doubly important given Singapore's reliance on trade.

FDI was valued as a source of technology transfer more than as a means of supporting the balance of payments. Foreign companies were urged to train workers in new techniques, particularly in electronics during the 1970s and early 1980s. With UNDP assistance the National University of Singapore was relocated from its old buildings at Bukit Timah to a new campus at Kent Ridge. Links between academia and business have always been encouraged. Singapore has sought to attract what it terms 'foreign talent'. Multinationals face few limits on the number of foreign employees, work permits are granted quickly, and taxes are set deliberately low to attract highly skilled overseas workers, who help keep selected members of the local workforce at the forefront of global technological developments.

7.2.3 How Singapore followed its own path

Yet for all the attempts to gain international confidence and attract FDI, Singapore followed a strongly self-determined development path. Para-doxically, appearing to do what the outside world wanted did not mean surrendering control over the machinery of economic governance. Hav-ing achieved international confidence, Singapore retained the policy space in which to tailor development strategy to national circumstances. Hon's 1978 budget statement probably has diplomatic undertones – aiming, as always, to maintain international support. It also hints that Singapore followed only general suggestions, leaving the details to locals and only taking advice where appropriate. A statement from Alan Choe, former head of the Urban Redevelopment Authority, provides a telling contradiction of the outward show of conformity:

> The Singapore context, since the day of the present Government – from 1959 onwards – is one of self-reliance. You cannot turn to any-body, any experts outside, because our problems are uniquely our own. First, Singapore was totally manned by expatriates; then the Singapore Government came in and Singaporeanized the whole lot. The Government was able to demonstrate what it could do with untried, unproven Singaporeans. Obviously, this got to the heads of the technocrats and professionals who thought: 'Look. Here's something to be proud of. We can do it on our own'.
>
> (Cited in Chow *et al.* 1997: 67)

This statement illustrates the importance of policy space, autonomy and self-belief, which allowed the development process to be customised to the national situation, in all probability making it more successful. The idea that Singapore must 'go it alone' in an often turbulent neighbourhood, retaining control over its domestic political and economic policy, has formed a central platform of national identity since independence.

Lee (2000) says that one of his government's first aims was achieving the financial independence to secure sovereignty over policy. He did not often request aid and minimised any sources of external financial leverage. By the 1990s Singapore had the largest per capita foreign exchange reserves of any country, with the total reaching US$113 billion in 2004 (although large reserves are to be expected in such an open economy). Foreign borrowing, especially from international institutions, has been largely unnecessary since the 1980s and overseas debt has always been minimal. The available data, shown in Figure 7.2, demonstrate that external debt comprised only 2.3 per cent of GDP in 1984 and fell to zero by 1995. Loans from the Asian Development Bank were never more than half of either bilateral British loan aid or loans from the

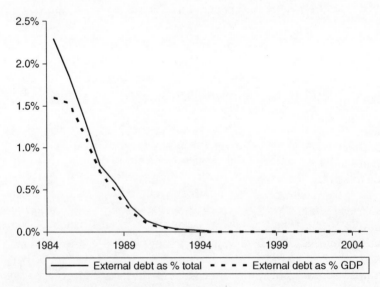

Figure 7.2   Singapore external debt, 1984–2004
Source: Monetary Authority of Singapore

World Bank. After 1995 the government was able to finance its borrowing through access to the substantial domestic savings. Because of international confidence and low domestic interest rates, it has never faced high debt-servicing costs.

A belief in the importance of national self-reliance had strong roots. The ruling People's Action Party had a socialist anti-colonial background. Former president Devan Nair edited a book in 1976 entitled 'Socialism that Works: the Singapore Way'. Elsewhere, in 'A socialist economy that works', Former Finance Minster Goh Keng Swee writes: 'Taking an overall view of Singapore's economic policy, we can see how radically it differed from the *laissez-faire* policies of the colonial era' (Goh 1995b: 105). The state has a history of directing public expenditure towards favoured areas, including infrastructure and 'complementary goods' (Shin 2005) that are not provided by the private sector. The government continues to 'pick winners' – in contrast to generally accepted modern policy wisdom.

Institutions such as the right-wing Heritage Foundation continue to rank Singapore as one of the two 'most free' economies in the world,[3] (Heritage Foundation 2007) relying amongst other things on the fact that at around 20 per cent of GDP the ratio of government expenditure to national income appears particularly low. Yet some commentators, such as Asher (1999), argue that proceeds from the lease of land, which is mostly government-owned, should be included in public revenues, bringing the total to 38.5 per cent of GDP, among the highest in the world. Low corporate taxes are compensated partly by expensive 10-year car ownership licences known as 'Certificates of Entitlement' and high taxes on alcohol and tobacco. Peebles and Wilson (2002: 122–3) suggest that when taxes and proceeds from the lease of land are combined with large regular budget surpluses the overall 'take' from the population is high. The proceeds from a compulsory savings scheme known as the Central Provident Fund must legally be used to buy government bonds, significantly reducing the cost of public borrowing and further reducing the role of the market in private savings.

The government retains strong links with, or partly owns, many of the large government-linked companies (GLCs), that dominate the economy. In 2000 these included a 79.7 per cent stake in Singapore Telecommunications, a 58.8 per cent share in SembCorporation Industries, 53.8 per cent of Singapore Airlines and 49 per cent of Singapore National Printers Corporation. Estimates suggest that the number of GLCs peaked at 720 in 1994 before later falling to below 600 (Peebles and Wilson 2000: 44). Government-linked corporations such as Temasek, a holding company, and Keppel Land, have invested significant sums overseas. Prior to corporatisation and privatisation government owned bigger stakes in the Development Bank of Singapore (which was partly privatised in the 1990s and was used to direct credit to desired areas), the Post Office Saving Bank, the Port Authority of Singapore and the Public Utilities Board. In addition the National Trades Union Council runs a powerful co-operative movement, which operates a supermarket chain, NTUC Fairprice. Policy in these areas has deviated heavily from the formula prescribed by the Washington Consensus.[4]

The state-led nature of the economy is not the result of ideological dogmatism. Singapore's authoritarian ruling party can be termed socialistic only in very specific macroeconomic terms, and then only until the 1980s, throughout courting foreign capital. Since independence the government has presided over an increase in inequality (Bhanoji Rao and Ramakrishnan 1980), a clampdown on press freedom, a reduction in freedom of speech and other democratic freedoms (in the 2001 and 2006 general elections only two opposition members of parliament were elected out of 84), and a draconian justice system. Policy has always been authoritarian and orientated towards control, yet the government has acted pragmatically, pursuing whatever course of action it believes best serves the long-term economic interests of the nation. The overriding objectives were not social but economic, tackled by technocrats who were ideologically constrained only by the desire to build wealth.

Former Finance Minister Goh perhaps sums up the Singaporean attitude to development: 'The selection of Western models needs careful study, diligent application and intelligent adjustment' (cited in Chow *et al.* 1997: 113), and: 'The book of rules tells you very little, and precedents borrowed from advanced countries have a nasty habit of coming apart in your hands' (Goh 1995b: x).

7.3   The importance of local context

Self-consciously and deliberately, Singaporean economic policymakers took account of particular and subjective local features. Policymaking has long been characterised by self-awareness. A monolithic state, unencumbered by dissent from an effective opposition, can reverse unsuccessful decisions without criticism.[5] An internationalist focus has put Singaporean successes and difficulties into perspective. Being small and potentially vulnerable reinforces the need for self-scrutiny, while being an island promotes cohesion. As shown below and in Appendix 2, this combination of features led to policies that diverged from the Washington Consensus.

7.3.1 Differences in institutions

Peculiarities among three sets of institutions – housing, education and the law – influenced economic development. Accommodating a diverse and relatively poor population on a small island represented a particular challenge at independence. The government considers universal public housing as one of its biggest achievements. Up to 90 per cent of Singaporeans live in public Housing Development Board (HDB) flats, which they buy on a 99-year leasehold agreement using a deposit from their Central Provident Fund account. Mortgages are guaranteed at 0.1 per cent above the rate of interest. The ability to link housing with savings enables the government simultaneously to appear as a benefactor and to exercise social control. A raft of rules governs behaviour in HDB flats, and occupants can be ejected for such trivial misdemeanours as placing pot plants in dangerous places or dropping litter in communal areas. Tremewan (op. cit.: 45–73) shows that housing is allocated to fragment communities and manipulate the vote. A strict ethnic quota system, justified on the grounds of racial harmony, is designed to split up the often rebellious Malay community as well as to divide generations. Social engineering initially helped co-opt the unions, then assisted in quelling dissent and driving down wages. Constituencies which vote against the People's Action Party are denied housing upgrades (Lydgate 2003), while the gerrymandering of electoral boundaries is frequent. The ability to exercise social control means the government is unlikely to reduce its influence over the housing system, and will tolerate minor microeconomic inefficiencies in the interests of maintaining social order.[6] Analyses such as the IMF country report by Cardarelli et al. (2000), which advocates increasing the role of the market in public savings, have had little effect on government policy because they ignore the political backdrop and treat the economy as an abstract entity isolated from these unique social and political realities.

The education system presented a peculiar challenge at independence because of the diverse ethnic and linguistic composition of the population. Approximately three-quarters of people are Chinese, whose mother tongue is English or one of at least seven other dialects. Malays, who speak English and Malay, make up 15 per cent of the population. Indians comprise around 6.5 per cent, and mostly speak English and Tamil, but there are five other language-groups. This diversity has been used as ideological justification for conformity in schools and in public. Variously Singapore has had campaigns to 'speak English' and 'speak Mandarin'. Malays who object are told that they must adapt to global economic conditions. Tremawan (op. cit.: 74–108) argues that the primary and secondary education system, based on rote-learning, helps generate conformity, a situation which is compounded by compulsory two-year military service immediately after school or university. Social control helps the government to direct workers into areas of the economy that it deems desirable. As with the housing system, education policy aims to create a compliant workforce, treating people as factors of production.[7]

It is well-known that Singapore's legal system is strict. Several crimes, including drug smuggling, carry a mandatory death sentence. Offences from petty theft to violent crime are punishable by caning. Under the Internal Security Act anyone can be detained indefinitely without trial. The PAP abolished trial by jury shortly after independence. Less frequently discussed are the economic ends of the law. More than in many wealthy nations, the law is directed at building wealth rather than securing individual or social rights. Business and the law have long been closely related. For example Yong Pung How, who had not practiced law for 18 years, in the late 1980s gave up a successful business career to become Chief Justice (ibid.: 193). The PAP also uses the law to criminalise the opposition, in 2000 finally bankrupting JB Jeyaretnam, the only successful long-term opposition member of parliament, after a series of legal cases dating back 20 years. The intimate connection between executive and judiciary is justified on the grounds that the opposition is 'incompetent' and that economic policy is best-served by political continuity.

These three sets of institutions – housing, education and law – played a strong role in the economic development experience, and, however *morally* problematic they may seem, the Singaporean government's *economic* prosperity hinged partly on its ability to harness and accommodate these subjective institutional features. Had the government been less able to exercise policy autonomy in these areas, it would probably have been less successful in growing the economy.

7.3.2   Differences in values

Singapore's government justifies its authoritarianism by suggesting that 'Asian' values are different to those in the liberal West and that Asians will tolerate the restriction of personal freedoms in return for more wealth. Lee Kuan Yew has argued that a regional Confucian ethic prioritises hard work, family ties, collectivism and personal responsibility. The East Asian economic boom lent weight to arguments that the region had a different way of doing things. Material prosperity, it was argued, outweighed secondary considerations of individuality and democracy. In a collection of essays titled 'Can Asians Think?' Kishore Mahbubani, a career diplomat who in 2004 was serving as Singaporean ambassador to the United Nations, argues that 'Asians and Westerners do think differently on some issues' (Mahbubani 2004: 8). His arguments are given qualified support by Sheridan (1999) amongst others.

Whilst the debate is wide-ranging, it is possible to identify differences in values that have affected economic development. A common Singaporean attitude is that 'I am prepared to put up with a few rules in order to stay wealthy'. People say that they are reluctant to experiment with a new government in case it induces instability. The national attitude is often summed up in the word 'Kiasu', dialect for 'fear of being left behind'. Family bonds are undoubtedly closer than in many Western countries, and despite the magnitude of the state savings system, the elderly remain dependent on subsequent generations.

Yet as with most cultural generalisations, examination of particular cases exposes problems. An increasingly independent-minded Singaporean youth expresses political apathy and cultural dissent as a mode of protest. Privately, many voice frustration with what they see as a heavy-handed, patriarchal regime. Younger people are increasingly reluctant to provide for their parents. The idea of an East Asian Confucianism is difficult to pin down in practice. Lee himself is arguably more British than Chinese. Southeast Asian cultures are largely Buddhist or Muslim rather than Confucian. Even supposed North Asian allies such as Taiwanese politicians have disavowed membership of any 'Confucian' community. Whilst Singaporean values are different, and they do have implications for economic development, they may be more pliable and multifaceted than political leaders suggest. It is doubtful whether these values extend far beyond the borders of Singapore.

7.3.3 Differences in behaviour

If there are differences in behaviour, they can be found in a willingness to tolerate authority for the sake of economic security. An 'economic' or developmentalist attitude pervades public discussion, and it is common to hear discussion of the state of the stock market or the trajectory of the economy. It is impossible to escape business life by, for example, retiring to the countryside. Singapore's leaders probably exaggerate the regional tendency towards political volatility and the history of domestic riots, but the potential for fragmentation is perhaps more prominent than in many older, more diverse countries. High economic growth is considered necessary in order to avoid these potential pitfalls.

A number of commentators argue that this unique sense of solidarity allows Singapore to pursue interventionist policies that would not work elsewhere. The country is often referred to as 'Singapore Inc' – like a large company where the government takes the place of directors, large corporations operate like managers, and others act as the workforce (Peebles and Wilson 2000; Low and Johnston 2001). During times of crisis people may act against their own immediate interests for the benefit of the common good, preferring long-term stability to short-term economic gain. 'In 1985, the workers accepted wage restraint, demonstrating once again a wiser, more mature and pragmatic work force placing national interest above that of self' (Chow et al. 1997: 7). This statement sounds propagandist (and it is true that the government wields a powerful propaganda campaign through the state-owned media) but there is no question that workers accepted wage cuts during the recession. During the late-1990s Asian economic crisis, and at other times, the government lowered the compulsory contributions of companies to the Central Provident Fund. It is hard to imagine such self-sacrifice in many Western countries.

There is a certain validity in the argument that smallness and a tendency towards conformity enabled Singapore to pursue interventionist economic policies. Smallness, and the particular values, institutions and behaviour in this context enabled the government to act somewhat like a large corporation. But this argument cannot be wholly correct since social cohesion was partly constructed by government as a conscious economic strategy. The 1950s and 1960s were a time of social disunity, while Singapore remains ethnically diverse. Social cohesion must be seen not as mere fortunate circumstance, nor as deep-rooted, but as part of economic policy. Because it is an active policy, rather than being unique to Singapore, similar options must be available to other small countries.

The cohesive veneer hides a more fragile reality. Election results, for example, may give the appearance of up to three-quarters support for the economic policies of the ruling PAP, but opposition candidates do not stand in every constituency. The number of unopposed seats rose to almost four-fifths in the 2001 general election, meaning that most people could not vote. Discontent is thus difficult to gauge but

may be higher than often supposed. Singaporeans are not more passive than people in any other culture, and dissent increasingly displays
itself through the arts, lifestyle and public debate. As Tremawan (op.
cit.) points out, when social control fails, the government is willing to
step in with powerful legal tools. Again, this shows that cohesion is not
necessarily natural, but is a result of government policies.

7.3.4 Summary

Had the government not been able to exercise policy autonomy, it
would have been less able to accommodate or create subjective reality. External analyses of the economy (such as the 2000 IMF country
report by Cardarelli et al.) often overlook subjective features, treating
the economy as an abstract entity isolated from particular social and
political realities.

Peculiarities of institutions, values and behaviour played a prominent
role in Singapore's economic development story. The government tried
to maintain control over policies which related to these characteristics,
including housing, education, law and the media. Generic macroeconomic policies, the like of which have been implemented during the
Washington Consensus era, would have stripped Singapore of its ability to accommodate these specific, contextual, subjective features. An
example is the important role played by the public housing system.
Although an IMF report recommended that it should be opened up further to market forces, the government realised that social cohesion had
wider-ranging macroeconomic implications than small microeconomic
gains. The government, contrary to Washington Consensus-style recommendations, operates a significant public spending programme which
enables it to maintain the particular brand of education and media
policies that it believes best serve national economic interests. The government also believed more strongly than most that people were factors
of production, used solely to make the economy grow, and individual
liberties assumed secondary importance.

The three features discussed above are linked. For example collectivist
values allow an authoritarian attitude towards public housing. An 'economic' mindset probably prompts some people to sacrifice legal freedoms which those in other countries would take for granted. Education
and media policies contribute to the stability of the collectivist value
system. Institutions, however, played a more prominent role in economic growth than different behavioural patterns, which in turn may
have been more important than values. Considerable doubt surrounds

the idea of any homogeneous 'Asian' set of values, and behavioural patterns, although important, are subject to change. Yet most commentators agree that the public housing system played an indispensable role in ensuring social and economic stability, while the unusual education and legal systems provided the raw materials and institutional backdrop for economic growth.

7.4 How economic tools, concepts and policies affected themselves

7.4.1 Industrial policy

As suggested in Chapter 4, reflexivity partly means accepting that policies or policy actions can backfire. The third point of the taxonomy argued that economic tools and concepts can undermine themselves, and that successful development experiences recognise the possibility of this kind of reflexivity. As in Vanuatu, Singapore's economy experienced feedback mechanisms during its development.

Singapore's recent history is often written as an unmitigated economic success, albeit with reservations about the social and political context. I have suggested that it is difficult to separate social norms and political processes from the economy, and plainly it would be possible to build a strong case against the authoritarianism of the ruling party (and many have, such as Tremawan, op. cit.; Alten 1995; Jeyaretnam 2003; Lydgate 2003). But even by its own, technocratic, economic criteria the government has experienced a number of failures – particularly in industrial policy – which were a product of the very success that those same policies enjoyed in the first place. This is more than just pointing out that governments sometimes get things wrong; it is an awareness that policies are rarely infallible and can contain with them the seeds of their own demise. This is one reason why it is so dangerous simply to transplant apparently successful policies from one country to another. Policies which are apparently successful may not be valid forever; they may work only in a particular time and context; and they may work differently when combined with other policies.

In his autobiography Lee Kuan Yew (2000: 69) discusses the failure of early government investments. During the 1960s the Economic Development Board, set up on UNDP advice, invested in joint ventures in paper recycling with a businessman who had no experience in the industry. A similar lack of experience underlay the failure of a ceramics business. A joint venture in shipbuilding failed because Singapore

had to import steel plates and engines. These failures were a consequence of the government's attempts to pick winners and to operate
businesses itself; given limitations of knowledge, success could not be
guaranteed. Early problems, however, did not deter it from adopting
a strongly interventionist stance throughout the development period,
with its successes outweighing the failures.

The government has suffered more recent business failures. In 1994 it
entered into a joint venture worth US$20 billion to build a government-
sponsored industrial park in Suzhou, west of Shanghai. After trumpeting
the deal as an example of how consensual 'Asian' business values could
lead to regional success, the Singaporean government was surprised to
find that a rival business park on the other side of the city was generating
unwanted competition. By 2001 sustained losses forced Singapore to cut
its stake to 35 per cent from an initial 65 per cent.

Lee is quoted as saying: 'We are not happy because we are not getting
the kind of attention we were assured we would get – special attention.
Indeed, what we are getting now is competition' (South China Morning Post, 29 June 1999). Subsequent experience supports evidence that
the Chinese authorities displayed no favouritism, with Singapore scal-
ing back its involvement in another government-sponsored zone in the
Chinese city of Wuxi. Chinese business people were more interested
in profits than any supposed common Asian ideals. Indeed observers
suggest that business cultures clashed, with Singaporeans touting transparency and accountability, which in China are often regarded as
'Western' values.

The Singaporean government, or government-linked corporations,
have often been unsuccessful in their foreign business operations. For
instance Temasek, the government holding company, paid what was
widely considered too high a price – in the biggest corporate deal in Thai
history – for the conglomerate Shincorp in early 2006. Government-
controlled Singapore Airlines bought a half-share in Virgin airlines
just before a widespread downturn in the industry. Other ventures in
telecoms and infrastructure have often been seen as attempts to use
spare cash rather than as strategic investments, while doubts surround
the historical returns achieved by the opaque Government Investment
Corporation, which invests public funds abroad.

As Lee's quote above suggests, the Singaporean government's domestic business success is due at least in part to the restriction of competition, often as part of a conscious infant-industry strategy. In a foreign
environment, with several competitors, success has proven more difficult. The government's industrial policy is not infallible, and although at

home government-linked companies do face global competition, abroad they find it more difficult to operate without government support. This is not a general criticism of domestic industrial policy but implies that as the economy has become more open, and as Singapore seeks to invest more overseas, its government-linked corporations cannot expect the same favourable conditions as they find at home.

7.4.2   Macroeconomic policy

In the years following independence the government conducted an import substitution policy and protected infant industries with a view to export promotion, although tariffs were low because the economy was so dependent on trade. As an extension of this protectionism, large domestic conglomerates were built up using special incentives, including subsidies and tax breaks. The additional heavy presence of major transnational corporations in such a small economy further reduced domestic competition.[8] High savings rates, largely due to the compulsory savings scheme, enabled high rates of capital accumulation.

This economic structure produced high growth until the 1990s. Subsequently, however, shortcomings began to surface. A debate over 'total factor productivity' in the mid-1990s highlighted the dependence of economic growth on the state mobilisation of savings. In an article entitled 'The Myth of Asia's Miracle' (1994), Paul Krugman used growth accounting work by Young (1992) and others in the new growth theory tradition to compare Singapore with the declining economy of the Soviet Union. The argument was that, as in command economies, current consumption was being sacrificed for future production, without corresponding improvements in labour or capital productivity. Given that this 'input-driven growth' was one-off, and such a massive increase in investment and education would be impossible to repeat, eventually GDP growth was likely to decline. Krugman and Young found that efficiency gains had been minimal throughout the recent history of the Asian 'tiger' economies. Many East Asian economies, and in particular Singapore, had simply been able to mobilise resources on a mass scale.

Krugman did not predict the Asian crisis, as has sometimes been claimed, and measurement problems with the growth accounting method have been exposed. As Keynes and Kalecki have shown, investment may determine savings rather than the other way around. But subsequent evidence provides qualified support to the total factor productivity argument. Table 7.2 shows that productivity growth slowed and became volatile during the 1990s, especially during the crisis. For most of the mid-1990s it grew slower than real wages, which declined

Table 7.2 Percentage change in real wages and productivity, Singapore, 1992–2003

Year	1992	1993	1994	1995	1996	1997	1998	1999	2000	2001	2002	2003
Real average wage change, %	5.8	5.3	5.4	5.2	5.3	3.5	–0.1	2.8	5.3	0.1	0.4	1.0
Productivity growth, %	3.4	8.7	6.6	2.9	1.8	2.3	–3.6	7.3	5.4	–5.2	3.6	2.3

Source: Singapore Ministry of Manpower 2003: 28

and remained particularly low after 2000. On average from 1992–2003 average annual productivity growth was 2.96 per cent, slightly below the average of 3.33 per cent for wages.

What was once a strength is now a weakness. The oligopolistic nature of the economy and high savings rates until the 1980s allowed resources to be directed into desired areas, particularly in heavy industry and export-orientated sectors. Subsequently the necessary lack of competition and government influence over the use of capital led to a decline in productivity, and a situation where productivity was unable to keep pace with wage growth. The entrenchment of the oligopolistic industrial structure is a major explanation for the levelling-off of GDP growth and per capita GDP seen since the late 1990s (shown in Figure 7.1). Whilst most governments would envy a situation where average economic growth dropped from 8 per cent to 5 per cent, in developmentalist Singapore, where high economic and wage growth has become expected, such a situation poses more of a problem.

A further dimension of the feedback mechanism at work here is that the social control necessary to achieve development has resulted in a paucity of entrepreneurs. As shown in Section 6.3.1 some commentators, such as Tremawan (op. cit.: 74–108), argue that the education system produces conformity rather than freedom of thought. Singaporean students perform very highly in technical subjects such as maths and engineering but relatively poorly in English and the arts. Subjects which require critical thinking and creativity, which are usually associated with entrepreneurship, have not been prioritised. The difficulty of generating domestic entrepreneurship further hampered the task of raising labour and capital productivity. The economy has become dependent on foreign workers, which the labour authorities work hard to attract, as shown in Section 6.2.2, but on which the economy depends increasingly as a source of entrepreneurship and risk-taking.

7.4.3   Summary

Whilst often painted as an unstoppable march to prosperity, the Singaporean economic development story has featured a series of difficulties, many of them a product of the very processes that led to success in the first place. Industrial policy, on balance successful, suffered a handful of domestic failures and more serious problems abroad. These failures stemmed partly from the lack of domestic competition, which was necessary to shift resources into appropriate areas but not conducive to producing enterprises which could succeed overseas. The most telling example of Singaporean over-confidence (and also a refutation of the idea of Asian values) was the failure of the industrial park in Suzhou. Again, this kind of failure was the other side of the coin to success.

Macroeconomic policy has arguably experienced a more serious problem of internal contradiction. To some extent it has become a victim of its own success. The conditions which led to rapid industrial growth between the 1960s and 1980s – high savings, heavy incoming foreign investment and a state-run oligopoly – became entrenched, leading to a decline in the productivity of labour and capital and producing a situation where wage growth outstripped labour productivity growth. While this situation has not resulted in a major economic downturn, and cannot be considered a serious problem in the short term, it has implications for long-term economic growth which the Singaporean government is working to address. These issues present bigger problems than usual in a nation with a developmentalist popular mindset which has become accustomed to continuous high levels of economic growth. The next section will deal with the issue of economic transformation.

7.5 The revision of theory as circumstances changed

The final section of the taxonomy developed in Chapter 4 suggested that successful development experiences involve the opportunity for self-revision. Rather than continually readjusting the same theory or model in the hope that it will eventually prove successful, or making minor changes from inside the same theoretical stance, wholesale theoretical revision can occur.

Following the Asian economic crisis which began in 1997 the Singapore government appeared to downplay its previously developmentalist theoretical perspective. Influenced by the US economic upturn and the stock-market boom of the 1990s, government officials began to talk of a transition to a more productivity-orientated, 'knowledge-based' economy. The new economic narrative was influenced by the new growth theory, with Paul Romer, one of its founders, visiting Singapore in 2000 to give a lecture and offer advice. This shift in theoretical perspective is an obvious response to the total factor productivity debate initiated by Young and Krugman a few years earlier. A further (contradictory) theoretical influence was the work of Schumpeter, which had also enjoyed a resurgence of popularity during the US economic upturn.

In 1998 *The Straits Times*, the government-owned newspaper, ran 41 stories about the 'new economy' compared with 12 the year before. The following year, use of the term in newspaper articles ran into the hundreds. Senior politicians began to use the term more and more often, with the following new year's message by the Prime Minister typical: 'We have the potential to become a globally competitive economy within a decade. We must embrace change, ride the new economic wave, innovate and create new wealth. Doing the same things better will not be good enough' (*The Straits Times*, 1 January 2000). Instead of portraying the growth process as one of gradual development towards a more prosperous future, government officials used terms like 'creative destruction' to suggest that future economic growth was expected to be more volatile.

To some extent such language is not unusual for Singapore, being a reflection of the attitude under which government encourages workers to remain flexible in the interests of what is held to be the more important goal of general prosperity. The kind of sentiment expressed here is redolent of the 1985 wage cuts described earlier, and unemployment did indeed hit historic highs following 2000. The emphasis on innovation, volatility and a 'new economic wave', however, reflects a major shift in public dialogue. Manufacturing came to be seen as less important, and services more so – in particular areas which were perceived to add more value such as biomedical sciences. In 2000 the government built a science park known as 'Biopolis' on which it hoped to position Singapore as a regional biomedical hub. The government was reported to be spending US$5 billion (US$2.8 billion) between 2004 and 2009 on research in the life sciences (*The Straits Times*, 4 January 2006). The scientist that led the team behind 'Dolly the Sheep' was only one of many well-known international scientists to be attracted to Singapore by high wages, liberal laws and good working conditions (he later left). The government built a new university in the centre of the city and invested more heavily in existing higher education, with a view to providing the human resources needed for the 'new economy'.

Some are sceptical about whether this apparent economic transition will work:

> Here again, we can see the traditional pattern of structural change. Public sector initiatives based on the advice of international advisors, a statutory board to provide the infrastructure, the public education system to try to guide Singaporeans into the relevant subjects and, no doubt, an international search for foreign scientists to fill the gap. This repeats the pattern that Alwyn Young hypothesized was the reason for Singapore's poor TFP performance: pushing the economy

into new fields without realizing the productivity gains of existing production.

(Peebles and Wilson, op. cit.: 265)

It is ironic that the government's professed desire to move towards a more 'competitive' and 'dynamic' economy involves the very elements of control that underpinned existing economic arrangements. It is hard to see an administration so orientated towards control being able to relinquish the strict economic policy management that proved successful until recent years. Official rhetoric may be different to reality. The national savings rate remained high, at 47 per cent of GDP in 2005 compared with 40 per cent four years earlier. The services sector accounted for 63 per cent of GDP in 2005, little different to the previous five years. Government reports claim that an increasing proportion of national output is generated by the biomedical sciences sector, but this is no indication of whether the sector is improving productivity. Managers at some of the major pharmaceutical companies suggest that their Singaporean operations focus only partly on research and development, and that they continue to manufacture low value-adding items such as pills. The attractions of the country do not differ markedly from a decade earlier, and include the high quality of infrastructure, political stability, good shipping links and quality of life.

Although official rhetoric may be clouding the true picture, there is little question that the administration must remain adaptable, because the economy is so small and open. The government clearly and self-consciously attempted to remould the economy. It has been able to do this because it has retained control over important policy levers, such as education and the provision of infrastructure, and it can exercise considerable influence over the destination of national savings. In the government's efforts to remake the economy it is able to take into account subjective national characteristics, including the institutional peculiarities discussed earlier. Such control is more easily achieved in a small state than a large one, and undoubtedly the often undemocratic nature of the political system makes the task easier.[9]

Whilst the implications of the quote above from Peebles and Wilson might be that Singapore should try to realise the productivity gains of existing production and not change its theoretical perspective or economic structure, in reality adaptability is an asset rather than a burden. Singapore's rapid economic growth has been due partly to its ability to remain flexible and not to become too embedded in one theoretical economic tradition. In the early stages of development finance ministers professed socialist beliefs; subsequently the growth process became more developmentalist; latterly, I have argued, the policy narrative could be described as being more influenced by the new growth theory and Schumpeterian-type ideas. It is possible to talk of the stages in Singapore's growth story in Hirschmanian terms: '...in the social world, things are...tangled and ambiguous. Here any connection we have established convincingly between events, as though it were a universally valid law, could be found simultaneously to hold and not to hold (or to hold in a very different form)...' (Hirschman 1995: 91). A plurality of theoretical perspectives, often overlapping and contradictory, have been conducive to economic growth.

7.6   Conclusion

The lionization of Singapore lies in its portrayal either as a development aberration which featured such special geographic, historical and cultural endowments that it holds no lessons for other countries; or as a heroic progression towards prosperity, with infallible technocrats at the helm. In reality neither view fully captures the development story. The country's spectacular economic growth can be explained both by objective geography and history *and* by subjective behaviour. The important point is that agency and structure are linked, in a manner suggested by Bourdieu. Whilst geography and history (which can be considered structural features) did matter, the government was able to assess how much they mattered, and consciously held on to the policy levers (which can be considered agential) that enabled it to carry out complementary policies to take account of national, subjective realities. Lucky endowments helped keep economic policymaking successful, but economic policymaking helped improve upon those initial lucky endowments.

Outside advisers with little knowledge of the domestic context could probably have suggested – and sometimes did suggest – policies which worked. Yet natural advantages could easily have been squandered. Government policymakers, who frequently shunned received economic wisdom, can take considerable credit for subsequent economic growth. In the years after independence good decision-making played an increasing role, so that politics collaborated with economics. In a sense Singapore contradicts the early determinism of early development professionals criticised by Arthur Lewis:

In 1950...economists and policy makers were sceptical of the capacity of LDCs to grow rapidly because of inappropriate attitudes, institutions or climates. The sun was thought to be too hot for hard

work, or the people too spendthrift, the government too corrupt, the
fertility rate too high, the religion too other worldly, and so on.
(Lewis, Nobel Lecture, cited in Singh 1994)

To what extent did Singapore's development fit with the taxonomy
proposed in Chapter 4? First, the government explicitly examined the
influence of external values and norms. One of the key principles of
Lee Kuan Yew's project was to win international confidence. To this
extent he followed certain international policy universals. The role of
outside advisors in Singapore's development is often ignored, but the
UNDP was involved in key early decisions, such as the creation of
the Economic Development Board. Attractiveness to the outside world
enabled Singapore to benefit from substantial incoming foreign direct
investment.

The government won international confidence partly in order to give
itself the space to carry out particular policies that might otherwise have
contradicted foreign advice. Singapore followed its own path, maintaining a prominent role for the state that contradicts the Washington
Consensus.[10] The public sector continues to account for over half of
GDP; the government still 'picks winners'; and public housing is provided by the state. A self-consciously autonomous mindset runs through
government thinking, and the national attitude is that Singapore should
'go it alone' in an often turbulent region.

Point two of the taxonomy, concerning an implicit assessment of
the extent to which local context is important, has particular relevance in Singapore. The government retained policy autonomy because
it wanted to accommodate peculiar national characteristics, including
institutions, values and behaviour – and in some cases to shape these
characteristics. Education, the law and public housing were all geared
towards economic growth, while values and behaviour helped condition the workforce to contribute to economic growth. Without the
policy autonomy to take account of these subjective national features,
the government would have been much less successful in growing the
economy.

Yet certain failures stand out. These failures were often a product of
early economic success, and thus constitute reflexive feedback mechanisms that may have been unavoidable but which pose future problems.
Industrial policy, whilst highly successful at home, led to difficulties
for Singaporean companies abroad. Macroeconomic policy faced the
criticism that it resulted mainly towards factor accumulation rather
than productivity growth, and on average between 1992 and 2003
labour productivity growth failed to match wage growth. To some

extent Singaporean business ventures abroad were a victim of domestic economic success.

The degree to which the government recognised the possibility that economic tools and concepts can undermine themselves is questionable. There is thus only partial support for this point of the taxonomy. But partly in acknowledgement of its shortcomings, and partly in response to changes in the international economy, the government changed the theoretical emphasis of its growth narrative, and began to talk of a 'new economy', adopting Schumpeterian terminology and responding to the criticisms levelled by certain critics. It is perhaps too early to tell whether the resulting public emphasis on flexibility, volatility and openness is yielding results. The People's Action Party may be unable to relinquish the tight grip it has held over economic policy and politics since independence, and according to Wilson and Young's argument productivity gains from the existing economic structure remain to be realised. But some control is still required in order to carry out the economic transition, and changes in the world economy required a response from small and open Singapore, which has always prospered because it is adaptable. This suggests that point four, an allowance for theory to be revised if it proves inadequate, has at least some relevance.

Throughout I have used words like 'prosperity' and 'success', focusing largely on the aggregate *economic* end results. This is justified because of Singapore's overwhelming orientation towards economic, rather than social or political development. But lower income-earners became poorer during the 1990s and early into the next decade. Wages for the worst-off are low compared with living costs. Even for the more affluent, strong reasons exist to question the benefits of more wealth when the costs are political authoritarianism, an unfree press, conformism in education and a draconian legal system. Despite Singapore's high performance in the Human Development Index, it is difficult to see the country as exemplifying Sen's vision. It would be possible to argue that relative to other countries, Singaporeans value wealth more highly than freedom. As I have suggested, not every Singaporean thinks like this. It is difficult to know, when the electoral system is rigged in favour of the ruling party and public dissent only selectively and grudgingly tolerated. In Sen's terms, despite Singapore's achievements in health and education, its contrasting lack of other freedoms – political, social, transparency-related and those related to protective security – throws into question whether the country is truly as developed as it appears to be.

Just as national perceptions of the economy depend on values and social influences, then so do foreign perceptions. Both outsider and insider views are essential in any final assessment of the development story. But at least from one perspective, if the price of prosperity is political repression and enforced conformity, then perhaps Singapore's economic growth has not been such a miracle after all.

The next chapter ties together the discussion of Vanuatu and Singapore, drawing some tentative conclusions from a comparison of the two countries and making some methodological points about the nature of comparison.

Appendix 2: Summary of how Singaporean development policies relate to the 10 points of the Washington Consensus

Washington Consensus (Williamson 2004–5: 196)	Singapore
1. 'Budget deficits should be small enough to be financed without recourse to the inflation tax.'	Budget deficits are rare, and the government has run an average surplus of 4.3 per cent of GDP since independence. Government expenditure is limited to only around 20 per cent of GDP while inflation has been consistently low. Asher (1999), however, argues that proceeds from the lease of land, which is mostly government-owned, should be included in public revenues, bringing the total to 38.5 per cent of GDP. Peebles and Wilson (2002: 122–3) suggest that combined with the high regular budget surpluses, this amounts to a high 'take' from the population. It is therefore a restriction of 'economic freedom' as measured by organisations such as the Heritage Foundation, which regularly ranks Singapore among the two freest economies in the world[11]. The proceeds from a compulsory savings scheme known as the Central Provident Fund legally must be used to buy government

(Continued)

Washington Consensus (Williamson 2004–5: 196)	Singapore
	bonds, significantly reducing the cost of public borrowing and further reducing the role of the market in private savings.
2. 'Public expenditure should be redirected from politically sensitive areas that receive more resources than their economic return can justify... toward neglected fields with high economic returns and the potential to improve income distribution...'	The government has a history of directing public expenditure towards areas that it deems desirable. In most cases the economic returns have justified this proactive stance. In a 1975 speech entitled 'Socialism in Singapore' Goh Keng Swee, Singapore's first Finance Minister, said that: 'The government's direct effort in promoting industrial growth is substantial... the industries initiated by government effort was [sic] as large as the *entire* sum of industries existing when we took office [in 1959]' (Goh 1995a: 105–6). Although data on income distribution are insufficient, little attempt appears to have been made to improve equality through public expenditure on areas with high economic returns. According to Pugh (1989), absolute poverty had increased to 35 per cent by the late 1980s from around a quarter of the population 20 years earlier. Peebles and Wilson (2002) show that the Gini coefficient increased (showing greater inequality) throughout the 1990s, while the incomes of the worst-off fell in absolute terms.
3. 'Tax reform... so as to broaden the tax base and cut marginal tax rates.'	Only around a third of the labour force and a quarter of companies pay taxes. A Goods and Services tax of 3 per cent was introduced in 1994, but it has not since been increased and direct tax rates are among the lowest in the world.

The government adjusts income taxes according to economic conditions, although the general trend has been for indirect taxes to comprise a larger proportion of public revenues.

4. 'Financial liberalisation, involving an ultimate objective of market-determined interest rates.'

The government has progressively liberalised financial markets since the 1980s and interest rates are largely market-determined. But these moves were gradual and occurred only after the economy had reached a certain stage of development. The domestic bond market remains relatively undeveloped, largely because of forced savings and the state-organised mortgage system.

5. 'A unified exchange rate at a level sufficiently competitive to induce a rapid growth in nontraditional exports.'

A currency board operated until the Singapore dollar floated in 1973. The currency has since been managed through central-bank intervention and taxes on interest earned on foreign holdings. There is no question that Singapore has pursued export-led growth, although the nominal and real exchange rates have appreciated over recent decades and some studies suggest that the Singapore dollar has been consistently overvalued.

6. 'Quantitative trade restrictions to be rapidly replaced by tariffs, which would be progressively reduced until a uniform low rate in the range of 10 to 20 per cent was achieved.'

The government pursued import substitution prior to independence and an infant-industry policy aimed at export promotion in subsequent years, although it imposed strict deadlines for the end of protection and import tariffs are now mostly close to zero. Quantitative restrictions have played little role in trade policy.

7. 'Abolition of barriers impeding the entry of FDI'

Singapore has made attracting inward FDI a central plank of economic policy since independence. Between 1980 and 2000

(Continued)

Washington Consensus (Williamson 2004–5: 196)	Singapore
	FDI averaged around 25 per cent of gross fixed capital formation, higher than any other East Asian economy.
8. 'Privatisation of state enterprises'	Privatisation began in 1985 with the sale of small- to medium-sized stakes in a number of government-linked corporations (GLCs). However the boundary between public and private often remains blurred, with senior government officials continuing to run major GLCs and statutory boards. Estimates of the share of GDP contributed by GLCs range from 45 per cent to 55 per cent (Peebles and Wilson 1996: 32).
9. 'Abolition of regulations that impede the entry of new firms or restrict competition'	Few regulations actively impede the entry of new firms. But the IMF considers local private companies, which are estimated to contribute only around 15 per cent of GDP, to be inefficient and small largely because they cannot compete in the oligopolistic market structure created by GLCs and multinational corporations (Cardarelli *et al.* 2000). Competition and the entry of new local firms are, in effect, restricted.
10. 'The provision of secure property rights, especially to the informal sector.'	Whilst most companies are guaranteed secure leasehold title and the government actively seeks to reassure foreign investors, the Land Acquisition Act (1966) allows the expropriation of private land. Using this law alongside the Planning Act (1970) and the Housing Development Board legislation, the government increased its land ownership from

26.1 per cent of land area in 1968, to 67
per cent in 1980 and 75 per cent in 1985.
(Lim 1989: 185; Wong and Ooi 1994: 791)
The government still owns most land.
Tremawan (op cit.: 53) points out that the
government specifically prevented
ordinary people from buying land.

Summary

Singapore partly followed policies that would be suggested by the
Washington Consensus. On points 3, 4 and 7 – tax reform, financial liberalisation and FDI – the government acted as liberally as the
Washington Consensus would have prescribed. Regarding points 1, 5,
6 and 9 – budget deficits, the exchange rate, trade policy and regulations on entry – the evidence is mixed. Budget surpluses can lead to
just as much crowding out as deficits. The exchange rate was floated
only in 1973, after the early stages of development; it remains actively
managed and exporters often complain that the currency is overvalued. A protectionist trade policy in the early stages encouraged import
substitution then export promotion. Inefficient local firms have always
found it difficult to compete with larger foreign and government-linked
corporations.

Regarding points 2, 8 and 10 – public spending, privatisation and
property rights – the government pursued policies which were directly
opposed to the Washington Consensus. It spent heavily in areas that
it deemed appropriate, 'picking winners'; it retains strong links with,
or partly owns, many of the large conglomerates that dominate the
domestic economy; and although it makes a point of guaranteeing leasehold for foreign companies it has used legal means to progressively
expropriate land.

In sum, for seven points out of 10 Singapore deviated from the Washington Consensus. As with many countries, it has proven impossible
to apply a fixed formula, and few points can be answered with a simple 'yes' or 'no'. Even if markets play a prominent role, they do so
in particular ways, often accompanied by government involvement.
At the risk of imputing beliefs to government that it does not truly
hold, it is possible to see that the government distinguished between
competition and ownership, promoting international competition yet

seeing private ownership as unnecessary as long as companies acted in a profit-orientated manner.

In the early stages of development Singapore considered itself a socialist system under which the government owned the largest share of the means of production. While the Washington Consensus has sought to downplay government's abilities, the Singapore state has continued to maintain a large, if unconventional role, seeking to harness the benefits of competition yet continuing to provide complementary goods (Shin 2005), build infrastructure and 'pick winners'.

8
Comparisons

8.1 Introduction

Having examined the taxonomy using two case studies, both of which provided some evidence in its favour, I now compare the experiences of Vanuatu and Singapore in order to establish whether any lessons can be learnt, and if so, what they are. As mentioned in the introduction and Chapter 5, I am comparing Singapore and Vanuatu because I lived and worked in them for three years and two years respectively and consider myself to have some degree of subjective knowledge about each. If post-modern relativism is to be avoided, it is important to try to establish lessons, however limited they may be.

Hopefully the use of comparative case studies has produced some interesting and surprising findings; for as Lawson suggests in *Reorienting Economics,* contrastive explanation is capable of producing valid results that may be provisionally true without using the kind of methods more appropriate to the natural sciences.

This chapter first discusses what sort of features might usefully be compared between Vanuatu and Singapore. After this comes a comparison of certain selected aspects of the development process in the each country, and finally a tentative attempt is made to draw lessons from the two development experiences.

8.2 A comparison of Singapore and Vanuatu

The two countries are so different that care must be taken with any comparison. Wealth is the most obvious point of contrast: it might be argued that discussing an economy with a GDP of US$160 billion alongside one of US$450 million is not meaningful, and that a wealth-per-person differential of 25 times is too great for useful comparison. Singapore ranks 28th out of the 179 countries in the 2008 Human Development Index. Vanuatu is in 123rd place.[1] Geographical location is another important factor: one of Vanuatu's major economic difficulties is the irregularity and high cost of international transport. Few countries are more favourably located than Singapore. A further point of difference is that Vanuatu is considered among the world's most vulnerable economies, while Singapore is reasonably secure. Education levels, ethnic composition and working habits in the two countries are also highly dissimilar.

Yet there are certain important resemblances. Both are recently independent British colonies and tropical island economies. Both can be classified as having a small population, although Singaporeans outnumber ni-Vanuatu by 20:1. Macroeconomic policy is similar in a number of areas. Each country enjoyed generally good fiscal management. Neither experienced significant inflation and their central banks were reasonably well-run. Unemployment was mostly not high in either country, although for different reasons. It is possible to argue that smallness and being islands created the opportunity in both countries for autonomous and centralised economic decision-making. Most importantly, Singapore can be considered a successful example of economic development that holds certain lessons for some other developing countries.

Following is a short comparison of certain pertinent features of policy in the two countries using the main points of the taxonomy in Chapter 4.

8.2.1 The influence of external values and norms

(i) The need for reform

In neither country was reform unnecessary, and nor was reform initiated entirely externally. In Vanuatu, however, change was more urgent and the outside institution took a greater role. Singapore was able to conduct its own reforms partly because it started with better endowments. It had an educated workforce and a strong tradition of trade and commerce, whilst independence proceeded relatively smoothly and with little animosity. These advantages were not present in Vanuatu, which suffered from low levels of education, a lack of a commercial tradition – the majority of its inhabitants are still subsistence farmers – and a relatively hurried transition to independence.

In 1997 Vanuatu's government was volatile and functioning poorly. Many parts of the civil service were also underperforming. This situation compounded the need for reform in a way that never existed in Singapore, which can be considered highly technocratic (Barr 2006).

Balance of payments problems formed another key reason why reform was more urgent in late-1990s Vanuatu than in post-independence Singapore. Vanuatu had suffered a structural trade deficit since independence, while Singapore enjoyed flexibility and a positive balance of payments position. Vanuatu's exports were limited and volatile, and it depended heavily on aid. Singapore, partly because of its location, exported a variety of products and services and received only a limited amount of aid during the years after independence.

The greater initial need for reform in Vanuatu meant that it negotiated external reform from a weaker position and was compelled to accept generic, outside reforms. This meant that policies were less appropriate to the national context. The lesser need for reform in Singapore, the continuing self-governance and the absence of crises enabled the government to retain autonomy over economic policy, making it more relevant to domestic circumstances.

(ii) The costs and benefits of universalism

The benefits of a universal approach to economic policy varied between the two countries. In the case of Vanuatu, 'governance' improved slightly after the CRP led to the introduction of a free press, made the government more accountable and reduced nepotism. Financial management also improved, while certain statistics were collected and analysed better. One of the key benefits of outside intervention was that it enabled the government to avoid the blame for unpopular decisions.

In Singapore, the act of conforming to policy universals carried the principal benefit of improving international confidence in a newly independent country with a government that considered itself socialist. Acting partly on UNDP advice, Singapore based its investment policy around attracting FDI, mainly to benefit from technology transfer but also as a source of capital, with Singapore gaining more FDI as a proportion of gross fixed capital formation than any other East Asian nation from 1980 to 2000. Having established outside confidence, Singapore proceeded to pursue many policies which were contrary to the Washington Consensus and which contradicted the kind of advice promoted internationally. Chapter 7 argued that one of the ingredients of Singapore's success was that it managed to cope with outside pressures for standard reforms, adding to its ability to tailor policy to domestic circumstances. Rapid economic growth further helped the government to operate independently of outside advice. Universalism in economic policy was therefore not a serious problem for Singapore.

Universal policy prescriptions created problems for Vanuatu, which was much more vulnerable, poor and dependent on aid. The Comprehensive Reform Programme was so laissez-faire that there appear to have been doubts about the effectiveness of *any* economic policy. This situation is profoundly different to Singapore, where the state assumed a prominent role, and where many of the recommendations of the Washington Consensus were ignored. The Vanuatu CRP focused excessively on specific institutional reform and governance, assuming that markets were so effective that they would solve most other problems. Unhelpful and misleading comparisons with East Asia led to an attempt to liberalise trade on a standardised basis, instead of attending to Vanuatu's particular situation. Corporatisation and privatisation proceeded too quickly, depriving the government of revenue and leaving it vastly more indebted than before the programme began. Singapore, on the other hand, was able to remain relatively free of debt and to pay off its loans to international institutions at an early stage.

8.2.2   The importance of local context

Vanuatu's government, because it was in a more vulnerable position and had less policy autonomy, was obliged largely to ignore local subjective circumstances. These included the unusual tax structure, in which 40 per cent of government revenue came from tariffs; the need for flexibility in trade policy; the cultural importance of land; and the role of money. In particular the absence of a commercial tradition and the unusual social role played by money meant that markets did not quickly assume functions previously performed by government. When government activity reduced, so did economic activity. The outside practitioners of the CRP, many of whom were short-term consultants, were free of any perspective which might have been considered self-reflexive. They therefore came under criticism. Rather than lay all blame at the feet of the Asian Development Bank, it is clear that the Vanuatu government did not initially devote much time to an assessment of the importance of local context, although this may have been because the political situation was particularly volatile and the civil service in a weakened position.

The case of Singapore was very different. The government consciously retained policy autonomy and could therefore take account of peculiar national characteristics. They included housing, education and the law, as well as a tendency to value material progress and to conform socially for the sake of financial security. In some cases the government shaped the outcome of these national characteristics. Whilst doubts have been raised about the 'Asian values' thesis, the government was at pains to promote economic growth by creating a malleable and cohesive workforce. The Singaporean state continues to shape policy towards the domestic context, which explains some of its economic success. There is therefore a link between this point and point four of the taxonomy, which suggests a revision of the theoretical perspective as appropriate. Retaining policy agency enabled the government to shift its overall stance so that it remained relevant to the existing economic situation.

8.2.3 How tools, concepts and policies affected themselves

Singapore's government was informed enough and exercised sufficient authority over companies and the workforce for industrial policy to be effective. In particular the government could put in place credible deadlines for the ending of infant-industry protection. These advantages were not present in Vanuatu, which gained independence at a later stage, and where a volatile political situation and weak administrative capacity meant that a small number of inefficient factories continued to receive major protection from government as late as 2004. In such a small country, with such high transport costs, infant-industry protection was always going to be a more precarious enterprise.

Singapore experienced a number of inevitable problems with industrial policy; problems that were a product of the very success that such policies delivered. Early government-run companies failed, while foreign ventures experienced more serious problems. But these failures were a necessary by-product of the generally successful interventionist industrial policy that operated at home. Macroeconomic policy in Singapore also featured a problem of internal contradiction, in that the high savings rates, high incoming FDI and state-run oligopoly necessary for growth became entrenched, reducing productivity over the long-term and probably lowering overall economic growth.

The reflexive feedback mechanisms at work in Vanuatu resulted largely from the structural adjustment programme, and proved more damaging. Public service reforms worsened the problem of institutional interference that they were aimed at solving. Quantifying the economy led to confusion and possibly worse policymaking. Trust in outside agencies declined. Making GDP the sole end of policy produced a reactionary body of local anti-development thinking.

Drawing attention to these reflexive feedback mechanisms shows not just that the policies had flaws; the discussion is intended to reinforce the idea that single policies aimed at curing all problems simultaneously tend to backfire, that policies must be amended to national contexts, and that policy recommendations are often partly self-defeating. Many parts of social reality affect themselves, and the relationship between entities in an economic system is not only one of cause-and-effect. Reflexivity means that entities such as policies impact upon themselves.

8.2.4   The revision of theory as circumstances changed

Because the Singaporean government remained adaptable and in control of overall strategy, it could alter the theoretical perspective through which it formulated policy. After the Asian crisis in 1997, Schumpeterian ideas began to inform public discussion. Another influence was the new growth theory which originates with Paul Romer, and which underpinned the work of Krugman, Young and others in the total factor productivity debate. It is too early to say whether this change has resulted in successful policy, and a considerable amount of cliché and rhetoric clouds the picture. But had the government preserved its old way of thinking, it is unlikely that the economy would have continued growing as quickly as it did.

Vanuatu suffered unnecessary restrictions on policy. The government was allowed little room to influence the theoretical perspective under which reform took place, still less the opportunity to change theory when it became clear that the original CRP was not working. This is not to suggest that an articulated or cohesive policy vision existed on which politicians planned to base future economic policy decisions, but that the international context and the CRP made the emergence of such a coherent vision less likely. Attempts to liberalise trade according to a generic plan threatened to drastically weaken government finances. A burgeoning public debt stock and aid conditionality further restricted government's room to manoeuvre, while instability in the public service at least temporarily weakened government capacity.

If agency is an important part of reflexivity, then on an economic path that is informed by reflexivity, governments must be left free to alter their theoretical perspectives. As suggested already, this became increasingly difficult under the Washington Consensus, and some commentators actually suggest that reducing flexibility can improve economic policy. Rodrik (2002b: 15), amongst others, has shown this view to be mistaken. Denying governments' access to policy tools such as changing public spending or to alter tariffs makes it more difficult to adapt during times of crisis or changes in the international environment. It is untrue that globalisation necessitates tight fiscal policy, since many small states, such as Singapore, run substantial counter-cyclical spending programmes. A non-positivist approach to knowledge implies that the implicit methodology of current practice in development economics is not final. States must be allowed to pursue policies that derive from an evolving theoretical path. Future policies and theoretical perspectives remain to be discovered.

8.3 Lessons

Singapore is neither in a unique and incomparable situation that holds no lessons for other countries, nor is it a model that must be copied identically. Few other developing countries have enjoyed such initial advantages, and as far as Singapore is a 'model' for development, it is one which must be adapted according to circumstances. Yet certain lessons can still be learnt.

Vanuatu is sometimes held to be so small and isolated that few lessons can be taken from other countries. This is also untrue, even if the country's unique characteristics must be taken into account. Limited, thoughtful comparison is always possible. This recognition derives from the vision of reflexivity as a step beyond either the modernist conception of science as a progressive, rationalistic endeavour which gradually unearths new discoveries, or the postmodern view which allows for no common foundations to truth, and under which history cannot progress.

8.3.1 Lessons from Singapore for Vanuatu

One of the most important findings from the two case studies is that policy space is essential, including the need for outside agencies to incorporate into any programme of economic assistance room for policies to be revised significantly at a future date. Just as someone may not appear allergic to dairy products for years, and the allergy may build up over time before suddenly producing a violent reaction, the impact of policies can change over time, *even if other things remain the same*. This is an epistemological lesson, which involves the way knowledge is conceptualised. If knowledge about developing countries is considered to be at an advanced stage, with any future developments likely to be mere refinements, the behaviour of outside agencies is less likely to allow for policy space. But because such questions were not addressed, Vanuatu came close to accepting an import tariff regime that would have severely limited its ability to raise revenues. It also suffered inappropriate restrictions on fiscal spending, when budgetary management was generally not a serious problem. The absence of such restrictions in Singapore contributed to its economic prosperity.

The idea of policy space does not mean allowing developing countries unlimited flexibility to change policy in any way they see fit. Outside intervention is valuable because it helps push through difficult reforms, counteracts corruption and can be a valuable source of knowledge about other development experiences. Policy agency, in other words, is not a free-standing entity that should be pursued at all costs. It is a process that exists amid a structure – which is shaped by the international context.

A further lesson from the comparison of Vanuatu and Singapore is that trying to impose blueprints from abroad made policy less useful. In Vanuatu, structural adjustment was generic, based on the standard Washington Consensus model and implemented in five other Pacific island states. Reform in Singapore proceeded gradually and with few impositions by the international community, meaning that ownership of policies was greater and that policy was more closely suited to local conditions. This is an epistemic issue, which involves the often implicit way in which the international institutions, and mainstream economics, used knowledge. In Vanuatu outside reformers did not consider it necessary to take into account subjective local details because, generally, it was believed that the answers were already known.

More specific lessons can be learnt. Perhaps one of the most important sources of Singapore's continuing success is its ability to retain international confidence, not just by accepting outside advice but by showing that it is open to foreign investment. Treating transnational corporations at least as favourably as domestic companies pre-empted such demands from international institutions and foreign governments. The Singaporean government could then pursue policies that might otherwise have provoked dissent. Being open to FDI in a small, open economy with no hinterland made much more sense in Singapore than in Vanuatu, but a similarly strategic approach to economic policy was much less evident in Vanuatu, which experienced political conflict with neighbouring countries and major aid donors. Choosing its battles, perhaps by reducing protection of certain inefficient local factories, would have meant that the government was free in other areas to enact policies that suited the domestic context.

Whilst under the CRP corruption was not the problem that it was alleged to be, the experience of Singapore holds lessons for Vanuatu. The government paid members of parliament and civil servants so much that engaging in corrupt activities was not worthwhile. Although Singapore remains more nepotistic than is sometimes acknowledged, it is far less corrupt than neighbouring countries. This perception of honesty contributes to international confidence. In Vanuatu MPs are paid little more than senior civil servants, who are themselves paid just above subsistence levels. The incentives for corruption are therefore significant. Whilst Vanuatu is more egalitarian than Singapore, and the budget is limited, paying MPs more, perhaps by reducing their number, would have helped reduce corruption and in turn improved the country's image abroad.

The notion of human agency, central to the concept of reflexivity, requires the presence of tools with which humans can collectively manage their economic affairs. The Washington Consensus and its successor attempted to deprive countries of policy tools, leaving as much as possible to market forces. This reduced the scope for agency. The example of Singapore shows that the opposite course of action – leaving a substantial proportion of economic policy and activity under the control of the state – produced more satisfactory economic outcomes. Singapore intentionally retained control over a considerable number of tools with which to manage the economy, such as government spending, import tariffs and subsidies. Protecting policy tools that had implications for social welfare, such as education, health and other social spending, as well as labour and consumer affairs, proved particularly important. The benefits of international competition were retained because the economy featured many transnational corporations and was open to the world economy.

8.3.2 Lessons from Vanuatu for Singapore

It might be expected that only Vanuatu can learn from Singapore. But lessons also apply in the other direction. The prevailing view is partly a product of the modernist view of economics, where an external development practitioner imagines that all countries should be remade in the image of the more prosperous economies. 'Experts' 'know' the answers to development and go to developing countries to carry them out. A reflexive stance, where the development economist or practitioner positioned herself as much as possible inside the country being examined, and used subjective data, might lead to an appreciation of local culture, values and norms, and in turn an understanding of ways in which developed country policymakers might learn from others. Development, and development theory, is a two-way process, rather than something that developed nations do to poor countries. It is interesting to note that Hirschman discovered something similar in generalising the underemployment argument, under which he argued that underdeveloped economies needed additional strategies to traditional Keynesian remedies aimed at reducing unemployment. Hirschman found that the same argument applied to developed countries. '… our understanding of the economic structures of the West will have been modified and enriched by the foray into other economies' (Hirschman 1980: 9). In the context of Vanuatu, learning from subsistence societies does not mean abandoning the pursuit of wealth, and neither does it legitimise malnutrition, poor education or inadequate health services, but it can refocus attention on non-material economic goals like happiness and social cohesion. Sen's arguments, amongst others, teach us that wealth is not the only end of development, and that an array of ends might exist in developing countries which have ceased to be available in materially wealthy societies.

While measuring happiness is notoriously difficult, a number of studies have suggested that Vanuatu has high levels of non-material prosperity. One of the most convincing, a report by the New Economics Foundation (2006), placed Vanuatu in first place on an index measuring happiness and environmental wellbeing in 178 countries. Using subjective and objective data, the report highlights Vanuatu's low 'ecological footprint' (meaning that it required a minimal land area to sustain the population at current levels of consumption, technological development and resource efficiency) reasonable life expectancy and sense of social welfare. The report disputes the use of GDP as a measure of progress and criticises alternative measures of progress that do not 'make explicit use of *subjective* data. In other words they do not include measures of how people actually feel about their lives' (ibid.: 9). In giving equal weight to subjective data and objective data such as material wellbeing the index follows an approach that might be considered reflexive.

In the same survey, Singapore came last among the 24 Asian nations surveyed, with a score almost half that of Vanuatu. Given this difference, Vanuatu's development experience holds lessons for Singapore. First, Vanuatu's 'ecological footprint' is very low. Singapore produces considerable waste per hectare. Whilst it would be unrealistic to imagine that Singapore might reverse its material gains, it can learn from the traditional ways in which people live in subsistence communities. The case of Vanuatu shows that sustainable interaction with the environment has intrinsic social worth, rather than being a cost that must be borne in order to stave off environmental damage. The Vanuatu government has consciously tried to preserve traditional society, limiting the adverse impact of commerce and conserving the environment.

Second, the New Economics Foundation index shows (ibid.: 35) that people in Vanuatu have a higher 'life satisfaction', meaning that they expressed reasonable happiness with their own lives. Although an attempt at explanation is conjectural and based on anecdotal observation, this difference could be connected with Vanuatu's lower population density, preservation of traditional values, subsistence lifestyle and generally low stress levels. Social cohesion in Vanuatu is not artificially constructed as it is in Singapore. A lesson here is that material gains can reduce life satisfaction. A more free and unrestricted society and a reassertion of certain traditions might improve the economic wellbeing of Singaporeans.

Third, the survey (ibid.: 35) further highlights the vibrancy of Vanuatu's democratic process, which is held to give people control over their lives, in turn making them feel more fulfilled. In Sen's terms, development is constituted here in political freedom. Fulfilment and personal autonomy are considered economic ends. The limitations of democracy in Singapore generate a sense of being subject to government decisions rather than in control of government, presumably leading to a lower sense of fulfilment and autonomy. Expanding democratic freedoms might improve economic welfare. Overall a closer interpretation of Sen's approach than the necessarily reductionist approach of the Human Development Index would probably place Vanuatu much closer to Singapore in terms of human development.

8.4 Conclusion

The comparison of the two countries presented here, although not exhaustive, highlights findings on several levels, including the methodological and the practical. An epistemological lesson from comparing Vanuatu and Singapore is the idea that policy space is important. Perceiving knowledge as open and changing leads to policy recommendations that are less specific and binding. A necessary subjectivity in economic knowledge also reduces the relevance of blueprints from abroad. Singapore, where economic growth was highest, maintained significant policy space and avoided international blueprints. Vanuatu, which was less successful, had less policy space and adopted a generic set of reforms.

Ontic lessons from the comparison of Vanuatu and Singapore mainly concern the need to adapt definitions of certain crucial concepts, such as money, to local conditions. Because in Vanuatu money and land ownership were dealt with and defined in the standard way, reforms were less suited to national circumstances. Singaporean policymakers managed to focus much more on the local context, implicitly ensuring that ontological specificities were taken into account.

The discussion was aimed not just at highlighting these methodological and practical lessons – doubtless there are more – but also that analysing international economic development involves *looking* for such lessons. The modernist framework of the Washington Consensus and its successor fail to do this.

Practical lessons from the case studies included the need to maintain international confidence; the validity of paying politicians more to avoid corruption; and the need for agency in order to have the ability to put in place tight deadlines for infant-industry protection. Lessons also apply the other way round, highlighting the problems with the modernist idea of development as something that rich countries perform on the poor. Development is a common endeavour, in which people on both sides of the income divide can learn from each other. Vanuatu's higher standards of non-material well being may have lessons for Singapore, where higher stress levels, a lower sense of personal autonomy and a bigger ecological footprint all reduce wellbeing.

Whilst certain policy universals were necessary in both countries, they had different costs and benefits. Singapore was more successful than Vanuatu in increasing the rate of economic growth because it adopted only those international policy universals that it believed were more appropriate. Seeking substantial FDI had intrinsic benefits, but it also satisfied outside donors and the international community, enabling the Singaporean government to pursue policies that contradicted conventional advice and which latterly conflicted with the Washington Consensus. While certain standard reforms held minor benefits for Vanuatu, on balance the policies recommended too closely resembled the generic prescriptions proposed throughout the region and beyond.

Theory and policy have intentionally been discussed in an interrelated way throughout this chapter. This is because, as argued by Bourdieu, theory and practice are inextricably related, and, to again cite a quote from Jenkins, '... only insofar as one does things is it possible to know about things' (Jenkins, op. cit.: 69). Critical realists have also drawn attention to the unnecessary separation of economic theory from reality, and this chapter suggested that countries which pursue economic policies that are more closely connected with reality are likely to be more successful. Not only does basing theory in reality help transcend the divide between modernism and postmodernism, but more importantly it may help discern economic interventions that are more humane and useful.

9
Conclusions

Both modernism and postmodernism suffer shortcomings as frameworks within which to study and practise development economics. The foundationalism, essentialism, determinism and scientism of modernism lead to an approach which is divorced from the real, changing conditions of human society. Many authors increasingly question the positivism that usually characterises modernist approaches, while problems arise from universalising the results of research conducted in one specific locale or period of time. Some postmodern approaches result in relativism, making development economics a difficult task. To this extent it is fortunate that only certain fringes of economics can be considered to have followed a strictly postmodern route. Yet the dialectical interaction between modernism and postmodernism is profitable, suggesting that economists, like any social theorists, should tackle the kind of questions thrown up by the discussion. It is unlikely that the kinds of questions asked by postmodernists will go away; issues of fragmentation, openness, unpredictability and subjectivity remain particularly relevant at a time when global economic crisis throws doubts over the mainstream project. A number of economic theorists, some of whom operated outside the mainstream, have long understood the importance of these kind of questions, and it may be time to resurrect some of their ideas.

Open-systems approaches respond to the dialectic between modernism and postmodernism, and some postmodernists can be seen to follow an open-systems approach. Critical realism, Keynes and the neo-Austrians have important differences but hold in common the idea that economics is about an ever-changing subject matter which is subject to unpredictability and uncertainty, even in a stochastic manner. These approaches tend to be sceptical about mechanism or atomism in social science, and allow the use of subjective evidence. Such approaches, particularly that of Keynes and the critical realists, are compatible with, and inform, the discussion of reflexivity.

Is reflexivity just an unexpected reversal of relations between two entities, as if a laboratory rat were training a scientist? The concept has further implications than this, as I hope to have shown. While modernism and postmodernism often assume a dualism between subject and object, and between structure and agency, certain versions of reflexivity, notably that of Bourdieu, try to move beyond this dualism. In simple terms Bourdieu's insight is to acknowledge the postmodern insistence on 'putting yourself in another person's shoes' but at the same time retains the modernist detachment of the external observer. The modernism of the Washington Consensus can be so externally detached as to ignore certain important features of the economic landscape in developing countries. The context-specificity of some postmodern approaches loses critical distance and can dissolve into relativity. By moving away from these two views, performing self-critique and conducting detailed analysis of the subjective features of developing countries, the researcher can portray a more insightful overall picture and in turn make economic policy recommendations that are more useful and relevant to real conditions in developing countries. Comparative research can also help establish results which are provisional and open to change, rather than permanent and static.

One of the key motivations of proponents of reflexivity is to move away from the kind of irrealism that characterises the approach of much mainstream economics, and to acknowledge that the subject matter of research may be difficult for outsiders to understand. This difficulty in comprehension arises in part because of the wide variations across societies and economies, as well as the inherent subjectivity of certain kinds of knowledge. Because of this openness and variation, economics is likely to be a process of investigation, not a set apparatus. The tradition of Marx, Mannheim, certain anthropologists, critical realism, Bourdieu and the science studies literature holds the common implication that economics is social theory, rather than the study of atomistic individuals acting in isolation from one another. Ideas spring from specific social circumstances, and thus the background from which ideas emerged is almost as important as the ideas themselves.

The first point of the taxonomy aims to acknowledge this. Development economics as practised under the Washington Consensus and its subsequent manifestation imagines itself to be the exercise of hard, natural science, much as a scientific technician studies a chemical reaction.

Yet in reality it reflects the predispositions and the economic interests of its practitioners. During economic reform or analysis it would therefore seem important to examine the influence of external values and norms, including the social context in which ideas or policies were generated. Highlighting context does not automatically make ideas or policies 'right' or 'wrong'; it simply puts them into perspective and may require them to be complemented by ideas or policies which come from within a different context. Global economic development is therefore a joint endeavour – aid agencies and governments need to act 'on' developing countries, and no country can develop without outside contact. But neither are developing countries passive objects with no autonomy. Developing countries can follow their own economic paths, and may even have lessons for the rich world. As suggested, Vanuatu perhaps has more to teach a wealthy country like Singapore than might at first be imagined.

National context therefore matters, and it is important to assess its significance. This means more than just taking account of economic institutions like the exchange-rate regime, central bank or property ownership, although these are important. Culture, values and social institutions all influence the way in which policies work, and how they are formulated. Economic policies which acknowledge this are likely to be stronger – and the cases of Vanuatu and Singapore aimed partly at illustrating this point. Singapore's history of economic reform was more successful because it took account of national context; Vanuatu's was less successful because it did not.

One of the basic meanings of reflexivity, which is perhaps more simple than that intended by Bourdieu or Giddens, is that things affect themselves. This point responds particularly to modernist confidence that economic science is proceeding in a teleological fashion and gradually builds up knowledge about developing economies. It is also a further response to the notion that subject and object are strictly separate. In reality policies or decisions can undermine the very goals that they aimed to achieve. Subject and object interact in a way that warrants caution about positivism.

Given that economic systems are open; that economic policy depends on social backdrop or interests; and that economic tools and concepts undermine themselves, it would appear necessary to re-examine the economic theory deployed in a development situation if it proves inadequate or as circumstances change. Following Kuhn, Feyerabend and Lakatos, many have questioned the notion that scientists are prepared to reject their own hypotheses in the face of contradictory evidence, and that we are progressively accumulating knowledge about the world. This is perhaps all the more true in social science, where the variegated and changing nature of the subject matter – human beings – makes it difficult finally to prove or disprove a hypothesis. What appear at first to be mutually exclusive ideas may be appropriate in the same situation, whilst theories may be falsified because social circumstances change rather than because new discoveries are made. Hirschman makes precisely this point in *A Propensity to Self-Subversion* (1995). The possibility that apparent 'laws' (or demi-regs) might be relevant in some areas but not others points towards the need for a frequent reassessment of the kind of theories employed in developing countries. The honest reappraisal of theory can have profound economic consequences, as shown in the cases of Singapore and Vanuatu.

I have argued here that Singapore's economic success came despite rejection of the Washington Consensus, and in this sense it broke out of the modernist mould. It retained substantial economic policy autonomy, it protected infant industries, the role of the government remained significant, while property ownership was different to that recommended by the international development institutions. The government's ability to fit policy to the national context formed a key explanation for its economic success. Its ability to remain nimble, to re-shape policy to the changing economic environment, further helped it remain economically successful.

Although it would be inappropriate to suggest that Vanuatu could ever exercise as much control over policy and therefore similarly shape policy to domestic circumstances, the government faced a situation in which important policies were effectively dictated by an outside agency. If this outside agency had known beforehand an infallible package of policy measures which was certain to succeed, perhaps the surrendering of policy autonomy might have been acceptable. But this was never likely to been the case because, as argued here, the ability to formulate knowledge about economic reality is imperfect. The ADB simply enacted a package of measures that had been conducted elsewhere in the Pacific region, and which was based on the same methodology that underlay structural adjustment packages elsewhere. The results of reform were disappointing, as shown in Chapter 7, and the legacy remains. I have implied that understanding the importance of outside influences and domestic social context, together with the possibility that tools, policies and concepts can affect themselves, and an allowance for more flexibility, would have led to more successful policies.

Hopefully the discussion has shown that economic methodology is important. Thinking about methodological issues helps inform discussions about policy and can have an impact on the results of economics as practised in developing countries. It appears that it is difficult to demarcate a rigid cut-off between methodology, method, theory and practice. Methodology is the approach to knowledge which underpins the selection and application of methods; theory changes according to which school of thought is chosen and influences how an economic problem is approached; practice is usually thought of as being the enactment of policy, which depends on theory, method and in turn methodology. Thinking first about methodology and theory would seem helpful in establishing useful policy measures that fit closely with national realities. It is unlikely that a blueprint for successful economic development exists.

After all this, can the taxonomy successfully claim to help overcome the methodological division between modernism and postmodernism in development economics? As suggested in the introduction, the discussion can only ever be partially and conditionally successful. One reason is that the idea of reflexivity warns against dogmatism in social science, and so cannot claim permanency itself. Hirschman and Kalecki both understood the difficulties of declaring oneself to have arrived at final answers, Hirschman because he believed that his thought progressed partly through self-criticism; Kalecki because he was an open-systems theorist who knew that economies evolve and change. Dialectical resolution is always to be valued, but a further reason for circumspection lies in the fact that any synthesis depends partly on what are the thesis and antithesis. Caution is therefore important, and in a realist vein, direct engagement with the real world would seem paramount.

Another reason why the taxonomy can only be considered provisionally 'successful' is that it was developed alongside the case studies. The case studies were revised in light of the taxonomy, and the taxonomy was altered as the case studies were written. Although this interaction between theory and practice can be considered an asset, it also throws doubt on the possibility that the case studies are a neutral 'test' of the taxonomy. But scepticism about the use of evidence is also warranted in the case of many apparently neutral and objective 'tests' in mainstream economics. Econometrics is frequently accused of being able to prove whatever point the statistician is aiming to prove, and the use of specific formal methods is likely to produce only a certain narrow range of answers. As Lawson points out, closed-systems methods presuppose an atomistic conception of the economy in which individuals interact in predictable ways. Running a regression rarely fully captures subjective evidence. The exclusive use of these kind of methods is unlikely to produce research which acknowledges the social and open-ended nature of the economy.

It would be self-contradictory to claim that reflexivity is somehow a total theory, capable of explaining much about development economics in the style of the grand narratives of Marx or Hegel. Part of the point is to avoid such grand narratives. Reflexivity might only give partial insights into the debate. But if it is not an all-encompassing solution, it at least inserts the researcher into the study of developing economies and provides a perspective on how some of the limitations of postmodernism and modernism might be avoided. In a world of economic 'expertise' and sweeping solutions, a certain critical self-reflection is perhaps warranted.

Recognising the self-referential and social nature of economics would not be self-defeating or generate despair. Instead, it should be possible to realise human agency as the old teleological and evolutionist views of history shrink away. We are no longer beholden to grand visions for our collective future, but neither must we 'salute Nietzsche and go our separate ways' as Giddens cautions. Liberating human agency from rigid visions of modernity that conceive of abstract individuals exercising free will in an idealised world would build a more realistic picture of how real people behave. Recognising that economics is *constructed*, and that it examines real *social* people, will help it achieve true scientific knowledge.

Notes

1 Introduction

1. The Liar's Paradox worried the poet Philetas of Cos to the extent that he stopped eating. He grew so thin he had to weigh his shoes down with lead to stop himself being blown away. The epitaph on his gravestone read: 'O Stranger: Philetas of Cos am I, 'Twas the Liar who made me die, And the bad nights caused thereby' (Gottlieb 1997).
2. In response to the accusation that 'those who can, do economics; those who can't, do methodology', I would question whether some of the more abstruse mathematical contortions really constitute 'doing' development economics.
3. http://www.imf.org/external/np/sec/pr/2009/pr0905.htm, date accessed 6 March 2009.
4. George Soros, although sometimes dismissed (for example in Krugman 1998) as not being a proper academic economist, suggests that: 'If Hegel's concept was the thesis and Marxism the antithesis, reflexivity is the synthesis' (Soros 1994: 365). Cross and Strachan (1997) and Bryant (2002) engage more with Soros's ideas.
5. Of the sort displayed in Woolgar (1988), and discussed in Chapter 4.

2 Beyond Modernism and Postmodernism

1. And hence vulnerable to Bertrand Russell's observation that this is a statement that cannot be tested.
2. Italics in original.
3. Kalecki is, however, widely considered to have pre-empted the General Theory by three years, in 1933 publishing work outlining a theory of effective demand and several other of the ideas later put forward by Keynes.
4. See Bhaskar (1978); Lawson (1997a, 2003); Downward *et al.* (2002); Fullbrook (2009).
5. For the moment I will substitute 'economics' for 'mainstream economics'.
6. Lawson also identifies it as the Popper-Hempel theory of explanation.
7. However Hume has been interpreted in ways that are incompatible with his portrayal as a simple enlightenment realist, for example in Dow (2002c).
8. An example from sociology of practical case-studies deriving from a critical realist position is Margaret Archer's *Structure, Agency and the Internal Conversation* (2003), which develops typologies of what she calls reflexive behaviour and examines several individual cases.
9. *Critique of Pure Reason*, preface to the second edition, B xxxv.

3   Theories of Reflexivity

1. Including Soros (1994, Archer (2003) and Cross and Strachan (1997).
2. For example see Bocock and Thompson (1985) and Eagleton (1991). It is further worth noting that although Marx considered religion to be ideological, he was not as critical of religion, or as dismissive of its followers, as is often suggested. The sentence before the famous quote that religion is the 'opium of the people' reads: '[It is] at one and the same time, the expression of real suffering and a protest against real suffering....the sigh of the oppressed creature, the heart of a heartless world, the soul of soulless conditions.'
3. As opposed to the structuralist school of development economics that began in Latin America in the 1940s.
4. This is a good example of why it would be inaccurate to suggest that no subjectivist economic approaches are Neoclassical, or that modernism is uniformly anti-subjectivist.
5. Some, such as Mouzelis (2000: 742), have questioned the possibility of 'transcending' the traditional divide between structure and agency.
6. World Bank and IMF economists continue to be criticised for flying in by business class to developing-world capitals, staying in five-star hotels for a week while they dispense advice, before leaving for another continent.
7. One implication of Woolgar and Ashmore's argument is that the issue of reflexivity may merit more treatment by critical realists than it has currently received.
8. This statement actually contradicts the subject of the book because Beck *et al.* obviously believe that the debate has produced a new way of looking at modernity – reflexive modernisation.
9. For a comparative discussion of Bourdieu and Giddens see Callinicos (1999).

4   Reflexivity and Development Economics

1. The two lengthy treatments of the methodology of development economics in the journals are the March 2007 issue of the Journal of Economic Methodology, where a version of this chapter is published, and the 1986 issue of World Development.
2. The kind of development addressed here is the active promotion of economic or social well-being, rather than autonomous change.
3. According to Zack-Williams (2000: 4) 32 of the 45 sub-Saharan countries were involved in World Bank or IMF programmes by the end of the 1980s, while 12 Central American economies signed emergency agreements with the IMF between 1980 and 1988. For an assessment of the impact of structural adjustment on poverty, see Killick (1995), while Zuckerman *et al.* (1991) considers the social impact. Lensink (1996) provides a discussion of the African experience. Callaghy and Ravenhill (1993) highlights the global context in which African countries began structural adjustment.
4. The IMF saw the creation of excess domestic credit as the key explanation of balance of payments problems. The following set of equations is known as the financial programming or Polak model (Killick 1995: 129; Easterly 2006).

R is the local-currency value of the net foreign assets of the banking system; M is the stock of money and D is domestic credit.

Money stock varies according to changes in the international and domestic money supply.

$$\Delta M = \Delta R + \Delta D \tag{1}$$

Equilibrium in the money market means that changes in the demand for money equal changes in the supply of money.

$$\Delta M = \Delta M_d \tag{2}$$

Money demand depends on changes in real income and prices. Real income is not affected by monetary variables.

$$\Delta M_d = f(\Delta Y, \Delta P) \tag{3}$$

Combining equations (1) (2) and (3) shows that balance of payments deficits, in other words losses of reserves, are caused by increases in domestic credit over and above increases in demand for money.

$$\Delta R = \Delta M - \Delta D = f(\Delta Y, \Delta P) - \Delta D \tag{4}$$

5. He often used the term 'underdeveloped'.
6. Cited in Malhotra (2008: 2). Public investment clearly also included spending on the other usual items such as infrastructure and research & development.
7. Including the notions of backward and forward linkages, the 'trickling down effect', the 'tunnel effect', the 'hiding hand' and many others.
8. The other reasons provided for the decline of development economics are, first, that the development 'disasters' of the 1970s led many to question the policy recommendations of development economists, and second, the disillusionment with aggregate economic growth as a panacea for underdevelopment. Hirschman believes that a concern with distributional effects and the breakdown of development practice into a variety of areas of expertise reduced the potency of development economics. This, Hirschman believed, was a reason for modesty among economists and an awareness of political realities: economics cannot 'slay the dragon of backwardness ... by itself' (Hirschman, ibid.: 23).
9. The IMF is traditionally run by a European; the World Bank by an American.
10. The Millennium Development Goals are: Eradicate extreme poverty and hunger; Achieve universal primary education; Promote gender equality and empower women; Reduce child mortality; Improve maternal health; Combat HIV/AIDS; Ensure environmental sustainability; Develop a global partnership for development.
11. Ha-Joon Chang (2007) rightly disputes the notion that cultural differences are all-important in determining development outcomes. He notes that prior to Japan's rapid economic growth in the twentieth century, outside commentators believed that Japanese people were too lazy to be economically

successful. Similar arguments were made about Korea and Germany. The lessons from this are that any group of people which is subjected to sufficient hardship or material incentive will work hard, and that institutions and policy may be more important in explaining economic success. Yet this is no argument for ignoring values and behaviour, which can still vary widely, in different ways affecting the implementation of policy.

5   Introduction to the Case Studies

1. A well-known development economist suggested to me at the beginning of my research that I should find two more similar economies as case studies because a comparison of Vanuatu and Singapore would not bear much fruit.
2. This happened in 2003. The data was re-checked, as Vanuatu has no garment factories, and it was discovered that the importer had marked down the incorrect code: VU for Vanuatu instead of VN for Vietnam.

6   Vanuatu: The Anti-crusoe Economy

1. See Appendix 1.
2. Vanuatu scores 46.4 on the UN Economic Vulnerability Index. Above 31 is considered vulnerable and above 36 highly vulnerable.
3. It is perhaps the ideal target of the literature on small and vulnerable economies that has emerged over the last 45 years. The first explicit treatments of small economies can be found in Kuznets (1960), Scitovsky (1960) and de Vries (1973); the literature has subsequently been developed in, amongst others, Srinivasan (1986); Easterly and Kraay (2000); Commonwealth Secretariat (2000); WTO (2002); Grynberg and Remy (2004).
4. Vanuatu (2004); Note on statistics. Most are unreliable, especially before 1997, although in general international data are more reliable than domestic. The issue of the reliability of statistics will be discussed further below.
5. See, for example, MacClancy (1981).
6. Economic structure is defined in the sense defined by Kuznets (1960) and used in Killick (1995b).
7. In 2006 US$1 was worth approximately VT 110. The exchange rate has been reasonably stable for many years. The vatu is fixed against a basket of the currencies of Vanuatu's major trading partners.
8. And the US current-account deficit partly underlay the 'global imbalances' that led to the economic crisis which began in 2008.
9. According to unpublished documents at the Parliamentary library, Vanuatu had 11 different governments between 1995 and 2006.
10. For recent discussions of fragmentation in Melanesian politics see Morgan (2004) and Powell (2004).
11. At the time of writing Vanuatu was predicted to graduate from LDC to developing status in 2014.
12. Reinert (2005) suggests that a lack of formal employment has always been an important reason for why many developing nations are locked into poverty.

13. The regional trading blocs are the Pacific Agreement on Closer Economic Relations, the Pacific Island Countries Trade Agreement and the Melanesian Spearhead Group Free Trade Area.
14. WTO (2001a); the average trade-weighted tariff in 2004 was 19 per cent. The average bound rate (upper limit) under the draft WTO offer was 40 per cent.
15. The WTO and most regional trade agreements do include clauses allowing for a limited tariff increase in an emergency.
16. For example see the front page of the Vanuatu *Daily Post*, 13 April 2004, 'Vanuatu seeks better deal on trade'.
17. Republic of Vanuatu, 31 May 2004, letter from Minister of Trade to US Trade Representative entitled 'Resumption of Vanuatu's accession to the WTO'.
18. The emphasis on quality of institutions is often cited as one of the main lessons of the experience of transition in Eastern Europe and the former Soviet Union. See, for example Williamson (1999); Stiglitz (2002). There is also literature on the importance of institutions for development, including Chang (2002, 2003a).
19. Source: Vanuatu Department of Finance and Economic Management.
20. Source: UN Online Network in Public Administration and Finance.
21. Vanuatu Department of Statistics.
22. According to Toye (2000), using IMF data, for the three years nearest 1987 the average proportion of revenue from trade taxes to GDP in non-industrialized developing countries was 5.13 per cent, compared with 0.72 per cent in industrialized countries.
23. Source: Vanuatu Department of Finance and Economic Management.
24. NB. Figures from 2004 are predictions.
25. Some have suggested that the rural communities face a backward-bending supply curve, but no empirical research has been done.
26. For example the Director of the Vanuatu Cultural Centre suggested that *Kastom* medicine and magic should be taught in schools as having equal validity to what he termed 'Western science'.
27. Vanuatu Daily Post, 12 October 2004.
28. Interview with Sowany Joseph, Principal Trade and Investment officer, Port Vila Chamber of Commerce, 2004.
29. Interview with Timothy Sisi, former Assistant Collector, Department of Customs and Inland Revenue, 2004. Now Principal Trade Officer, Department of Trade, Industry and Investment.
30. Articles I and III of the General Agreement on Tariffs and Trade refer to Most-Favoured Nation treatment and National Treatment, respectively.
31. Interview with Dickinson Tevi, Technical Assistant– Finance, Vanuatu Association of NGOs, 2004.
32. In practice the Washington Consensus has been shown to have worsened inequality. See Killick (1995a) and Zuckerman (1991).

7 Singapore: The Lionized City

1. It is worth noting that in the Washington Consensus era it is unlikely that the Bretton Woods institutions would advocate such an interventionist industrial policy or provide technical assistance for upgrading the manufacturing sector.

2. In 2004, the president was paid approximately US$1.5 million a year.
3. The other one is Hong Kong.
4. See Appendix 1. Some policies could even be called Keynesian, but the first Finance Minister, Goh Keng Swee, does not consider himself a follower of Keynes, giving credit to few economists later than Ricardo, apart from Arthur Lewis who gets half-marks (Goh 1995b: x).
5. Outside commentators sometimes appear to believe that the Singaporean government is infallible. Section 7.4.1 highlights some of the investment and policy mistakes it has made since independence.
6. 'I am often accused of interfering in the private lives of citizens. Yet, if I did not, had I not done that, we wouldn't be here today. And I say without the slightest remorse, that we wouldn't be here, we would not have made economic progress, if we had not intervened on very personal matters – who your neighbour is, how you live, the noise you make, how you spit, or what language you use. We decide what is right. Never mind what the people think. That's another problem' (From Lee Kuan Yew's speech at the 1986 National Day Rally, quoted in the Straits Times, 20 April 1987).
7. Since early in Singapore's history, politicians have shown a desire to promote conformity and contempt for ordinary people. Lee Kuan Yew addressed a community centre meeting in 1967 thus: 'We will be to blame if youngsters ten years from now become hooligans, ruffians and sluts. They can be trained to be otherwise. Even dogs can be trained as proved by the Police Training School where dogs, at a whistle, jump through a hoop, sit down or attack those who need to be attacked' (quoted in George 1984: 194).
8. 'A rough rule of thumb used by the United States Embassy in its reports on Singapore is that about 60 per cent of the economy is represented by the public sector, 25 per cent by MNCs and so only 15 per cent by private businesses' (Peebles and Wilson 1996: 32).
9. This raises interesting questions about the kind of political state necessary for economic development, but which are not discussed here.
10. See Appendix 2
11. It should be noted that 'economic freedom' is an ideological notion which has little grounding in theory. The Heritage Foundation is a right-wing American think-tank funded by private donations.

8   Comparisons

1. Source: http://hdr.undp.org/en/statistics/, date accessed 6 March 2009.

Bibliography

Alten, F. (1995) *The Role of the Government in the Singapore Economy* (Frankfurt am Main: Peter Lang).

Althusser, L. (1996) *For Marx* (London: Verso).

———(2001) *Lenin and Philosophy and Other Essays* (New York: Monthly Review Press).

Amariglio, J. and D. Ruccio (1993) 'Keynes, Postmodernism, Uncertainty', in Dow, S.C. and Hillard, J. (eds.) *Keynes, Knowledge and Uncertainty* (Cheltenham: Edward Elgar).

Angner, E. (2006) 'Overconfidence in Theory and Practice', *Journal of Economic Methodology*, 13(1): 1–24.

Archer, M. (2003) *Structure, Agency and the Internal Conversation* (Cambridge: Cambridge University Press).

Asher, M.G. (1999) 'An Analysis of Singapore's 1994–95 Budget', in Anthony Chin and Ngiam Kee Jin (eds.) *Outlook for the Singapore Economy* (Singapore: Trans Global Publishing).

Asian Development Bank (1996) *Vanuatu: Economic Performance, Policy and Reform Issues* (Manila: Asian Development Bank Pacific Studies Series).

———(2002) *Vanuatu: Economic Performance and Challenges Ahead* (Manila: Asian Development Bank Pacific Studies Series).

Asiaweek (2001) 'The Neighbourhood's on Fire', 4 May, Daniel Gay.

AsiaWise (2001a) 'Singapore's Start-Up Scene', 19 February, Daniel Gay.

AsiaWise (2001b) 'Singapore's Pharmaceutical Dreams', Daniel Gay.

Atkins, J.P., S.A. Mazzi and C.D. Easter (2000) 'Commonwealth Vulnerability Index for Developing Countries: The Position of Small States', Economic Paper No. 40 (Commonwealth Secretariat: London).

Barr, D.M. (2006) 'Beyond Technocracy: The Culture of Elite Governance in Lee Hsien Loong's Singapore', *Asian Studies Review*, March 2006 (30): 1–17.

Beck, U., A. Giddens and S. Lash (1994) *Reflexive Modernisation* (Cambridge: Polity Press).

Bergeron, S. (2006) *Fragments of Development* (Ann Arbor: University of Michigan Press).

Bernal, R.L. (2001) 'Small Developing Economics in the World Trade Organisation', Paper Presented at World Bank Conference "Leveraging Trade, Global Market Integration and the New WTO Negotiations for Development," Washington, DC, July 23–4, http://www.richardbernal.net/Small%20Developing%20Economies%20in%20the%20WTO%20Ver%202%20by%20Richard%20Bernal.pdf, date accessed 26 February 2009.

Bhanoji Rao, V.V. and M.K. Ramakrishnan (1980) *Income Inequality in Singapore* (Singapore: Singapore University Press).

Bhaskar, R (1978) *A Realist Theory of Science* (Sussex: Harvester).

Billig, M. (2000) 'Institutions and Culture: Neo-Weberian Economic Anthropology', *Journal of Economic Issues*, December 2000, 34(4).

Bloor, D. (1976) *Knowledge and Social Imagery* (London: Routledge).

Bøås, M. and D. McNeil (eds.) (2004) *Global Institutions and Development: Framing the World?* (London: Routledge).

Bocock, R. and K. Thompson (1985) *Religion and Ideology* (Manchester: Manchester University Press).

Bohm-Bawerk, E. (1970) *Capital and Interest: A Critical History of Economical Theory* (New York: August M. Kelley).

Bourdieu, P. (1972) *Algeria 1960* (Cambridge: Cambridge University Press).

———(1988) *Homo Academicus* (Stanford: Stanford University Press).

———(1990a) *In Other Words* (Cambridge: Polity Press).

———(1990b) *The Logic of Practice* (Cambridge: Polity Press).

———(2005) *The Social Structures of the Economy* (Cambridge: Polity Press).

Bourdieu, P. and L. Wacquant (1992) *An Invitation to Reflexive Sociology* (Cambridge: Polity Press).

Brander, J. and B. Spencer (1985) 'Export Subsidies and International Market Share Rivalry' *Journal of International Economics*, 18: 83–100.

Brewster, H. (2003) 'On Linking Trade and Development in Economic Partnership Agreements', *Commonwealth LTT Working Party*, Washington, DC.

Bryant, C.G.A. (2002) 'George Soros's Theory of Reflexivity: A Comparison with the Theories of Giddens and Beck and a Consideration of its Practical Value', *Economy and Society*, 31(1): 112.

Caldwell, B. (2009) 'Some Comments on Lawson's *Reorienting Economics*', in Fullbrook, E. (ed.) *Ontology and Economics: Tony Lawson and his Critics* (Abingdon: Routledge), 13–19.

Callaghy, T.M. and J. Ravenhill (1993) *Hemmed In: Responses to Africa's Economic Decline* (Columbia: Columbia University Press).

Callinicos, A. (1999) 'Social Theory Put to the Test: Pierre Bourdieu and Anthony Giddens', *New Left Review*, July/August, 236: 77–102.

Cammack, P. (2002) 'Attacking the Poor', *New Left Review*, 13, January–February 2002: 125–34.

Cardarelli, R., J. Gobat and J. Lee (2000) *Singapore: Selected Issues,* International Monetary Fund, Staff Country Report No. 00/83, Washington, DC.

Castells, M. (1988) *The Developmental City-State in an Open World Economy: The Singapore Experience*, Berkeley Roundtable on International Economy Working Paper no.31.

Chang, H.J. (2002) *Kicking Away the Ladder* (London: Anthem Press).

———(2003a) *Globalisation, Economic Development and the Role of the State* (London: Zed Books).

———(ed.) (2003b) *Rethinking Development Economics* (London: Anthem Press).

———(2007) *Bad Samaritans* (London: Random House).

Chick, V. and S. Dow (2001) 'Formalism, Logic and Reality: A Keynesian Analysis', *Cambridge Journal of Economics*, 25: 705–21.

———(2005) 'The Meaning of Open Systems', *Journal of Economic Methodology*, 12(3), September: 363–81.

Chow, K.B., M.L. Chew and E. Su (1997) *One Partnership in Development: UNDP and Singapore* (Singapore: United Nations Association of Singapore).

Commonwealth Secretariat, World Bank (2000) 'Small States: Meeting Challenges in the Global Economy', Report of the Commonwealth Secretariat/World Bank Joint Task Force on Small States.

Comprehensive Reform Programme (1997) Port Vila, Comprehensive Reform Programme Co-ordination Office.

Connell, J. and R. Curtain (1982) 'The Political Economy of Urbanization in Melanesia', *Singapore Journal of Tropical Geography*, 3(2), December: 119–36.

Cross, R. and D. Strachan (1997) 'On George Soros and Economic Analysis', *Kyklos*, 50: 561–74.

Cullenberg, S., J. Amariglio and D. Ruccio (2001) *Postmodernism, Economics and Knowledge* (London: Routledge).

Danby, C. (2002) 'The Curse of the Modern: A Post Keynesian Critique of the Gift/ Exchange Dichotomy', *Research in Economic Anthropology*, 21: 13–42.

Davidsen, B. (2005) 'Critical Realism in Economics – A Different View', *Post-Autistic Economics Review* (33), 14 September 2005, 36–50, http://www.paecon.net/PAEReview/issue33/Davidsen33.htm, date accessed 26 February 2009.

Davidson, P. (2004–5) 'A Post-Keynesian View of the Washington Consensus and How to Improve it', *Journal of Post-Keynesian Economics*, 27(2): 273–91.

Davis, J., D.W. Hands and U. Mäki (1998) *The Handbook of Economic Methodology* (Cheltenham: Edward Elgar).

Davis, J. and M. Klaes (2003) 'Reflexivity: Curse or Cure?', *Journal of Economic Methodology*, 10(3): 329–53.

De Vries, B.A. (1973) 'The Plight of Small Countries', *Finance and Development*, 10(3): 6–8.

Dow, S.C. (1990) 'Beyond Dualism', *Cambridge Journal of Economics*, 14(2): 143–57.

——(1991) 'Are There any Signs of Postmodernism within Economics?', *Methodus*, 1(3): 81.

——(1996) *The Methodology of Macroeconomic Thought* (Cheltenham: Edward Elgar).

——(2001) 'Modernism and Postmodernism: A Dialectical Analysis', in Cullenberg, S., J. Amariglio and D.F. Ruccio (eds.), *Postmodernism, Economics and Knowledge* (London: Routledge).

——(2002a) 'Postmodernism and Analysis of the Development Process', *International Journal of Development Issues*, 1(1): 27–34.

——(2002b) *Economic Methodology: An Enquiry* (Oxford: Oxford University Press).

——(2002c) 'Interpretation: The Case of David Hume', *History of Political Economy*, 34(2): 399–420.

Dow, A. and S.C. Dow (2005a) 'The Importance of Context for Theory and Policy Development in Adjusting Economies: The Case of Scotland', in Haroon Akram-Lodhi, A., R. Hardoon, R. Chernomas and A. Sepheri (eds.) *Globalization, Neo-Conservative Policies and Democratic Alternatives: Essays in Honour of John Loxley* (Winnipeg: Arbeiter Ring Publishing).

Dow, A. and S.C. Dow (2005b) 'The Application of Development Economics: General Principles and Context Specificity', *Cambridge Journal of Economics*, 29(6): 1129.

Downward, P. and A. Mearman (2009) 'Reorienting Economics through Triangulation of Methods', in Fullbrook, E. (ed.) *Ontology and Economics: Tony Lawson and his Critics* (Abingdon: Routledge), 130–41.

Downward, P., J.H. Finch and J. Ramsay (2002) 'Critical Realism, Empirical Methods and Inference', *Cambridge Journal of Economics*, 26: 481–500.

Dow, S.C. and J. Hillard (1995) *Keynes, Knowledge and Uncertainty* (Cheltenham: Edward Elgar).

Duncan, R. and S. Chand (2002) 'The Economics of the "Arc of Instability"',
Journal of Asian-Pacific Economic Literature, 16(1): 1–9.

Eagleton, T. (1991) *Ideology: An Introduction* (London: Verso).

Easterly, W. (2006) 'An Identity Crisis? Examining IMF Financial Programming',
World Development, 34(6): 964.

Easterly, W. and A. Kraay (2000) 'Small States, Small Problems? Income, Growth
and Volatility in Small States', *World Development*, 28(11): 2013–27.

Economic Development Board (1994) *Singapore Unlimited* (Singapore: Economic
Development Board).

Escobar, A. (1995) *Encountering Development: The Making and Unmaking of the
Third World* (Princeton: Princeton University Press).

Fama, E.F. (1970) 'Efficient Capital Markets: A Review of Theory and Empirical
Work', *Journal of Finance*, 25: 383–417.

Ferguson, J. (1990) *The Anti-Politics Machine* (Cambridge: Cambridge University
Press).

Feyerabend, P. (1975) *Against Method: Outline of an Anarchistic Theory of Knowledge*
(London: New Left Books).

Fine, B. (2004) 'Addressing the Critical and the Real in Critical Realism', in Lewis,
P. (ed.) *Transforming Economics* (London: Routledge), 202–26.

Fine, B., C. Lapavitsas and J. Pincus (2003) *Development Policy in the Twenty-First
Century* (London: Routledge).

Fleetwood, S. (ed.) (1999) *Critical Realism in Economics: Development and Debate*
(London: Routledge).

Foucault, M. (1972) *The Archaeology of Knowledge* (London: Routledge).

———(1980) *Power/Knowledge* (London: Harvester Wheatsheaf).

Freeman, N.J. (2003) *Financing Southeast Asia's Economic Development* (Singapore:
Institute of Southeast Asian Studies).

Friedman, M. (1953) 'The Methodology of Positive Economics', in *Essays in
Positive Economics* (Chicago: Chicago University Press), 3–43.

Friedman, T. (1999) *The Lexus and the Olive Tree* (London: Harper Collins).

Fullbrook, E. (ed.) (2009) *Ontology and Economics: Tony Lawson and His Critics*
(Abingdon: Routledge).

Galbraith, J.K. (1974) *Economics and the Public Purpose* (London: André Deutsch).

———(2004) *The Economics of Innocent Fraud: Truth for our Time* (London: Allen
Lane).

Gay, D. (2003) 'Vanuatu', *The Doha Development Agenda: Perspectives from the
ESCAP region*, UNESCAP Studies in Trade and Investment, 51: 275–305.

———(2004) 'The Emperor's Tailor: An Assessment of Vanuatu's Comprehensive
Reform Programme', *Pacific Economic Bulletin*, 19(3): 22–39.

———(2005) 'Vanuatu', in Gallagher, P. (ed.) *Managing the Challenges of WTO
Participation* (Cambridge: Cambridge University Press).

Geertz, C. (1976) 'From Nature's Point of View: On the Nature of Anthropological
Understanding', in Basso, K.M. and H.A. Selby (eds.), *Meaning in Anthropology*
(Albuquerque: University of New Mexico Press).

———(2004) 'Interview of Clifford Geertz by Alan Macfarlane, 5th May 2004',
http://www.alanmacfarlane.com/ancestors/geertz.htm, date accessed 26
February 2009.

George, T.J.S. (1984) *Lee Kuan Yew's Singapore* (Singapore: Eastern Universities
Press).

Giddens, A. (1984) *The Constitution of Society: Outline of a Theory of Structuration* (Cambridge: Polity Press).

———(1990) *The Consequences of Modernity* (Stanford: Stanford University Press).

———(1994a) *Beyond Left and Right* (Cambridge: Polity Press).

———(1994b) 'Brave New World: The Context of a New Politics', in Miliband, D. (ed.) (1994) *Reinventing the Left* (Cambridge: Polity Press).

Goh, K.S. (1995a) *The Economics of Modernisation* (Singapore: Federal Publications).

———(1995b) *The Practice of Economic Growth* (Singapore: Federal Publications).

Gore, C. (2000) 'The Rise and Fall of the Washington Consensus as a Paradigm for Developing Countries', *World Development*, 28(5): 789–804.

Gottleib, A. (1997) *Socrates* (London: Phoenix).

Gounder, R. and V. Xavayong (2001) 'Globalisation and the Island Economies of the South Pacific', Discussion Paper no. 2001/41, World Institute for Development Economics Research.

Greene, G. (1978) *Brighton Rock* (Harmondsworth: Penguin).

Griffiths, P. (2003) *The Economist's Tale: A Consultant Encounters Hunger and the World Bank* (London: Zed Books).

Grynberg, R. and R.M. Joy (2000) 'The Accession of Vanuatu to the WTO– Lessons for the Multilateral Trading System', *Journal of World Trade*, 34(6): 159–73.

Grynberg, R. and J.Y. Remy (2004) 'Small Vulnerable Economy Issues and the WTO', Data Paper, 24th Commonwealth Parliamentary Conference of Members from Small Countries, Quebec City, Canada.

Guerrien, B. (2009) 'Irrelevance and Ideology', in Fullbrook, E. (ed.) *Ontology and Economics: Tony Lawson and his Critics* (Abingdon: Routledge), 158–61.

Guitian, M. (1981) 'Fund Conditionality: Evolution of Principles and Practices' (Washington, DC: IMF pamphlet no. 38).

Hands, D.W. (2001) *Reflections without Rules* (Cambridge: Cambridge University Press).

Harcourt, G.C. (1996) 'How I Do Economics', in Harcourt, G.C. (2001) *50 Years a Keynesian and Other Essays* (New York: Palgrave).

Harriss, J. (2002) 'The Case for Cross-disciplinary Approaches in International Development', *World Development*, 30(3): 487–96.

Harrod, R. (1972) *The Life of John Maynard Keynes* (Middlesex: Penguin).

Hayami, Y. (2003) 'From the Washington Consensus to the Post-Washington Consensus: Retrospect and Prospect', *Asian Development Review*, 20(2): 40–65.

Hayek, F.A. (1944) *The Road to Serfdom* (London: Routledge).

———(1945) 'The Use of Knowledge in Society', *American Economic Review*, 35(3): 519–30.

———(1966) *Monetary Theory and the Trade Cycle* trans. N. Kaldor and H.M. Croome (New York: A.M. Kelley).

Hefner, R.W. (1990) *The Political Economy of Mountain Java* (Berkeley: University of California Press).

Held, D. (2004) *Global Covenant: The Social Democratic Alternative to the Washington Consensus* (London: Polity Press).

Heritage Foundation (2007) *Index of Economic Freedom 2007* http://www.heritage.org/research/features/index/index.cfm, date accessed 14 May 2007.

Hirschman, A. (1958) *The Strategy of Economic Development* (Yale: Yale University Press).

———(1980) *Essays in Trespassing: Economics to Politics and Beyond* (Cambridge: Cambridge University Press).

———(1995) *A Propensity to Self-subversion* (London: Harvard University Press).

———(1998) *Crossing Boundaries: Selected Writings* (New York: Zone Books).

Hodgson, G. (1999) *Economics and Utopia: Why the Learning Economy is not the End of History* (London: Routledge).

———(2009) 'On the Problem of Formalism in Economics', in Fullbrook, E. (ed.) *Ontology and Economics: Tony Lawson and His Critics* (Abingdon: Routledge), 175–88.

Hoksbergen, R. (1994) 'Postmodernism and Institutionalism: Toward a Resolution of the Debate on Relativism' *Journal of Economic Issues*, 28(3): 679–714.

Honderich, T. (ed.) (1995) *The Oxford Companion to Philosophy* (Oxford: Oxford University Press).

Horkheimer, M. (1937) 'Traditional and Critical Theory', *Critical Theory: Selected Essays* (New York: Continuum).

Horscroft, V. (2005) 'Small Economies And Special And Differential Treatment: Strengthening The Evidence, Countering The Fallacies', Paper prepared for the Commonwealth Secretariat, 16 March.

Huff, W.G. (1995) 'What is the Singapore Model of Economic Development?', *Cambridge Journal of Economics*, 19: 735–59.

———(1997) *The Economic Growth of Singapore* (Cambridge: Cambridge University Press).

———(1999) 'Singapore's Economic Development: Four Lessons and Some Doubts', *Oxford Development Studies*, 27(1): 33–55.

Huffer, E. and G. Molisa (1999) 'Governance in Vanuatu', *Pacific Economic Bulletin*, 14(1): 101–12.

Hughes, H. (1984) *The Singapore Economy: The Next 25 Years* (Singapore: National University of Singapore).

Hurt, S.T. (2003) 'Cooperation and Coercion? The Cotonou Agreement between the European Union and ACP States and the End of the Lomé Convention', *Third World Quarterly*, 24(1): 161–76.

Jameson, F. (1991) *Postmodernism, or, The Cultural Logic of Late Capitalism* (London: Verso).

Jenkins, R. (1992) *Pierre Bourdieu* (London: Routledge).

Jeyaretnam, J.B. (2003) *The Hatchet Man of Singapore* (Singapore: Jeya Publishers).

Kalecki, M. (1976) *Essays on Developing Economies* (Brighton: Harvester).

Kanbur, R. (2002) 'Economics, Social Science and Development', *World Development*, 30(3): 477–86.

Kanth, R. (1999) 'Against Eurocentred Epistemologies', in Fleetwood, S. (ed.) *Critical Realism in Economics* (London: Routledge).

Keynes, J.M. (1921) *A Treatise on Probability* (New York: Macmillan).

———(1936) *The General Theory of Employment, Interest and Money* (London: Macmillan).

———(1937) 'The General Theory of Employment', *Quarterly Journal of Economics*, 51(2): 209–23.

———(1973) 'The Collected Writings of John Maynard Keynes: The General Theory and After: Part II, Defence and Development', *Royal Economic Society* XIV.

Killick, T. (1993) *The Adaptive Economy: Adjustment Policies in Small, Low-Income Countries* (Washington: World Bank).

———(1995a) 'Structural Adjustment and Poverty Alleviation: An Interpretative Survey', *Development and Change*, 26(2): 305–31.

———(1995b) *IMF Programmes in Developing Countries: Design and Impact* (London: Routledge).

———(1998) *Aid and the Political Economy of Policy Change* (London: Routledge).

King, J.E. (2002) *A History of Post-Keynesian Economics Since 1936* (Cheltenham: Edward Elgar).

Klaes, M. (2006) 'Keynes Between Modernism and Postmodernism', in Backhouse, R. and B. Bateman (eds.) *The Cambridge Companion to Keynes* (Cambridge: Cambridge University Press).

Klamer, A. (1995) 'The Conception of Modernism in Economics', in Dow, S.C. and J. Hillard (eds.) *Keynes, Knowledge and Uncertainty* (Cheltenham: Edward Elgar).

———(2002) 'Late Modernism and the Loss of Character in Economics', in Cullenberg, S., J. Amariglio and D.F. Ruccio (eds.) *Postmodernism, Economics and Knowledge* (London: Routledge).

Knapman, B. and C.D. Saldanha (1999) *Reforms in the Pacific, An Assessment of the ADB's Assistance for Reform Programmes in the Pacific* (Manila: Asian Development Bank).

Krause, L., A.T. Koh and Y. Lee (1987) *The Singapore Economy Reconsidered* (Singapore: Institute of Southeast Asian Studies).

Kruger, A. (2004) 'Lessons from the Asian Crisis', Keynote Address, International Monetary Fund SEACEN Meeting, Sri Lanka, February 12.

Krugman, P. (1984) 'Import Protection as Export Promotion: International Competition in the Presence of Oligopoly and Economies of Scale', in Kierzowski (ed.) *Monopolistic Competition and International Trade* (Oxford: Oxford University Press).

———(1998) 'Soros' Plea', http://web.mit.edu/krugman/www/soros.html, date accessed 26 February 2009.

———(1994) 'The Myth of Asia's Miracle', *Foreign Affairs*, 73(6), November/December: 62–79.

Kuhn, T.S. (1962) *The Structure of Scientific Revolutions* (Chicago: University of Chicago Press).

Kuznets, S. (1960) 'Economic Growth of Small Nations', in Robinson, E.A.G. (ed.) *The Economic Consequences of the Size of Nations: Proceedings of a Conference Held by the International Economic Association* (Toronto: MacMillan).

———(1971) 'Modern Economic Growth: Findings and Reflections', in Lindbeck, A. (ed.) *Nobel Lectures, Economics 1969–80* (Singapore: World Scientific Publishing Co., 1992).

Lakatos, I. (1976) *Proofs and Refutations* (Cambridge: Cambridge University Press).

Lal, D (2000) *The Poverty of Development Economics* (Oxford: Oxford University Press).

Lamy, P. (2004) 'The Emergence of Collective Preferences in International Trade: Implications for Regulating Globalisation', Conference on collective preferences and global governance: What future for the multilateral trading system?, Brussels, 15 September 2004, http://europa.eu.int/comm/archives/commission_1999_2004/lamy/speeches_articles/spla242_en.htm, date accessed 26 February 2009.

Lange, O. and F.M. Taylor (1938) *On the Economic Theory of Socialism* (Minneapolis: University of Minnesota Press).

Lawson, T. (1997a) *Economics and Reality* (London: Routledge).

———(1997b) 'Horses for Courses', in Arestis, P., G. Palma and M. Sawyer (eds.) *Markets, Unemployment and Economic Policy* (London: Routledge).

———(2003) *Reorienting Economics* (London: Routledge).

Lee, K.Y. (1998) *The Singapore Story: Memoirs of Lee Kuan Yew* (Singapore: Singapore Press Holdings).

———(2000) *From Third World to First – The Singapore Story 1965–2000: Memoirs of Lee Kuan Yew* (New York: HarperCollins).

Lee, R. (1994) 'Modernization, Postmodernism and the Third World', *Current Sociology*, 42(2): 1–63.

Lensink, R. (1996) *Structural Adjustment in Sub-Saharan Africa* (London: Longman).

Levi-Strauss, C. (1964) *Structural Anthropology* (New York: Basic Books).

Lim, L.Y.-C. (1989) 'Social Welfare', in Sandhu, K.S. and Wheatley, Paul (eds.) *Management of Success: The Moulding of Modern Singapore* (Singapore: Institute of Southeast Asian Studies), 171–97.

Low, L. (1998) *The Political Economy of a City-State: Government-Made Singapore* (Singapore: Oxford University Press).

Low, L. and D.M. Johnston (eds.) (2001) *Singapore Inc.* (Singapore: Asia Pacific Press).

Low, L. and L.B. Lum (eds.) (1997) *Strategies of Singapore's Economic Success* (Singapore: Federal Publications).

Lucas, R. (1976) 'Econometric Policy Evaluation: A Critique', Carnegie-Rochester Conference Series on Public Policy 1: 19–46.

———(2003) 'Macroeconomic Priorities', *American Economic Review*, March, 93(1): 1–14.

Lydgate, C. (2003) *Lee's Law: How Singapore Crushes Dissent* (Victoria: Scribe Publications).

Lyotard, J. (1984) *The Postmodern Condition: A Report on Knowledge* (Minneapolis: University of Minnesota Press).

MacClancy, J. (1981) *To Kill a Bird with Two Stones* (Port Vila: Vanuatu Cultural Centre Publications).

Machlup, F. (1978) *Methodology of Economic and Other Social Sciences* (New York: Anthem Press).

Mahbubani, K. (2004) *Can Asians Think?* (Singapore: Marshall Cavendish).

Mair, D. and A.G Miller (1991) *A Modern Guide to Economic Thought* (Aldershot: Edward Elgar).

Malhotra, K. (2008) 'National Trade and Development Strategies: Suggested Policy Directions' (New York: UNDP).

Malinowski, B. (1978) *Argonauts of the Western Pacific* (London: Routledge and Kegan Paul).

Mankiw, N.G. (1994) *Macroeconomics* (New York: Worth) (Second edition).

Mannheim, K. (1936) *Ideology and Utopia. An Introduction to the Sociology of Knowledge* (London: Routledge).

Marx, K. (1974) *The German Ideology* (London: Laurence and Wishart) (Second edition).

McCloskey, D. (1985) *The Rhetoric of Economics* (Wisconsin: University of Wisconsin Press).

————(2001) 'The Genealogy of Postmodernism: An Economist's Guide', in Cullenberg, S., J. Amariglio and D.F. Ruccio (eds.) *Postmodernism, Economics and Knowledge* (London: Routledge).

Menger, K. (1963) *Problems of Economics and Sociology* (Urbana: University of Illinois Press).

Miles, W. (1998) *Bridging Mental Boundaries: Identity and Development in Vanuatu* (Honolulu: University of Hawaii Press).

Ministry of Manpower (2003) *Report on Wages in Singapore* (Singapore: Manpower Research and Statistics Department).

Ministry of Trade and Industry (1998–2005) *Economic Survey of Singapore* (Singapore: Singapore Press Holdings).

Mises, L. (1962) *The Ultimate Foundation of Economic Science* (London: Allen and Unwin).

Morgan, M.G. (2004) 'Political Fragmentation and the Policy Environment in Vanuatu, 1980–2004', *Pacific Economic Bulletin*, 19(3): 40–8.

Mouzelis, N. (2000) 'The Subjectivist-Objectivist Divide: Against Transcendence', *Sociology*, 34(4): 741–62.

Nair, D. (ed.) (1976) *Socialism That Works: The Singapore Way* (Singapore: Federal Publications).

Narsey, W. (2004) 'PICTA, PACER and EPAs: Weaknesses in Pacific Island Countries' Trade Policies', *Pacific Economic Bulletin*, 19(3): 74–101.

New Economics Foundation (2006) 'The Happy Planet Index: An Index of Human Wellbeing and Environmental Impact', http://www.neweconomics.org/gen/uploads/dl44k145g5scuy453044gqbu11072006194758.pdf, date accessed 26 February 2009.

Ormerod, P. (1994) *The Death of Economics* (London: Faber and Faber).

————(2005) *Why Most Things Fail: Evolution, Extinction and Economics* (London: Faber and Faber).

Page, S. (1994) *How Developing Countries Trade: The Institutional Constraints* (London: Routledge).

Parfitt, T. (2002) *The End of Development: Modernity, Post-Modernity and Development* (London: Pluto).

Parpart, J.L. (1995) 'Deconstructing the Development "Expert": Gender, Development and the "Vulnerable Groups"', in M.H. Marchand and J.L. Parpart (eds.) *Feminism, Postmodernism and Development* (London: Routledge), 221–43.

Peebles, G. and P. Wilson (1996) *The Singapore Economy* (Cheltenham: Edward Elgar).

————(2002) *Economic Growth and Development in Singapore* (Cheltenham: Edward Elgar).

Powell, P.T. (2004) 'A Theory of Atomistic Federalism for Melanesia' *Pacific Economic Bulletin*, 19(3): 49–63.

Premdas, R. (1987) 'Melanesian Socialism', *Journal of Commonwealth and Comparative Politics*, July: 141–60.

Preston, P.W. (1989) *Rethinking Development: Essays on Development and Southeast Asia* (London and New York: Routledge and Kegan Paul).

Pugh, C. (1989) 'The Political Economy of Public Housing', in Sandhu, K.S. and Wheatley, P. (eds.) *Management of Success: The Moulding of Modern Singapore* (Singapore: Institute of Southeast Asian Studies), 833–59.

Ranis, G., F. Stewart and A. Ramirez (2000) 'Economic Growth and Human Development' *World Development*, 28: 197–219.

Reinert, E.S. (2005) 'Development and Social Goals: Balancing Aid and Development to Prevent "Welfare Colonialism"', Post-Autistic Economics Review (30), 21 March, article 1, http://www.btinternet.com/~pae_news/review/issue30.htm, date accessed 26 February 2009.

Republic of Vanuatu (2004) *Fiscal Strategy Report*, Budget 2004, Vol. 1, Department of Finance and Economic Management, Government of the Republic of Vanuatu, Port Vila.

Rio, K. (2003) 'The Third Man: Manifestations of Agency on Ambrym Island, Vanuatu', PhD thesis, Department of Social Anthropology, University of Bergen.

Rodrik, D. (2002a) 'After Neoliberalism, What?', http://ksghome.harvard.edu/~drodrik/after%20neoliberalism.pdf, date accessed 31 March 2009.

———(2002b) 'Feasible Globalisations', http://ksghome.harvard.edu/~drodrik/Feasglob.pdf, date accessed 31 March 2009.

———(2007) *One Econonomics, Many Recipes: Globalisation, Institutions and Economic Growth* (Princeton: Princeton University Press).

Ruby, J. (1980) 'Exposing Yourself: Reflexivity, Anthropology, and Film' *Semiotica*, 30: 153–79.

Ruccio, D. (2009) '(Un)real Criticism', in Fullbrook, E. (ed.) *Ontology and Economics: Tony Lawson and His Critics* (Abingdon: Routledge), 263–74.

Ruccio, D. and Amariglio, J. (2003) *Postmodern Moments in Economics* (Princeton: Princeton University Press).

Russell, B. (1991) *A History of Western Philosophy* (London: Routledge).

Sachs, I. (1977) 'Kalecki and Development Planning', *Oxford Bulletin of Economics and Statistics*, 39(1): 47–56.

Sachs, J. (2005) *The End of Poverty: How We Can Make it Happen in Our Lifetime* (London: Penguin).

Sachs, J. and A. Warner (1995) 'Economic Reform and the Process of Global Integration', *Brookings Papers on Economic Activity*, 1: 1–118.

Said, E. (2003) *Orientalism* (London: Penguin).

Salong, J.D. (1998) 'Reform or Recolonisation: Vanuatu's Comprehensive Reform Programme under the Microscope', *Tok Blong Pasifik*, March/June: 17–18.

Samuelson, P. (1947) *Foundations of Economic Analysis* (Cambridge: Harvard University Press).

Santiso, J. (2000) 'Hirschman's View of Development, or the Art of Trespassing and Self-Subversion', CEPAL Review 70: 92–109, April, http://mpra.ub.uni-muenchen.de/12906/, date accessed 17 February 2009.

Sawyer, M. (1985) *The Economics of Michal Kalecki* (London, Macmillan).

Schmid, A. (2005) 'An Institutional Economics Perspective on Economic Growth', May 23 draft, Paper presented to Seventh International Worksop on Institutional Economics, Hertfordshire, 22–4 June 2005.

Schumacher, E.F. (1974) *Small is Beautiful: A Study of Economics as if People Mattered* (London: Abacus).

Scitovsky, T. (1960) 'International Trade and Economic Integration as a Means of Overcoming the Disadvantage of a Small Nation', in Robinson, E.A.G. (ed.) *The Economic Consequences of the Size on Nations: Proceedings of a Conference Held by the International Economic Association* (Toronto: Macmillan).

Scollay, R. (1998) 'MFN (Non-Preferential) Liberalisation by Forum Island Countries, Commentary on Computable General Equilibrium (CGE), Analysis of Economic Effects' Unpublished report for Pacific Islands Forum Secretariat, Fiji.

Schumpeter, J. (1944) *Capitalism, Socialism and Democracy* (London: Allen and Unwin).

See, Brigitte K.H. (1997) *Singapore, A Modern Asian City-State: Relationship Between Cultural and Economic Development*, PhD dissertation, Nijmegen University.

Sen, A. (2000) *Development as Freedom* (New York: Anchor Books).

Sent, E. (1998) *The Evolving Rationality of Rational Expectations* (Cambridge: Cambridge University Press).

Sheridan, G. (1999) *Asian Values, Western Dreams* (St. Leonards: Allen and Unwin).

Shin, J.S. (2005) 'The Role of the State in the Increasingly Globalised Economy: Implications for Singapore', *The Singapore Economic Review*, 50(1): 1–13.

Singapore Department of Statistics (1974–2005) *Yearbook of Statistics Singapore* (Singapore: Singapore Department of Statistics).

Singh, A. (1994) 'The Present State of Industry in the Third World: Analytical and Policy Issues', in Chada, G.K. (ed.) *Sectoral Issues in the Indian Economy: Policy and Perspectives* (New Delhi: Har-Anand Publications), 104–55.

Skidelsky, R. (2003) *John Maynard Keynes* (London: Macmillan).

Soros, G. (1994) *The Alchemy of Finance* (New York: John Wiley and Sons).

South China Morning Post (29 June 1999) 'Singapore Drops Control of Suzhou Park', Porter, B.

Srinivasan, T.N. (1986) 'The Costs and Benefits of Being a Small, Remote, Island Landlocked, or Ministate Economy', *Research Observer*, 1(2): 205–18.

Staveren, I. Van (2009) 'Feminism and Realism: A Contested Relationship', in Fullbrook, E. (ed.) *Ontology and Economics: Tony Lawson and His Critics* (Abingdon: Routledge): 297–310.

Stiglitz, J. (1991) 'Another Century of Economic Science', *Economic Journal*, 101(404): 134–41.

———(1998a) 'More Instruments and Broader Goals: Moving toward the Post Washington Consensus', http://www.globalpolicy.org/socecon/bwi-wto/stig.htm, date accessed 31 March 2009.

———(1998b) 'Towards a New Paradigm for Development: Strategies, Policies and Processes', http://siteresources.worldbank.org/CDF/ Resources/prebisch98.pdf, date accessed 31 March 2009.

———(2002) *Globalisation and its Discontents* (London: Penguin).

The Straits Times (1 January 2000) 'A Great Start to New Year, Says PM'.

———(4 January 2006) 'Mega R&D Funds for Two New Sectors', Chang, A.-L. and N. Soh.

———(20 January 2006) 'Managing Political Dissent', Lim, C.

Thynne, I and M. Ariff (eds.) (1989) *Privatisation: Singapore's Experience in Perspective* (Singapore: Longman).

Toye, J. (2000) 'Fiscal Crisis and Fiscal Reform in Developing Countries', *Cambridge Journal of Economics*, 24: 21–44.

Tremewan, C. (1994) *The Political Economy of Social Control in Singapore* (London: Macmillan).

Tucker, R.C. (1972) *The Marx-Engels Reader* (London: Norton).

United Nations (1961) *A Proposed Industrialisation Programme for the State of Singapore* (New York: UN Commission for Technical Assistance).

United Nations Conference on Trade and Development (2004) *The Least Developed Countries Report* (New York and Geneva: United Nations).

United Nations Development Programme (1990) *Human Development Report 1990* (New York and Geneva: United Nations).

———(2004) *Human Development Report 2004* (New York and Geneva: United Nations).

United Nations Economic and Social Commission for Asia and the Pacific (2002) *Project Completion Report in Respect of the Comprehensive Reform Programme*, Pal, S.H. (Port Vila: United Nations Economic and Social Commission for Asia and the Pacific, Pacific Operations Centre).

Van Trease (1987) *The Politics of Land in Vanuatu: From Colony to Independence* (Suva, Fiji, Institute of Pacific Studies: University of the South Pacific).

Veblen, T. (1899) *The Theory of the Leisure Class: An Economic Study of the Evolution of Institutions* (New York: Macmillan).

Wade, R. (1990) *Governing the Market: Economic Theory and the Role of Government in East Asian Industrialisation* (Princeton: Princeton University Press).

———(2001) 'Showdown at the World Bank', *New Left Review*, 7, January-February 2001: 124–37.

Walters, A. (1994) 'Do We Need the IMF and the World Bank?' *Current Controversies* No. 10. (London: Institute of Economic Affairs).

Wedel, J. (1998) 'The Harvard Boys Do Russia', *The Nation*, June 1998.

Williamson, J. (1990) 'What Washington Means by Policy Reform', in John Williamson (ed.) ch.2 of *Latin American Adjustment: How much has happened?* April 1990 (Washington, D.C.: Institute for International Economics).

———(1993) Democracy and the 'Washington Consensus', World Development, 21(8): 1329–36.

———(1999) 'What Should the Bank Think about the Washington Consensus', *Institute for International Economics*, paper prepared as background to the World Bank's *World Development report 2000*, July 1999.

———(2002) 'Did the Washington Consensus fail?', http://www.iie.com/publications/papers/paper.cfm?ResearchID=488, date accessed 31 March 2009.

———(2003) 'The Washington Consensus and Beyond', *Economic and Political Weekly*, April 12: 1475–81.

———(2004–5) 'The Strange History of the Washington Consensus', *Journal of Post-Keynesian Economics*, 27(2): 195–206.

———(2004a) 'The Washington Consensus as Policy Prescription for Development', http://www.iie.com/publications/papers/williamson0204.pdf, date accessed 31 March 2009.

———(2004b) 'A Short History of the Washington Consensus', http://www.iie.com/publications/papers/williamson0904-2.pdf, date accessed 31 March 2009.

Wilson, P. (2000) 'The Dilemma of a more Advanced Developing Country: Conflicting Views on the Development Strategy of Singapore', *The Developing Economies*, XXXVIII-1: 105–34.

Wong, A.K. and Ooi, G.L. (1994) 'Chng Suan Tze v The Minister of Home Affairs & Ors and Other Appeals', *Malayan Law Journal*, 1: 69–90.

Woolgar, S. (ed.) (1988) *Knowledge and Reflexivity* (London: Sage).

———(1992) 'Some Remarks about Positionism: A Reply to Collins and Yearly,' in A. Pickering (ed.) *Science as Practice and Culture* (Chicago: University of Chicago): 327–42.

World Bank (1993) *The East Asian Miracle: Economic Growth and Public Policy* (New York: Oxford University Press).

———(2002) 'Embarking on a Global Voyage: Trade Liberalization and Complementary Reforms in the Pacific', Report No. 24417-EAP, Poverty Reduction and Economic Management Unit, East Asia and Pacific Region.

World Trade Organisation (2001a) 'Draft Report of the Working Party on the Accession of Vanuatu', document WT/ACC/VUT/13 (restricted).

———(2001b) 'Draft Report of the Working Party on the Accession of Vanuatu, Part II – Draft schedule of Specific Commitments on Services, Draft List of Article II MFN Exemptions', document WT/ACC/VUT/13/Add.2 (restricted).

———(2002) 'Small Economies: A Literature Review', Document WT/COMTD/SE/W/4.

Young, A. (1992) 'A Tale of Two Cities: Factor Accumulation and Technical Change in Hong Kong and Singapore', http://www.nber.org/chapters/c10990.pdf, date accessed 31 March 2009.

Zack-Williams, A.B., E. Brown and G. Mohan (2000) 'The Long Road to Structural Adjustment', in Mohan, G., E. Brown, B. Milward and A.B. Zack-Williams (eds.) *Structural Adjustment:Ttheory, Practice and Impacts* (Routledge: London).

Zuckerman, E. (1991) 'The Social Costs of Adjustment', in Thomas, V., A. Chhibber, M. Delami and J. de Melo (eds.) *Restructuring Economies in Distress: Policy Reform and the World Bank* (Oxford: Oxford University Press).

Index